TIMES BOOKS

ARE WE AT WAR?

ARE WE AT WAR?
LETTERS TO THE TIMES 1939 – 1945

edited by

ANTHONY LIVESEY

TIMES BOOKS

Published in 1989 by
TIMES BOOKS LIMITED
16 Golden Square
London W1R 4BN

Copyright © 1989
Times Books Limited

British Library Cataloguing in Publication Data

Are we at war?: letters to *The Times*
1. Great Britain. Social life, 1936–1945
I. Livesey, Anthony   II. *The Times*
941.084

ISBN 0 7230 0332 7

Typeset by Rowland Phototypesetting Limited,
Bury St Edmunds, Suffolk

Printed in Great Britain by
Richard Clay Limited, Bungay, Suffolk

CONTENTS

ACKNOWLEDGEMENTS   page 7

FOREWORD by Leon Pilpel   9

INTRODUCTION by Anthony Livesey   11

1939   15

The importance of national recreation – ARP – The black-out –
Gas-masks – Air-raid warnings – Evacuation – Domestic measures –
The aesthetics of war – Official measures – Horses, wives and bats –
Kilts and casualties – Gloves and flannels – The end of the *Graf Spee* –
German rulers and people – Temperance in war-time

1940   49

The English accent – Sugar and butter – Street beggars – Alternative
food – The black-out – A voice from East Africa – Waste – Treatment
of aliens – National defence – Are we at war? – The stiletto – The
householder's pig – Budget suggestions – News broadcasts – Tobacco
for soldiers – Camouflage of cars – The British spirit – Air-raid stories
– Reprisals – *Jervis Bay* – Binoculars

1941   97

Man management – Buckets – Hermann the irascible – Food for hens –
Summer Time – Vermin – Rare birds as food – Why racing? – In place
of tobacco – More cases of waste – Conscientious objectors on the land
– Gas-masks – Petrol – The Hess affair – Bureaucracy – "Esquire" –
"Taxi!"

1942   127

BBC bulletins – Wheat shipments – Good Friday – Cats and milk –
Simpler clothes – Store cupboards – Waste of paper – The head-louse –

Flowers or food? – Dogs and the war – Poultry rations – "You've had
it" – The five-inch bath – The birth-rate and regulation 33B – War
films – Black-out again

1943   159

Drains and brains – The arch-fiend – The price of vegetables –
Economy in ink – Mr Churchill's broadcast – Trying it on the dog –
The crawling bus – Waste of effort – The bombing of Rome –
War-time manners – The population of Britain – War crimes –
400,000,000 cigarettes – A maternity hospital – Lost luggage – Rural
needs

1944   181

A Trinity jump – A "no treating" order – "A jolly factory" – Flying
bombs – A city hoarding – Rabbits – The Home Guard – Noise of
aircraft – A service club sign – Poultry keeping – Horse marines

1945   199

Identity cards – Boarding the bus – Hitler – Eire and Hitler – Italians
and Mussolini – Too true to be good – A railway poster – The
execution of German boys – Not on the register – Trunk call delays –
Victory broadcasts – War damage insurance – Epilogue

INDEX OF SUBJECTS   219

INDEX OF CORRESPONDENTS   222

ACKNOWLEDGEMENTS

The editor and publishers would like to thank all those who have so readily given permission for inclusion of the letters which appear in this volume. Every effort has been made to trace the writers of the letters or their heirs and executors. To those whom it has proved impossible to trace we would offer our sincerest apologies. Note: the letters which appear in this volume faithfully reproduce the way in which they originally appeared in the columns of *The Times*. Certain letters, which exclude the words "Yours faithfully" etc., appeared in edited form under the heading "Points from Letters".

FOREWORD

BY LEON PILPEL
Letters Editor, *The Times*

When John Walter I launched *The Daily Universal Register*, later renamed *The Times*, on January 1, 1785, his notice "To the Public" proclaimed, among other things, that "A News-Paper . . . like a well-covered table, . . . should contain something suited to every palate . . ." Such a spread, in his view, must have included correspondence, for a somewhat suspect letter, "signed" Gregory Gazette, occupied one of the 16 columns in that day's four-page paper, crying down the opposition, puffing the *Universal Register*, and reiterating that "a newspaper may be considered – as a political salmagundy, or a feast furnished to suit every palate".

In essence, that is what the correspondence columns have remained, ranging from the weightiest, most serious, and frequently best-written contributions at the top of the page, down to the bottom-right "tailpiece" letter, providing, as Robert Morley once put it, a "special sense of idiocy".

What John Walter could not have foreseen was the development of letters to the Editor in their influence, variety, and almost conversational quality, as though to his well-spread table had been added the well-fed diners themselves. The correspondence columns today can sustain themes and balance arguments promptly, particularly since the facsimile machine has come into general use, by-passing postal delays.

Influence is debatable, but a former Editor, Sir William Haley, was able to pinpoint a specific example of the formation of public opinion, leading directly to the Children Act of 1948, by a letter, published on July 15, 1944, by Lady Alan of Hurtwood, then chairman of the Nursery Schools' Association. She had observed the condition of slum children who became evacuees and was concerned at the apparent failure to take account of social deprivation in post-war reconstruction plans. Her letter produced a deluge, which continued daily, week after week. Similar outpourings followed the Suez crisis, Mr Enoch Powell's speeches on coloured immigration, the post-war uprisings in Hungary and Czechoslovakia, and the Falklands war, but the results, if any, cannot be so confidently traced.

Dickens inveighed in the columns against public executions, but several years elapsed before the hanging of Michael Barrett, author of the Fenians' explosion at Clerkenwell prison, put an end to that grisly sequence in May, 1868. Queen Victoria wrote anonymously in April, 1864, to complaints about her withdrawal from public life after Prince Albert's death, but only undertook to meet "the loyal wishes of her subjects" in the manner "least trying to her health, strength, and spirits".

Anonymity disappeared from the columns after the Second World War and now all letters bear a full authenticating address, except in cases of possible danger and the like. Letters are required to be exclusive, factually accurate – a good deal of attention goes to that – and addressed more *ad rem* than *ad hominem*, though that need not reduce their vigour. They tend in length towards a maximum of 300 words, but even so only about a tenth of the many tens of thousands received each year find a platform. A consoling reply goes to the less fortunate, but those who expect a detailed criticism, in the manner of a form examination paper, will be disappointed.

Some complain at their own exclusion and the repeated preference given to others, sometimes on the same subject. To them it is explained that many correspondents have similar ideas, but some express them better and more pithily; yet even those are rationed to perhaps a total of six appearances a year. There is also a well-marked distinction between a right of reply and the desire to have the last word, but it sometimes takes a longish telephone conversation or an exchange of (non-published) correspondence to get the point home. And frequently a letter perfectly acceptable at one time will fail to make it because that particular topic has gone off the boil.

That said, there never appears the notice: "This correspondence is now closed". Letters editors are constantly surprised at the ingenuity of writers in finding some new angle, just as they are constantly confounded by the reluctance of a correspondence to "start up". An occasional sprat may be required to catch the lurking mackerel. And there is always a new generation unfamiliar with the earlier debates of their elders. So the arguments, or better, discussions, about economy, temperance, food, defence, Summer Time, and the state of the nation, so well displayed in this collection, continue down to the present day, and no doubt beyond. As Sir Max Beerbohm cogently put it, in "A Letter That Was Not Written" (1914): "There sprang from my lips that fiery formula which has sprung from the lips of so many old choleric gentlemen in the course of the past hundred years and more: 'I shall write to *The Times*' ".

INTRODUCTION

Letters published in *The Times* evoke the atmosphere of a period in a way that newspaper reporting cannot. War-time instructions on how to wear a gas mask, for example, may enlighten a later reader, but a letter from a maladroit correspondent, whose bemusement puts his life potentially at risk, tells us more.

An alien from outer space, or a human revived from a long coma, need read only the 'Letters to the Editor' to appreciate what subjects currently exercise the minds of the British. More than 16,000 letters were published during the war years; many more were submitted. The prevailing impression is of British good-humoured resignation in the face of countless nuisances.

Subjects, as ever, ranged from the trivial to the profound and complex —how to save ink but also grand strategy, the country's economic policy and how best to organise the world after Allied victory, in which outcome no correspondent doubted.

The selection that follows cannot encompass so many and such diverse subjects. Some readers may feel that a number of topics are too insignificant for a period of global tragedy. Yet paradoxically it was precisely the pinprick inconveniences and frustrations that most infuriated the British. To be 'bombed out' was certainly a greater misfortune than having one's letters misdirected, but the former experience was both unavoidable and shared by neighbours and friends, while the latter arose from incompetence and seemingly inconvenienced only oneself.

Thus inconsequential subjects dominated much of the correspondence throughout the war. This pattern emerged early. In May 1940, a correspondent wrote to *The Times* of his amazement and disgust that able-bodied people were still employed in frivolous activities; he particularly cited racing. 'Have they nothing better to do?' he demanded. 'Are we at war?'

A considerable correspondence ensued and, on 28 May, *The Times* published an article under that heading in its Home News page. The article bears reproducing, for it lists some of the 'trivial' matters that preoccupied the British as the war approached its second year. Many of the subjects —trifling and unprofitable employment of labour, bureaucracy, food rationing, waste of paper and other commodities—were to become recurring themes:

ARE WE AT WAR?

Readers continue to press for the stopping of pursuits which they consider inappropriate at this time—horse and greyhound racing, for example, and football pools, which, they state, employ people who might be doing useful productive work, waste paper, and throw unnecessary work on the postal service without helping the national war effort. Those who in these days of paper scarcity have wondered at the continued appearance of some of the more trifling journals produced for women will have noticed that yesterday evening newspapers came into line with morning papers in not issuing contents bills.

Many urge that no one should at this time eat or drink more than is good for him or the country, and there is a widely held view that less sugar should be diverted to the making of alcoholic liquors, especially when little or none may be available for preserving fruit. Unnecessary building, such as the erection of cinemas, is condemned, particularly when there are so many empty showrooms, shops, and offices available. At the same time there is much unemployment in the building industry, and it will be for the new Labour Supply Board to place these idle workers where they can make the contribution each is only too anxious to give.

One instance of wasted effort and transport is to be seen daily all over the country. Perhaps as many as six different milkmen will call each at one or two houses in a short street. There will be a similar abundance of bakers, greengrocers, coalmen, and other tradesmen, and some will be consuming valuable petrol. A pooling of effort seems to be an urgent need here.

Press photographers went the other day to take pictures of the new Minister of Supply, whose controllers keep a strict watch on essential commodities. Mr. Herbert Morrison went on working amid the flashlights, but suddenly paused to ask: "Who controls those bulbs you are wasting? . . . I shall have to make inquiries. . . ."

Inquiries yesterday showed that many shop assistants would gladly be doing something more useful, but dread leaving their families without enough to live on. One said:—"I am buying a small house, and could not possibly keep up the payments to the building society out of Army pay." Others said: "I should not be able to pay the rent and continue other standing payments." Some veterans of the last War, men with the M.M., are holding back from service with the anti-parachutists for similar reasons; they dare not risk losing their jobs as hairdressers, in shops and so on, unless arrangements are made for the security of their families. Many of those who volunteered for service at once have, it seems, heard nothing since.

Many of the younger men engaged in non-essential work are keen to serve, but are waiting their turn. Three waiters at a small restaurant in London yesterday said that they were eager to join the Forces, had registered in March—one for the Navy, one for the R.A.F., and the other for the Army—and were simply waiting to be called up.

A business man said: "We have a big wireless department and employ skilled wireless operators. The manager, aged about 32, saw me last November about joining the R.A.F. and I heartily agreed. After tedious delay he went into the Force as a wireless operator, and I send his wife an allowance of £8 monthly. The first hand was promoted manager, and three months ago he suggested giving his name to the R.A.F. and again I agreed. Again tedious delays, a week at a station, then home again. The man was told he would receive his papers in a short time. So I engaged another manager, but the second one has still not been called up. Meanwhile I am paying an allowance to the wife of the first man, the second is still receiving a manager's salary, and there is a third manager in. A few days ago an assistant in our linen department made application to the R.A.F., and has left to take up duties as a wireless operator; yet the trained wireless operator is still waiting here."

The letters in the following pages have been chosen to reflect the British war-time mood. I hope that collectively they prove redolent for those who lived in the British Isles during that time, enlighten those who did not, and that they may perhaps, now and again, amuse both.

Anthony Livesey
July 1989

1939

THE IMPORTANCE OF
NATIONAL RECREATION

◆

At the outbreak of war, the British Government closed theatres, picture houses and other places of public entertainment. This met—not least from George Bernard Shaw—with an immediate and hostile response.

SEPT. 4

Sir,—Entertainment is necessary to the moral of the people. Crowd psychology is a potent influence. Remember "Are we downhearted?" Remember Sir James Barrie's "Der Tag!" Remember the film *Four Years in Germany*, initiated by the American Ambassador to Berlin. Remember the community songs and singers of soldiers and people. Remember, too, that it is not logical to close theatres and cinemas and to open churches to crowds. None can foresee where bombs will fall and whether by night or day. The people are willing to take them as they come, under ordinary precautions or intermittently extraordinary precautions. While freely acknowledging the efficiency of our system of black-outs, as such, in hiding the country from air-raiders, I submit humbly but with conviction, that complete black-outs, from sunset to sunrise, are excessive; that they should be imposed only when actual air raids are signalled; that the conversion of semi-black-outs into complete ones is quick and easy work, if top lights are at all times obscured; that, without this necessary modification, black-outs are already converting assets into liabilities faster than the enemy could; and, finally, that, with this modification, no lives were lost in theatres during the last war.

Yours truly, OSWALD STOLL
Carlton House, Putney Hill, S.W.

SEPT. 5

Sir,—May I be allowed to protest vehemently against the order to close all theatres and picture-houses during the war? It seems to me a masterstroke of unimaginative stupidity.

During the last War we had 80,000 soldiers on leave to amuse every night. There were not enough theatres for them: and theatre rents rose to fabulous figures. Are there to be no theatres for them this time? We have

15

hundreds of thousands of evacuated children to be kept out of mischief and traffic dangers. Are there to be no pictures for them?

The authorities, now all-powerful, should at once set to work to provide new theatres and picture-houses where these are lacking.

All actors, variety artists, musicians, and entertainers of all sorts should be exempted from every form of service except their own all-important professional one.

What agent of Chancellor Hitler is it who has suggested that we should all cower in darkness and terror "for the duration"?

"Why brother soldiers, why
   Should we be melancholy, boys?"
Faithfully, G. BERNARD SHAW

SEPT. 6

Sir,—I would like to associate myself with Mr. Bernard Shaw, who writes protesting against the order to close theatres and picture-houses. I do not write this because my son is a film producer, but because of my experience in the years of 1914 to 1918. War is not only dangerous but dull, and it is as important to keep civilians amused as it is to keep them occupied. War work and anxiety are exhausting, and for those who have been through the last War—and hardly recovered from it—I think as much diversion as possible is necessary. I would go further, and say that music should be played in the parks and in the streets; nor should mourning be worn for those who have died for their King and for their country.
Yours faithfully, MARGOT OXFORD

SEPT. 6

Sir,—It is not "illogical," as Sir Oswald Stoll suggests, to keep churches open while closing places of entertainment. For the great body of Catholic Christians, whether of the Roman or Anglican Communion, it is not a mere question of "keeping up one's spirits", it is a paramount moral duty to attend Divine Service on days of obligation. Further, services of obligation are held in the daytime, when the task of removing people quickly to shelters or getting them home again is easier than during the hours of evening performances. Later on it will doubtless be found possible to reopen theatres and cinemas at any rate in the daytime. Meanwhile, Christians of all denominations must agree that worship and entertainment are not exactly parallel cases.
Yours faithfully, DOROTHY L. SAYERS, HELEN SIMPSON
24, Great James Street

SEPT. 6

Sir,—I hope that the manufacture of crosswords will be regarded as work of national importance and their ingenious authors not claimed for other service. What a boon they would have been in the last War! What better to fill in the inevitable lacunae of a martial career or the weary hours in hospital? May we ask that henceforth and for "the duration" the clues should rely on wit and not give way overmuch to dictionary references? Perhaps it would be possible to confine lights to the words in "the Little Oxford Dictionary," which, although surprisingly comprehensive, can easily be slipped in the pocket or haversack.—LIEUTENANT-COLONEL H. P. GARWOOD, Hurlingham Court, S.W.

SEPT. 11

Sir,—Although fully appreciating the risk of danger caused by large numbers of people congregating in one place, the case made by several of your correspondents who are urging the necessity for entertainment in time of war is sound.

So far the correspondence has referred mainly to the professional theatre, but I believe the need for national recreation goes further. At this time home-made entertainment, whether of a musical or dramatic nature, has an important part to play.

Considerable experience in recent years has brought me in contact with amateur dramatic activities of all kinds, be it with groups of unemployed people or in rural communities, and the social value of much of this has been proved abundantly. There is still a need for it to-day. In certain areas the need is perhaps greater than ever before.

I am convinced that people (both young and old) in the new reception areas would not find the substitution of a rural for an urban background quite so strange if they could take part in some elementary musical or dramatic activity alongside their new neighbours. Should it be impossible to make any elaborate plans, social evenings of community-singing or improvised drama will help to break down the social difficulties that must occur when a large section of the community is placed in an environment with which it is totally unfamiliar.

Yours faithfully, ROBERT G. NEWTON
Hazelwick Grange, Crawley

Note: Theatres were reopened by Sept. 18 1939. Other sources of entertainment were swiftly identified as providing a vital contribution to the war-winning effort.

OCT. 27

Sir,—Will you permit me, through the medium of your columns, to appeal to other lovers of *The Times* crossword puzzle not to collaborate audibly with friends or neighbours in railway carriages, or announce to their fellow-travellers, unasked, the guesses which they have made? I have little doubt that there are many, like myself, for whom the pleasure of solving the puzzle is almost wholly destroyed if they are given the answer to even a single clue. Yesterday, after vainly trying to stop my ears, I had to withdraw to the corridor with my copy of *The Times* in order to continue the solution of the puzzle without unwanted assistance from two fellow-travellers who were collaborating. The puzzle is so precious a relaxation in these trying days that—selfishly perhaps—I grudge any lessening of the pleasure of solving it, or at any rate trying to do so, on my own.—MR. C. B. COXWELL, Admiralty, S.W.1

NOV. 2

Sir,—May I add a rider to Mr. Coxwell's appeal? Would you also ask other lovers of *The Times* crossword puzzles to print their answers in characters as large as the spaces permit? It is most annoying to sit next to a perfect stranger who feels no difficulties over words which have left one completely stuck, and not be able to read his solution—quite apart from the eye strain imposed.—MR. F. R. MATTHEWS, Twyford, Berks

Note: The Times *had published its first crossword on Feb. 1, 1930 and it proved an instant success.*

ARP

Fear of a German pre-emptive air strike against the British Isles led to numerous measures being taken by order of the Government, ARP (Air Raid Precautions), which were implemented by patrols raised from the civilian population. One, the 'black-out', was thought by many to be imposed with bureaucratic officiousness, often to the risk of life and limb.

SEPT. 9

Sir,—Many "lights o' London" are still showing despite the drastic black-out regulations.

From the roof garden of my house—one of the highest in the West End—I can make an after-dark inspection of London and most of the suburbs. I still see many top-storey lights which are difficult to detect from the streets. Some of them are showing through thin curtains; a few from apparently unprotected windows.

These lights could be seen for miles from an approaching aeroplane and would thus nullify the effect of the black-out.

In the interests of every Londoner I invite any police officer to visit my roof garden after black-out time to locate some of the offenders.

Yours, &c., DECIES

Sir,—The great defect in the present A.R.P. regulations is that no distinction has been drawn between towns and country districts. It is very obvious that different considerations should apply to them, but some of the obvious distinctions I will point out.

Any town forms a possible mark for bombs, and the larger the town the greater the likelihood? In any town there is a chance of crowds collecting, with the consequent possibility of panic. In the case of any bomb falling, either high explosive, gas, or incendiary, the damage might spread easily and rapidly and the destruction of valuable property and heavy loss of life follow.

In the country (on the other hand) things are entirely different. The chance of bombs falling is remote and the likelihood of any individual cottage or haystack being hit is negligible. The damage caused (if damage there is) will be small and quite local.

It follows that the paraphernalia of whistles, bells, rattles, gas masks, and the rest, while advisable in towns, is quite unnecessary in the country. Country people who sleep soundly should be left to sleep, and if a bomb should hit their cottage they may never know it. Fire brigades and first-aid parties should be available.

One final point: How is the distinction to be drawn? I can make only one suggestion. "Built-up areas" are well known and distinctly marked. They might be treated as danger areas and air-raid warnings arranged for them only.

Yours faithfully, WARDEN

Sir,—Assuredly it is time that Air Raid authorities began to cultivate a sense of proportion, or a little sense even. In this remote corner of England the zeal of our wardens is provoking mild disaffection. Seeing that by night trains on the electrified Southern Railway illuminate the whole of our valleys with streaks of lightning, we rustics are not so simple as to suppose that a German aviator, should he have the whimsical notion of entering England by Beachy Head en route for London, would pry out from his lofty station a chink in a blind the size of a sixpence, when his trail was blazed for him by a stream of flashes. Nevertheless, ploughmen and shepherds, eating their suppers after a prolonged day's work, are being harassed and rebuked because a quarter of an inch of light shows beneath the kitchen door or because the blind fails to render the window lower in tone than the side of the house. The wardens themselves, sensible and unpaid, agree with their victims that the whole thing is absurd, but plead instructions from higher authority. And the "higher authority," when discoverable, can think of no better excuse than that he is so pestered by busybodies and informers that he must do something to placate them. Meanwhile, though living in a part of England on which no one in his senses would waste a bomb, solitary ploughboys working in the heart of the Downs and children scaring birds have been warned that they are liable to a fine of 10s. for going to work without gas-masks.

Yours faithfully, CLIVE BELL

Charleston, Firle, Lewes, Sussex

SEPT. 16

Sir,—We wish to protest most emphatically against the failure of many Government Departments with regard to the lighting restrictions.

Civilians in our sector have made, and are making, great efforts to do their part, and have always immediately remedied any defects. It is, therefore, all the more regrettable that the Government offices, particularly those in Great George Street, King Charles Street, and the immediate vicinity, seem to take no trouble to ensure that their windows are light proof.

If we had a lead from them in this respect, civilians in general would be more willing to listen to requests from their wardens.

We are yours faithfully,

R. J. McNALLY, Sector Warden, A. J. GILDROY, CHARLES PROBERT

7, Queen Anne's Gate, S.W.1

SEPT. 21

Sir,—I was very glad to read the protest made by Admiral Dewar against the absurd waste of money and man-power that is being caused by the fantastic preparations that are made to protect us from air raids. The head of a large firm of builders who are doing some trifling repairs for me, informed me to-day that most of his business is disorganized because some of his principal men, who had put down their names for voluntary work, have been called up, and are being kept in idleness as air-raid wardens or auxiliary firemen, while the useful work on which they were engaged has had to be discontinued, and other men are thrown out of work in consequence.

This is by no means a single instance. Everywhere you hear the same story of men and women being taken from their ordinary occupations, even in remote country districts, and walking about night after night with bands round their arms looking out for little chinks of light in order to protect people from possible air raids, most of which, it is safe to say, will never occur.

Air raids, no doubt, are terrible things: but is not this panic fear of them rather deplorable?

I am, &c., PHILIP MORRELL

10, Gower Street, W.C.1

Sir,—It is good to see that a number of weighty protests have been made in your columns against the appalling waste of public money which has been taking place over A.R.P. The trouble started at the beginning, when no difference was made between the scale of preparations in the countryside and in vulnerable areas. During the crisis of September, 1938, the same measures were being taken in the Island of Skye as in London. There has been an improvement in this respect, but it has not gone nearly far enough.

Another cause of waste has been the excessive fear of gas bombardment in country districts. Thousands of pounds have been wasted on useless equipment.

Urged from above, a vast and expensive organization has been set up all over the country, and in every headquarters of local government large staffs have been formed to deal with A.R.P. These vie with one another in putting into force expensive and complicated precautions, the majority of which will probably never be called into use. In a village near here a motor-van with stretchers and a driver stand by continually. In several villages spaced about the district fire-engine stations have been set up, each with its detachment of highly paid firemen. Innumerable telephones are supposed to be manned continually.

Payment of wages of £2 or £3 a week to men to stand about doing nothing is causing noticeable resentment among genuine workers in the country, whose ordinary wages are under £2. Incidentally the same feeling is aroused with regard to the excessive wages which are being paid by contractors to workmen on huts, &c., under construction for the Government in many places.

Most people are agreed that the best air-raid warning for country districts is the sound of our own anti-aircraft gunfire. Based on this premise the whole of our A.R.P. organization outside really important areas should be drastically cut down, especially as regards its paid personnel.

If voluntary unpaid service does not produce what is required, some form of compulsory service under the new National Register should be resorted to. A man can be compelled to go into the trenches, but cannot be compelled to work a fire-engine occasionally, or a telephone.

We certainly cannot afford to go on wasting our substance as we are doing, and carry on a war of exhaustion against the greatest military Power in the world.

I am, Sir, your obedient servant, H. DE PREE
Beckley

Sir,—As one personally interested may I ask you to suggest that all householders should have their chimneys swept at once, and repeat the process every three months? A fire often breaks out at night, and the flames are likely entirely to do away with the black-out.—MR. E. McCONNELL, 9, Roland Gardens, S.W.7

OCT. 27

Sir,—Visitors to the House of Commons are raising the difficulties of getting in touch with their members owing to what many of us consider the absurd system of blacking-out in the Central Hall. This perhaps was not so noticeable when days were longer, but now that daylight is becoming less it will soon be impossible for any caller to see his or her member or for the member to see his caller after 4 o'clock. I can understand the necessity for a reasonable amount of blacking-out, but surely there ought to be sufficient inventiveness to enable a measure of light to be diffused round the barrier where visitors call. Every other room in the House of Commons apparently enjoys complete illumination, but the one place which is available to the public is in absolute darkness, since no one can suggest that the miserable floor lamps which are employed are of any help to anybody.—MR. ROBERT H. MORGAN, M.P., House of Commons, S.W.

OCT. 27

Sir,—Sir John Anderson has stated that all A.R.P. workers are to be provided with a suit, price 11s. As a head warden I can state that in my opinion this is a quite unnecessary extravagance; an armlet plus the badge is all that is necessary. I am quite sure that none of my wardens will ever wear the suit.—MR. J. B. HOARE, Meole Brace Hall, Shrewsbury

---

THE BLACK-OUT

The black-out made life particularly dangerous on the streets and roads. Many accidents occurred—and many suggestions offered on how they might be avoided.

SEPT. 9

Sir,—Would it not be possible to make a regulation that all pedestrians should wear a patch of white in front and at the back, not higher than the waist-line, after dark? Discs of paper, white handkerchiefs, and white belts are within the reach of all.—MR. M. H. LLOYD DAVIES, Orchard Hill, Netherbury, Dorset

---

SEPT. 16

Sir,—Another aspect of A.R.P. precautions is the plight of country doctors whose practices lie in remote areas, far from any strategic or military points likely to be attacked from the air. To ask the doctors to drive their cars along dangerous narrow roads such as one still encounters in many parts of England, Scotland, and Wales with dimmed lamps is unreasonable and unnecessary.

The work of doctors has been increased by the advent of hundreds of evacuated children, especially in the Highlands; and with winter not far off, how can these children be looked after properly if the doctor is compelled to drive at the imminent risk of losing his own life in carrying out his duties? Lighting restrictions, at least for doctors' cars, should be abolished immediately in areas where such are totally unnecessary.

Yours faithfully, M. R. MACKAY

Caerleon

SEPT. 19

Sir,—It has been authoritatively stated that in the first week of war road accidents trebled. If comparison is made with the weekly average of September last year this means that over 400 persons have been killed and between 3,000 and 4,000 seriously injured on the roads of this country.

The announcement of the modification of the lighting restrictions is very welcome, but may I appeal to the Government to go a step further and to restore in some modified form the operation of systems of street lighting that are switch controlled? So long as the present conditions exist, whatever devices are used, the risks of the road at night remain greatly increased for all classes of road users. Provided that the present restrictions on the lighting of buildings are maintained, a small volume of shielded light from street lamps should be sufficient to guide road users, and the lights could be switched off two minutes after an air raid warning had been sounded.

The restoration of street lighting on the lines indicated would probably do more to relieve the nervous strain on the civil population than any other single measure, and unless this is done the reopening of places of entertainment at night can only result in a further increase of street accidents.

Yours faithfully, F. C. FOLEY, Secretary

The Pedestrians' Association, 3, Tudor Street, E.C.4

SEPT. 20

Sir,—When out of doors during the black-out I find it very useful to carry a walking-stick. With it I can walk nearly as quickly and safely as in a lighted street. An occasional touch on walls and fences enables one to keep in the middle of the pavement, and when crossing the road it is easy to find the kerbs. Further, a few taps on the ground when another pedestrian is near gives a quiet but sufficiently audible warning of one's presence.—MR. JOHN DE B. LANCASTER, Courtrai, Evesham Road, Reigate

NOV. 2

Sir,—I read in *The Times* of October 31 the report of an accident in which a motor lorry ran into the rear of a detachment of soldiers marching on the road after dark; apparently eight of them were seriously injured. Having had a similar experience myself, on the first night of the black-out, luckily escaping the accident by inches, I am amazed to find such risks still being allowed to exist. Surely the carrying of a small red light by one of the rear file would at least lessen the chances of such a thing happening? Before long we may need every one who can be trained, yet we are so prodigal with our man-power that we permit similar accidents still to be possible.—MR. J. W. DOHERTY, 140, Harley Street, W.1

NOV. 14

Sir,—The number of pedestrians killed by motor-cars before the war was bad enough: now it is appalling. The chief reason for the present drastic restrictions on vehicular and street lighting is, I presume, to prevent loss of human life in air raids; but it may be gravely doubted if the deaths by such means would, in two months, have resulted in this holocaust caused by the black-out. In fact, the "Safety First" Association reaches the grim conclusion that, in a three years' war, unless things are altered, 40,000 people will have died as a result of this attempt to protect the civil population against enemy aircraft.

It looks as though the remedy may turn out to be worse than the disease. Yours faithfully, J. REID MOIR

NOV. 16

Sir,—Motoring along the Kingston by-pass last night about 6 o'clock I overtook hundreds of cyclists, some of them riding four or five abreast, and perhaps 30 per cent. of them without rear lights. Some, in dark clothes and without lights, crossed in front of me, so close that I avoided them only with difficulty. It was unsafe to drive at more than 10 miles an hour. This experience is only too common.

These cyclists, of course, were not only courting disaster for themselves and creating danger for others, but they were breaking the law. No doubt the police are doing all that they can in the matter, but still scores of cyclists are killed and injured every month, and many motorists and others are killed or hurt in trying to avoid them.

Would it not be possible for employers to help the police in this matter? If all employers would impress upon their workpeople the danger (and the violation of law) involved in cycling without rear lights many accidents might be avoided. If they would go farther and refuse to allow on their premises any cycles not properly provided with rear and front lights, it is probable that quite 95 per cent. of those cyclists who use the roads on these dark nights would be compelled to comply with the law, and many lives would be saved. I suppose an employer would be within his rights in taking such action.

I am aware of the difficulty of obtaining rear lights at present; but if sufficient pressure were brought to bear the shortage would soon be made good.

I am, Sir, yours faithfully, F. G. CREED
24, Dingwall Road, Croydon

NOV. 21

Sir,—If I take my car out at night I hang a very large sheet of white cardboard on the back and on the front of the car. If people cycling on dark roads would hang on their backs a large sheet of cardboard, they would, I think, be very easily seen.—MR. W. HOWARD BADGER, The Union Society, Oxford

---

GAS MASKS

◆

The compulsory carrying of gas masks was thought by some to be imposed by A.R.P. workers with an 'excess of zeal'.

SEPT. 28

Sir,—The Home Office last week issued a statement on the carrying of gas masks recommending that they should be carried only when one was likely to be more than seven minutes' distance from home. Since the issue of this recommendation, there has been in London and its suburbs a marked decrease in the number of those carrying their masks unnecessarily, and in consequence considerably less risk of damage to the masks and their containers.

I have just returned from London to my work at a school situated in a reception area some eight miles from Reading. Here, though I live less than two minutes' distance from my place of work, I am expected by the local air raid Wardens to carry my gas mask at all times to and from school. Here is yet another instance of that excess of zeal on the part of local A.R.P. workers which is rapidly making the nation a laughing-stock. It seems that, while the Home Office is wisely striving to relax its precautionary measures so far as is compatible with public safety, its efforts in this direction are being obstructed by the over-officiousness of local authorities.

I am, Sir, yours faithfully, RONALD WOODHAM

AIR-RAID WARNINGS

◆

*The need for effective warnings to indicate the approach of
enemy bombers was a major problem. The calls of roosting
pheasants came close to solving it.*

NOV. 8

Sir,—It would be interesting to know if any of your correspondents have
noticed any disturbed calling of pheasants at night when aircraft fly over
the woods they are roosting in. During the last War, whenever Zeppelins
flew over the woods in Hertfordshire at night on their way to or from
London the pheasants made such a noise that we always went out to look,
hoping to pick out the Zeppelins against the starry sky.—MR. D. M.
LIGHTBODY, Addiscombe Lodge, Harpenden Road, St. Albans

NOV. 17

Sir,—During night duty in lonely outposts on the fringe of the Thames
Estuary in the Great War I frequently heard the crowing of pheasants
between the bursts of gunfire during air raids. On a number of occasions
restless rooks and cuckoos would also display their respective vocal pro-
clivities, probably for the same reason as the pheasants; but it was the
booming of the first distant gun that shattered the stillness of those
memorable moonlight nights.—MR. G. J. SCHOLEY, 38, Dysart Avenue,
Kingston-on-Thames

Sir,—With reference to Mr. Lightbody's letter, I should like to say that
during the 1914–18 War in East Anglia I noticed that the pheasants in the
neighbouring covers invariably "gave voice" on the approach of Zeppelins:
it appeared to me, from repeated observations, that the pheasants "sensed"
the distant low-pitch vibrations before the human ear (referring only to my
own) recognized the cause.—DR. J. R. WHITWELL, 43, Lancaster Close,
W.2

EVACUATION

◆

*The most disruptive safety measure taken in the first months of
the war was evacuation. Many thousands, mainly children, were*

*removed from British towns and cities (and their families) to be
billeted in 'safe' areas. The results were not always agreeable to
evacuee or host.*

SEPT. 15
Sir,—As an emergency plan for a few weeks the evacuation of all city
children to country homes would be beyond criticism. As a scheme to be
carried through for several years it simply bristles with difficulties.

Take the small middle-class home where the income largely disappeared
from the moment war was declared. Here the billeted children have meals
with the kitchen staff if we are fortunate enough to have one. But we cannot
feed our maids on 8s. 6d. a week per head. The children must have the same
food, and they eat more.

But our kitchen staff has probably gone home either because their own
mothers have children billeted on them, or they do not like the extra work in
our homes. Many of us are either elderly, not overstrong, or busy with our
own small children, and unable to do the extra work of cooking, cleaning,
washing, and mending, unable to afford the extra expenses and the wear
and tear to our homes and gardens for more than a short time. Yet many
fathers of evacuated children are in good jobs and the mothers are now free
to go out to work. Might not the broadcast appeals to the charitable public
for clothing, also remind the parents to do their share at any rate in this
respect?

Then, where the mothers are billeted with smaller children, in some cases
they do not lift a finger to help, and expect to have everything done for
them, and the women naturally dislike being in other people's houses. The
teachers, too, are not at all easy or contented.

Now that the children are safely out of the cities, is it not possible to
organize empty houses as camps, with teachers, mothers, and children
running them themselves with voluntary helpers? Happy billets could be
left undisturbed, but a heavy burden would be lifted from many homes
where the strain of living is already great.

Yours, &c., E. M. CURTIS

Alton House, Redhill

SEPT. 11
Sir,—May I suggest that all we who have evacuees in our villages should
take this great opportunity of giving instruction to the mothers in simple
cookery, hygiene, &c.? It is a lamentable fact to find so many of these
mothers devoid of any sense as regards the care and feeding of their
children.—MISS VIOLET E. OATES, Gestingthorpe Hall, Castle Hedingham,
Essex

Sir,—While from all my friends in the country comes praise of many town-children evacuees—and, without exception, praise of all the secondary schoolchildren—complaints are pouring in about the half-savage, verminous, and wholly illiterate children from some slums who have been billeted on clean homes. Stories with which one cannot but sympathize are told of mattresses and carpets polluted, of wilful despoliation and dirt that one would associate only with untrained animals. The authorities, with plenty of time to prepare, seem to have failed both in the physical and psychological examination of the evacuees, although the mechanics of the great trek have been so well ordered.

Now one hears that both women and children of the roughest and uncleanest types are going back to their own "homes." At the present time, when Britain is fighting for liberty, no Briton would suggest dictatorship methods, but surely something short of these can be evolved to prevent these unfortunate children from being allowed to return to the appalling conditions whence they have been rescued. It is not fair that they should disrupt small houses; but is it not possible to cause (to coin a phrase) grass orphanages, under the care of skilled and sympathetic teachers, to come into being? Let the mothers go back if they will. It does not matter so much what happens to adults, but surely children should not be allowed to go back to conditions which shame a nation fighting for civilization.

In the course of my work I have, in the last few years, attended many trials at the Central Criminal Court, and am nearly always horrified by the low physical and mental standards of the accused persons. Stunted, misshapen creatures, only capable of understanding the very simplest language and quite incapable of thought, moved by impulses at the best sentimental, at the worst brutal. During a trial when accused and witnesses are of this sub-human sort, it is as though a flat stone in the garden had been raised and pale, wriggling things, that had never seen the light, were exposed. No one who knows anything of criminal courts would contradict me.

These children, of whom the country residents so reasonably complain, are bound to grow up into just such sub-human savages, unless we seize this opportunity of saving them. I do not, of course, say that all crime is due to the appalling conditions in which most men and women who find their way to our courts live when young—there have been several trials in the last two years which have shown that men, who have had every advantage in youth, can be brutal, treacherous, and base. But I do say that no child, who has not been shown the rudiments of decency, and in whom imagination has not been encouraged, stands a chance of being a good and happy citizen.

War has lifted the flat stone—these disgraces to our educational system have been forced out into the light. Do not let us, even though a certain amount of arbitrary arrangements may be needed, let them creep back beneath their stone. This is, and I repeat it with every emphasis of passion at my command, an opportunity which, if we miss it, we do not deserve to have given to us again.

Yours faithfully, F. TENNYSON JESSE

11, Melina Place, N.W.8

OCT. 5

Sir,—The second wave of evacuation is about to break, so may I suggest that not only—as Lord Dorchester recommended the other day—should more common sense be applied to A.R.P. in general, but a greater sense of proportion to evacuation in particular?

The arrangement is voluntary and no one is forced to send his children. But my own and other local experience suggests that evacuation authorities should explain to parents that good manners are the least return they can make for the very real effort and unselfishness on the part of householders of all conditions—especially in houses where there is a trained and often reduced domestic staff and where extra work has been cheerfully undertaken and where children live on a scale above the weekly 8s. 6d. and generally above their own home standard. They are, after all, on the footing of guests, and it is no bad training in the spirit of cooperation and good fellowship so vital to our future to behave as such and to remember that houses where children are billeted are private houses, which cannot be entered, inspected, and criticized without at least some reference to the owner.

I think I am not alone in feeling that those parents who for reasons of impatience or prejudice take their children back must not claim re-evacuation at the taxpayers' expense.

Yours faithfully, BEATRIX CROFTON

Berwick St. John Manor, Wilts

DOMESTIC MEASURES

◆

The need to economise became quickly apparent. Suggestions proliferated for re-using envelopes, saving domestic electricity and gas with 'haybox' cookery and avoiding nutritional waste by preparing potatoes in their 'jackets'.

OCT. 6

Sir,—We are asked to save paper. In the last War gummed labels and strips were available to make possible the re-use of old envelopes. Many people receive quantities of gummed half-penny envelopes through the post containing circulars, bills, and receipts. A., B., and C. are three correspondents; let them each collect these envelopes in packets of 25; A. sends his to B. and C.; B. sends to A. and C.; C. sends to A. and B. Thus all three have ready addressed envelopes for use when corresponding with each other. The packets of envelopes (with any number of addresses) can be covered with a slip of paper with the name of addressee in block letters for easy reference; a kind of card-index box can be easily made out of the numerous cardboard boxes which nearly every one has, and the packets stored in this.—MISS OLAVE N. PALMES, The Mount, Witley

---

OCT. 21

Sir,—In the drive against waste I wonder if the waste-paper baskets of the mushroom departments which spring up as a result of war will have a watchful eye turned upon them? Throughout the last War I worked in a department manned by a temporary clerical staff, which, intoxicated by the easy lavishness of supplies, squandered the products of the Stationery Office wholesale, blithely filling its waste-paper baskets with the results of careless work. It was no uncommon thing to see five or more carbon copies, complete with fresh carbons of exquisite quality, ripped from a machine and hurled into the nearest basket, for one typing error. It was not until the start of the third year of war that the iron hand of authority descended upon us.—MRS. JOHN RIDGE, Les Hêches, St. Peters, Guernsey

---

OCT. 5

Sir,—Cooking potatoes in their jackets may be an economy from the point of view of food, but such cooking takes longer and is not, therefore, an economy as regards fuel. Those of us who do all our cooking by gas or electricity are properly between the devil and the deep. I believe that fuel economy can be effected by cooking certain dishes, such as porridge or stews, in a haybox, but I have no idea how to construct a haybox nor how long the various dishes take to cook.—MRS. D. M. SILVER, 57, Brancaster Lane, Purley, Surrey

---

OCT. 10

Sir,—With reference to Mrs. D. M. Silver's inquiry, this form of cooking is on the same principle as the thermos flask—*i.e.* insulation to conserve heat. Hayboxes are easily made with a stout wooden box with no open cracks and a good lid, the box measuring not less than 3ft. by 3ft. by 2ft. wide. Line the box with several layers of stout newspapers covered with brown paper. Fill the box half full of hay, making wells or spaces in the hay to contain the cooking vessels. Each vessel must fit exactly, as even small empty spaces involve loss of heat; each vessel must also have a tight fitting lid and no lip. Food should be partly cooked and the vessel then transferred to the well made in the hay and covered immediately with cushions made with hay. Leave no empty spaces but fill up with hay (preferably in cushions). The lid of the box must fit well and be fastened down either with clasps or with weights. Food cooked for roughly a third of the usual time and transferred to a haybox will be perfectly cooked in three to four hours. The contents of each vessel must be boiling before it is transferred to the haybox, and each vessel must be as full as possible, otherwise the air-space results in cooling of contents. Porridge can be left overnight and brought to boiling point next morning.—MISS ELEANOUR SINCLAIR ROHDE, Cranham Lodge, Reigate, Surrey

NOV. 2

Sir,—When hay cannot be had newspaper makes an efficient substitute. Tear the paper in pieces about the size of a pocket handkerchief, crumple it, and pack the box tightly with it, leaving a nest to fit the saucepan or stewpan intended to be used. A thick, flat layer of newspaper should be placed over the stewpan, and over it a cover of felt or blanketing; then shut the lid. All this should be done as quickly as possible to avoid loss of heat.—LADY STEPHEN, Hale, Fordingbridge, Hants

OCT. 6

Sir,—May I add the useful point that the "noses" of the potatoes to be boiled in their jackets should be cut, so that the salt may the better penetrate, thus greatly enhancing the natural flavour of the potato.—MISS SARAH A. WHITE, Birchenholt, Crowthorne, Berks

OCT. 17

Sir,—If a thin strip of peel is taken round the potato at its greatest length, the two elliptical pieces of skin remaining are easily removed after boiling. The mealiness is unimpaired and the salt penetrates.—MRS. MARY WID-DOWSON, Kingswood Training School, near Bristol

NOV. 6

Sir,—In connexion with your recent article about a use for dead michael-mas daisy stems, it may interest your readers to know that these, when dry, make first class kindling wood. This I learned in Germany a good many years ago and have gratefully practised it ever since.—LADY PENTON, Wyke House, Walton-on-the-Hill

THE AESTHETICS OF WAR

A further economic proposal—to do away with municipal flower beds—fell on stony ground. Indeed, some felt that certain unsightly defensive measures should be aesthetically en-ʰ⸱nced.

OCT. 28

Sir,—I have read with regret that it is proposed to do away with the flower-beds in a number of the public parks in our big cities, owing to the shortage of labour.

Is this not a job which could be undertaken by the Girl Guide Association and other such junior organizations? It may well be found on consideration to be of national importance: the provision of some colour and beauty will surely have much influence on the moral of those who, owing to their work, have to remain in the cities, and all such aids to moral may become increasingly necessary within the next few months.

It must also be remembered that drastic restrictions are bound to cause much hardship among many unfortunate tradesmen, most of whom have already enough loss of custom to face.

I am, Sir, yours faithfully, GUENDOLEN WILKINSON
8, Queen Anne Street, Cavendish Square, W.1

NOV. 3

Sir,—Cannot some steps be taken to improve the present squalid appearance of the main streets caused by the protective coverings of the pavement lights? In many cases these consist of sprawling piles of rotting sandbags, a danger to pedestrian and a source of damp. May I suggest that these be replaced by wooden boxes, creosoted internally and painted on the outside? They could then be filled with the sand and earth from the displaced sandbags, thus forming large window boxes. With sufficient cross members dividing them into compartments, these should prove fully as strong and considerably more permanent than sandbags, besides providing surfaces on which a touch of cheerful colour might be introduced.—MR. G. L. CADELL

OFFICIAL MEASURES

The sheer number of emergency regulations introduced by the government produced some confusion.

OCT. 9

Sir,—In his letter published in your issue of yesterday Major H. N. Robertson attacks the "blind and pompous folly of inflated functionaries" at our seaports; but we must give them their due, for they can show a fine and devastating contempt for our great enemy.

I landed at Folkestone at the beginning of this week, and after waiting two hours in a queue to have my passport examined I had my baggage searched. I was deprived of my Dutch grammar, my Homer and Horace in the original, a book of reproductions of Dutch paintings and another of Utrillo, my personal diary, my address-book, Ludecke's attack on the Führer, "I knew Hitler," and Sinclair Lewis's "It Can't Happen Here," which I had bought to read on my journey. All this dangerous literature, together with a half-exposed film which I was made to take out of my camera, was sent to the Chief Censor at Liverpool, and I was reassuringly told that I would probably get it back if I applied to him. But "Mein Kampf," the German edition, was left with me, with a proud disdain for Hitler's persuasive powers which augurs ill for the Nazi cause!

Incidentally, such activities as this may be damaging to our self-respect. You published towards the beginning of the war a letter from a learned reader who had delved into his Tacitus and discovered some satisfyingly wholesale condemnations of the German character (though Mr. Chamberlain has told both countries that our quarrel is not with the German people, but with the Nazi Government). But, after all, two can play at that game, and if these ridiculous restrictions come to German ears, some equally learned Nazi might delve into his still unconfiscated Horace and write to the *Voelkischer Beobachter* to denounce us as "Britannos hospitibus feros." Which would be mortifying for us, wouldn't it?

I am, Sir, your obedient servant, H. M. THRELFALL

Grosvenor Hotel, S.W.1

OCT. 30

Sir,—If there are regulations for the carrying of cameras in built-up areas of no military importance, should not they be made known? One afternoon recently my wife and I were walking from our home to Bournemouth through the residential district of Branksome Park. Opposite a bus station a man came up in plain clothes and from his cycle said to my wife: "I want you. I have been observing you for the past 15 minutes. I am a police officer. You are carrying a camera in a prohibited area." My wife was carrying over her shoulder in a leatherette case a small "popular" camera. I immediately had my solicitors write the police for explanation and there the matter rests at the moment. But it appears that regulations on the carrying of cameras should be made known throughout the country forthwith, otherwise many innocent persons will have to face, as we did, the annoyance and degradation of being questioned by the police in public places.—MR. J. ERIC PUTNAM, Westdene, Canford Cliffs Road, Westbourne

OCT. 31

Sir,—I read with admiring wonder that the Customs are soon to announce a scheme under which the minimum number of duty-free cigarettes allowed in a single parcel sent to a soldier in France will be reduced from 2,500–3,000 to 1,000. Such sympathetic official condescension is sure to be gratefully appreciated by the vast majority of private soldiers' wives, who will then, of course, be able to send regular 25s. parcels out of their weekly allowance of 17s.—MR. SIMPSON STOKES, 156 Park Road, W.4

HORSES, WIVES AND BATS

Throughout the war, correspondents found occasion to write, and The Times *space to print, letters on inconsequential matters. Early subjects included concern for homesick horses, the sale of wives and suggestions on how to remove bats from barns.*

HOMESICK HORSES   OCT. 28

Sir,—I was interested in your story of the homesick Belgian horse, because, years ago, I had to leave my old home, and Tommy my pony had to go, too. He was sold to a friend, miles away, where he would have a good home; but Tommy was homesick, and the very next morning he was discovered quietly grazing in his own field. It was always a mystery how he escaped, and made the journey without being seen, and how he managed to get back into his own field, which had good hedges and a strong gate.—MRS. CECIL SANDWITH, 26, Canynge Square, Bristol, 8

NOV. 2

Sir,—May I cap the tales about the homing instinct in horses by one which can be guaranteed by several people to be true? A mare we sold at Nanoose Bay, Vancouver Island, from a ranch on a promontory in Puget Sound, to a buyer at Wellington, a small mining settlement 14 miles away, quickly returned, making her way along the track through bush country and actually swimming across the narrow end of the bay, so saving herself further miles round by the road-track. A cow we sold to the same place returned in a similar way, also swimming the end of Nanoose Bay and scrambling up the bank. But this cow had a calf left at the place she had been sold to—and we received a bill for milk consumed by the calf in its mother's absence!—MRS. SCARBOROUGH JOHNSON, Hydro Hotel, Eastbourne

---

NOV. 7

Sir,—May I, in turn, cap the tale about the homing instinct of horses in your issue of November 2? Before the last War I was farming in Saskatchewan, and as part of my stock bred about 80 Clydesdales. When winter arrived in November, I, in common with other farmers, turned out to graze all those horses not required for winter work. The undisputed "boss" of the "bunch" was a 14.2 bronco mare. She would lead them to a stamping ground some 40 miles away, where they would paw the snow to reach the abundant supply of "prairie wool." About the middle of March she would lead them home, all with long shaggy coats and butter feet. I did not brand my horses, but never lost one.—MR. H. S. COTTERILL, Junior Army and Navy Club, Horse Guards Avenue, S.W.1

NOV. 9

Sir,—I knew a mare bred on the Kamloops Ranch, B.C., belonging to the Canadian Western Ranching Company, which was taken to their Gang Ranch over 150 miles up-country, necessitating the swimming of two rapid rivers. This mare returned on her own account in less than six months to the Kamloops Ranch.—MR. W. WHITEHEAD, 3, Copthall Court, Throgmorton Street, E.C.2

SALE OF A WIFE
OCT. 18

Sir,—In the little notice of Weyhill Fair in *The Times* a reference was made to the sale of a wife. As a living link with the past I might perhaps be allowed to say that when I was rector of Dodbrooke, Devon, in 1882, I knew an old lady there who told me that, as a young woman, she had been led into Tavistock Market with a rope round her neck by her husband and sold to another man for 2s. 6d., the recognized way in those days of settling matrimonial matters of that kind.—CANON A. F. NORTHCOTE, Parklands, Bradninch, Devon

---

OCT. 24

Sir,—In "The Churchwardens' Presentments of the Oxfordshire Peculiars of Dorchester, Thame and Banbury," which cover the period of 1620–1770, there are two cases of husbands disposing of their wives to others. One man sold his wife at 2¼d. a pound, and the sum paid was 29s. 0½d. (155lb., or 11st. 1lb.!). These presentments were formal complaints made by parish authorities to the Bishop or Archdeacon at his visitation.—MR. ALBERT WADE, 8, Brydeck Avenue, Penwortham, near Preston

OCT. 27
Sir,—In the autumn of 1852 a man led his wife into the market at
Aylesford, near Maidstone, with a rope round her neck and sold her for
half-a-crown. My sister knew the woman, who continued to live in the
village. It would be interesting to know how far west the practice extended,
and the latest recorded date of such a transaction.—THE REV. H. P. BETTS,
Upper Durford, Petersfield

OCT. 31
Sir,—In reply to Mr. Betts's query, this practice seems to have continued to
our own day. In "English Folklore," by A. R. Wright (Benn, 1928), a whole
list of cases are given. Thus the Leeds magistrates had evidence in 1926 of
the sale of a wife for £10, apparently with her full consent. And in May,
1928, there was a similar case at Blackwood (Mon). The husband said he
did not sell his baby "because it was my own flesh and blood."—MISS
CICELY M. BOTLEY, Guidables, 17, Holmesdale Gardens, Hastings

OCT. 31
Sir,—I was much interested in the letters which have appeared on this
subject. A far more modern case can be quoted. I often met a man on the
roads in our village about 1900, and was told he sold his wife, who was so
little esteemed that a pair of boots had to be thrown in to make the bargain
of far greater value.—MISS SYLVIA M. WOOD, Steeple Ashton

BATS IN THE BARN   OCT. 23
Sir,—Can any of your readers tell me how to get rid of bats? I have a Tudor
barn, and for the last 2½ years they have become troublesome, making it
impossible to store odd furniture, &c. Fumigating would not be of any use
on account of the many crevices in the wooden structure and the thatch
roof.—MR. E. DONNISON, Dibleys, Blewbury, Berks

OCT. 26
Sir,—It was interesting to me to read the request of one of your correspondents as to how to get rid of bats, because I once experienced the same
trouble. Some years ago, when I was living somewhere near the Equator,
bats made sleep impossible by spending much of their time between the roof
of the house and the ceiling of my bedroom. I fixed near the respective
entrances branches from a thorn tree. The bats flew against them, got
pricked, and found a home elsewhere. Your correspondent may be able to
apply a similar remedy by driving long pins through thin slats of wood and
hanging them where necessary.—MR. W. ADDISON, Victoria Hotel, Deal,
Kent

Sir,—There are two methods worth trying to rid one's house of the bat nuisance. One was described in *The Times* of October 26—that is, find out their exits and entrances and cover these holes with bunches of prickly thorns. Another, and perhaps more satisfactory way, is to let in light; this can be done by making 6in. diameter holes along the eaves, covering the holes with wire, and fixing a light in the roof by means of a louvre, sky-lights, or glass tiles.—MR. H. J. H. STEDMAN, Hyde Barton, Winchester

Sir,—Would it not be possible to dislodge the bats first and then use the spray (as used by Mr. A. L. Howard) to prevent them from returning to the roof? It seems a pity to destroy the bats, especially as they eat so many insects, &c.—MRS. E. C. MOULE, Junior School, Weymouth College, Dorset

KILTS AND CASUALTIES

Many writers were concerned that kilts, generally worn by Scottish soldiers, offered fertile breeding grounds for pediculus vestimenti, *the body louse so vexatious to First World War troops in the trenches.*

Sir,—The division in which I served as a chaplain during the War of 1914–18 contained two kilted battalions. I noted that during the winter of 1917–18, when we were for over four months in the mud of Passchendaele, all the senior officers of these battalions wore breeches in the line. And I remember well how the commanding officer and the adjutant of one of them told me that they ascribed much of the sickness in their battalion to the wearing of the kilt by men who were unaccustomed to its use in peace-time (which at that stage of the War meant the vast majority).—CANON E. L. MARSDEN, The Vicarage, Grimsby, Lincs.

Sir,—In support of the wearing of the kilt on active service, as raised by Sir Ian Malcolm of Poltalloch, it may be of interest to give my experience during the last War. A battalion of The London Scottish, whose members always wore kilts, was a unit of the 60th Division, which saw service in France, Macedonia, Egypt, and Palestine, and although I have not now the exact statistics available I can safely say that I, who had medical charge of that division, always looked upon The London Scottish Battalion as the most healthy unit in the whole division. Moreover, these men were London Territorials, who never wore kilts in civil life.—COLONEL E. B. DOWSETT, Thames Eyot, Twickenham

---

NOV. 22

Sir,—I hope it will not be considered impertinent of a mere southerner to take part in the interesting correspondence in *The Times* about the kilt. I venture to do so because there is another side of the question which should be ventilated, even at the risk of being considered indelicate. May I be personal for a moment?

During the late Great War it was the writer's unique privilege to hold the rank of Rat Officer to the Second Army of the B.E.F. in France. His activities were not however entirely devoted to the theoretical and practical extermination of trench rats. Occasionally other tasks came his way.

One day a large wooden crate arrived from the War Office. On prising open the lid it was discovered to contain a quantity of garments—gents' underwear—and with them emerged a peculiar odour of chemicals. The crate was shortly followed by official instructions. In these it was explained that the vests and pants had been impregnated with certain poisonous chemicals which were thought to be fatal to the body louse—*pediculus vestimenti*—the scourge of all armies.

It was the interesting duty allotted to the present writer to carry out experiments with these garments. A small camp of bell tents was erected not too near to Poperinghe, and then came the question of obtaining the human subjects for the experiment. First of all 12 volunteers, without lice, were asked for from an infantry battalion in the line. Most of the battalion volunteered, and after some close scrutiny 12 were selected, guaranteed free from infection. Then 12 thoroughly lousy soldiers were indented for, and 12 kilted Highlanders reported themselves at the camp. These heroes in the cause of science, who were to wear the underclothes, had not been selected; they happened to be the first 12 numbered off by the sergeant-major.

The experiment proved interesting if futile, but this is neither the place nor the time to enter into details. The point is that every kilted soldier in the trenches was thoroughly lousy, not, let it be clearly stated, through any fault of his own, but of the pleats of his kilt, which made ideal lurking places for the loathsome parasites, from which safe retreats it was impossible for the unwilling host to evacuate them.

Once again, Sir, I apologize for dwelling on so repellent a subject in the

columns of *The Times*, but we all must bravely face what the late Professor A. E. Shipley termed "the Minor Horrors of War."
Yours, &c., PHILIP GOSSE
Steyning, Sussex

NOV. 23

Sir,—My experience as medical officer to a Territorial battalion of The Seaforth Highlanders in the Great War is the reverse of Canon Marsden's. The rate of sickness was very small, and the general health of the men under all conditions was as good as any of the non-kilted regiments. It is difficult to see why the kilt should now be banned when the war is likely to be fought under circumstances similar to the last. The under-garments and long hose tops are a protection against gas. And the kilt has a definite psychological effect on the Highlander in particular. It is a manly dress, historic and romantic, and it is the dress of his forefathers who were a brave fighting race.—DR. M. R. MACKAY, Caerleon, Newport

---

NOV. 25

Sir,—In contrast to that of Colonel Dowsett, my experience as medical officer to a Highland Division on the Western Front, 1915–18, led me to disapprove of the kilt for active service for two reasons. (*a*) During six months of the year sick parades included cases of chilblains of varying degrees of severity, and of chafing and excoriation by the hem, wet with mud around the knee. Healing was a slow process and entailed many days of light duty. (*b*) Difficulty in delousing the many pleats. Much time was spent on this task in rest billets, until provision of an ironing room was made at the Divisional baths.—MR. P. WITHERS GREEN, 5, Cheyne Gardens, S.W.3

NOV. 27

Sir,—In the manuscript journal kept by Colonel Malcolm Fraser, then a lieutenant in the 78th Foot (Fraser's Highlanders) during the operations before Quebec, 1759 to 1760, the following details are given under date December 20: "The winter is becoming insupportably cold. . . . The garrison in general are but indifferently cloathed, but our regiment in particular is in a pityful situation, having no breeches, and the Phillibeg is not at all calculated for this terrible climate. Colonel Fraser is doing all in his power to provide trousers for them, and we hope soon to be on a footing with other regiments in this respect." It is known that the nuns in the Ursulines Convent in Quebec knitted homespun stockings for the regiment.—CAPTAIN R. V. STEELE, Penrhyn Lodge, Gloucester Gate, N.W.1

Sir,—If Dr. Gosse had had to deal with men from a regiment dressed not in the kilt but in its original, the belted plaid, he would have found no lice. This is the genuine Highland dress. It consisted of as many yards as accorded with the wearer's taste and means, of saffron linen.

About the end of the fifteenth century, woollen material woven in the patterns now called tartan replaced the linen. As much as 24 yards of material is recorded as a chief's wear. The length was pleated under the owner's belt, leaving a lot of material falling outside the belt, which was drawn on to the wearer's shoulders and was used as cloak and hood when required.

On going into bivouac the belt was released, the man rolled himself in his plaid, and slept warmly. In bitter winds the plaid was soaked in the nearest burn and made a cold compress, through which no wind could get. Troops so clothed were notoriously healthy. A fine, sunny day and the plaids spread out to sun—a bitter winter wind and the plaid well soaked—a good shake every morning—what louse could stand it?

The belted plaid is ideal for soldiers. It takes but a moment to take on or off; it is cloak, leg clothing, and blanket in one. It will outlast dozens of pairs of trousers and several kilts. It is comfortable, sanitary, and the handsomest of all male dresses.

As usual primitive simplicity is better than civilized complexity. There is an old German print of the days of the 30-year war showing Mackay's Highlanders in belted plaids, with a legend explaining that these Scots troops could march 70 miles in a night. They could and did, at a run, which they could not have done in trousers or modern kilts.

Yours faithfully, M. M. HALDANE
2, Plantin House, Ashford, Kent

GLOVES AND FLANNELS

◆

Re-using old materials for novel purposes was a recurring theme. Turning gloves into waistcoats receive a more enthusiastic response, however, than making hot-water bottle covers from cricketers' flannel trousers.

Sir,—As a lifelong reader of *The Times* I venture to bring to your notice an appeal I am making for old kid and other leather gloves, of any colour, to be made into wind-proof waistcoats. These were much appreciated by the men on the East Coast defences and other exposed places during the Great War.

I should be grateful to any readers who will send me their old gloves for this purpose.—MISS ETHEL A. PURCELL, Glebe Lodge, Blackheath, S.E.3

Sir,—You were good enough to insert a letter from me in *The Times* of November 6 appealing for old gloves to be made into wind-proof waistcoats. I write now to thank you and to tell you that the response has surpassed my expectations. I have already received over 500 pairs of gloves, several old golfing and leather coats, and some parcels of cuttings from leather-work—all most useful for my purpose. My friends and I hope to make many waistcoats as a result.—MISS ETHEL A. PURCELL, Glebe Lodge, Blackheath, S.E.3

DEC. 12

Sir,—Now that cricket is out of season there must be many pairs of flannel trousers which will not be needed. A member of my detachment has made most excellent covers for hot-water bottles for hospitals from the legs of grey and white flannels. Hundreds of these are required, and ladies can help British Red Cross supplies in this way.—MRS. E. B. CHILDS, Commandant, East Croydon and Addiscombe Division, British Red Cross Society

---

DEC. 16

Sir,—May I protest against flannel trousers, of any colour, being cut up into hot-water bottle covers, as suggested in your issue of December 12. They have only to be repaired or remodelled to be a godsend to destitute Polish refugees, and there are also thousands of British settlers in Canada, whose wheat crop has again failed, who would be thankful for such garments for any age. The address of the Polish Relief Fund is 10, Grosvenor Place, S.W.1. Clothes for Canada should be sent to the Maple Leaf Fellowship, 63, Tufton Street, S.W.1.—MISS C. H. WASHINGTON, Lolmans, Jarvis Brook, Crowborough, Sussex.

THE END OF THE *GRAF SPEE*

◆

Following a successful rampage through Allied merchant shipping in the South Atlantic and Indian Oceans, the German pocket battleship Graf Spee was severely damaged by a British cruiser force off the River Plate estuary on Dec. 13, 1939. She then found herself trapped in Montevideo harbour, where she

*sought refuge in neutral waters. To avoid the ignominy of being
sunk by the enemy, the* **Graf Spee** *was scuttled on Hitler's
orders on Dec. 17. Many sanguine correspondents took this as a
conclusive sign that Hitler had already lost all hope of winning
the war.*

DEC. 20

Sir,—Two features of the ignominious end of the Admiral Graf Spee
—which were doubtless the subject of express instructions—seem to
indicate that the enemy Government, in choosing that particular end, was
actuated by despair:—

(1) If the ship had submitted to internment, Germany would have been
entitled to resume possession of her if and when Germany won the war. Is
it, therefore, too much to infer that the German Government despair of
winning the war?

(2) If the ship had steamed out courageously and had magnificently
risked battle, there was at least the bare possibility that, with her great
speed, she might have got away. Is it, therefore, too much to infer that the
inconceivable audacity which drove her into Montevideo harbour, also
drove the Government for which she fought to despair of her success—even
in running away!

What would Nelson not have done in command of the Graf Spee! War
not being a sport, we are encouraged by every fresh instance of the enemy's
despair; especially despair of fastening on us "the evil thing" for which he
fights.

Yours, &c., HECTOR HUGHES
1, Garden Court, Temple, E.C.4

———————————

DEC. 20

Sir,—Surely the most significant implication of the scuttling of the Admiral
Graf Spee on Herr Hitler's direct order is its evidence that the Führer now
no longer hopes for victory in the war? Had he expected to win, he would
have told the captain of his finest pocket battleship to submit to internment
for the duration, if escape was impossible. That course would have
preserved the ship for Germany to recover at the end of the conflict. That
instead of this he ordered her to be scuttled, proves he has virtually
abandoned hope of triumph, and anticipates the end of the struggle will see
any interned German naval vessels appropriated by the enemy; hence this
somewhat premature imitation of the Scapa Flow incident of June 21,
1919.

For us the tattered hulk off Montevideo is a happy augury of ultimate
success. Cannot its implications be "put across" in our foreign broadcasts
with something of the vigour and forcefulness with which, had the case

been reversed, one can imagine "Lord Haw-Haw" dealing with this admission of despair by the enemy?
Yours, &c., MALCOLM THOMPSON
27, Willow Road, Hampstead, N.W.3

DEC. 28

Sir,—It may not be known to all of your readers that the German wireless belied in advance the horrid scurrility in regard to the dead of the Graf Spee which is now being put abroad by the German News Agency. Listeners on Friday or Saturday night heard a description of the funeral broadcast from Hamburg and Bremen according to which the route was lined throughout by sorrowing and sympathetic inhabitants of Montevideo who were declared to have made many manifestations of sympathy. That being so it would have been quite impossible for anyone to have carried out the outrages mentioned.—MR. DONALD M. O'CONNOR, Lincoln House, 2, Red Post Hill, S.E.21

GERMAN RULERS AND PEOPLE

Many correspondents sought to understand the enemy's mind and account for the fanaticism of German youth.

OCT. 30

Sir,—I appreciate the courteous letter of Lord Horder in your issue of October 21, and agree with much of it, especially as to the importance of a study of the psychology of the German people (a large subject!), but I cannot admit any inconsistency in my praise of Herr Hitler's services to the German nation which appeared in your columns two years ago and my psychological analysis of his character which you published last week. The hysterical and paranoid tendencies which I now mention were apparent in Hitler's mental make-up years ago—in my opinion—and could be identified on careful study in his book and in his broadcast speeches—not to mention his personal interviews with friends and foes, which could not be kept entirely secret. But these tendencies are not incompatible with great gifts of oratory and exhortation, of leadership and organization, especially if the followers are themselves in an abnormal mental condition, as were the German people at the end of the last War—so changed from the people such as I knew in my student days in Germany over 30 years ago.

Even in the manifestations of full-blown paranoia the development of the *Wahnsystem*, or delusional system, proceeds "with complete preservation of clearness in thinking, willing, and acting" (Kraepelin), and in the more widespread but less serious "paranoid tendency" the individual's mental clearness and vigour persist unimpaired. It is the later development of fanatical self-confidence and megalomania which can bring catastrophe and pull down what has been so brilliantly and skilfully built up.

The overt error of judgment and the political false step, in Herr Hitler's case, occurred last March, with the annexation of Bohemia and Moravia, and I endeavoured in my letter of October 19 to give a psychological explanation of his turning to Russia at that time (although not known to us until August), in spite of his strong anti-Communist complex. I think a psychological explanation of his own action then is required, even though I agree with Lieutenant-Commander Elwell-Sutton that there has always been a group in Germany in favour of a pact or an actual alliance with Russia.

Of course I am speaking only for myself in my brief analysis of Herr Hitler's character and I do not pose as a representative of any school or section of British psychologists in this matter. I have been fortunate in obtaining reliable private information through friends and acquaintances over a number of years which has supplemented and illumined the evidence accessible to the general public.

Finally, may I add that I do not give a diagnosis of Herr Hitler's personality. That is only possible, in the case of anyone, after a period of close personal observation.

Yours faithfully, WILLIAM BROWN
The Athenaeum, Pall Mall, S.W.1

DEC. 1

Sir,—Dr. Edwyn Bevan, in his thoughtful letter in your issue of November 28, omits one sad but all-important consideration. I am in continuous contact with Germans in this country, many of them of the civilized and liberal-minded type he describes, but one and all agree in saying that it is the young people who are Hitler's most enthusiastic supporters. There are probably some 13,000,000 young Germans between the ages of 16 and 24 to whom Hitler is God, Himmler is his prophet, and the noblest task of a good Nazi is to beat up Jews and anti-Nazis in a concentration camp. Thirteen million young fanatics take a deal of crushing, but until they have learnt their lesson there is no hope of a reasonable Germany. And that is why this war will be long and bitter.

I am, &c., GEORGE R. CLERK
Turf Club, W.1

DEC. 5

Sir,—I was interested in that portion of Field-Marshal Lord Milne's speech in the House of Lords in which he said, "We are said not to be fighting the

German people. That is a very dangerous theory—the youth of the German nation are thoroughly behind their leader." With respect, I entirely agree with the Field-Marshal. The youth of Germany are intoxicated with success and are encouraged to believe in the certainty of world domination. They believe themselves to be fighting for the sacred cause of self-preservation and for many years have been taught to believe in "encirclement." The Field-Marshal truly says that the youth of Germany must receive blow after blow on land, sea, and air before they are likely to sue for peace.

Herr Hitler raised Germany from the degradation of defeat to a position of European dominance and, in the words of Shakespeare "in the bright lexicon of youth there is no such word as failure." There are many eminent men in Germany, however, of mature age and discretion who, to my knowledge, never desired this war and did their best to prevent it. At the moment they are impotent, and not until the youth of Germany receive a severe reverse and are permitted to know the truth will such men be in a position to exercise their influence towards peace. In my humble opinion the Prime Minister is right and always has been right in making it manifest that we have no territorial ambitions and do not desire to crush the German people, but to persuade them to the point of view that Germany has been for many years and is to-day a disturber not only of the peace of Europe but of the civilized world.

Therefore, I think that the Field-Marshal's speech is in no way inconsistent with the policy of the Prime Minister. Germany on sea has violated every code of international law to which she herself has been a signatory, in the same way that she violated the neutrality of Belgium, which she had guaranteed, in 1914. What does youth know of international law and treaties which should be sacred? At the moment the youth of Germany only desire to kill, kill, kill the accursed nation which has designed their encirclement and intends their destruction.

The German Government do not intend the youth of Germany to know the truth because they know full well that if the truth were known the opportunity would arise when those thinking men in Germany, who never desired this war, would be able to secure a hearing without the risk of certain and immediate assassination. I therefore venture to support the policies of both the Prime Minister and the Field-Marshal on the grounds that they are in no way inconsistent—indeed they indicate an intention to pursue a logical (and indeed inevitable) programme.

Yours, &c., R. E. W. CHILDS

Marlborough Club, Pall Mall

TEMPERANCE IN WAR-TIME

—◆—

The consumption of alcohol, its debilitating effects and relatively low cost, elicited numerous calls for war-time abstinence.

NOV. 6

Sir,—Every patriotic person will applaud the appeal which you publish from the Joint Presidents and Chairman of the Temperance Council of the Christian Churches, for the exercise of self-restraint in drink during the war. Their belief, however, that the Government are considering "the restriction on sale and supply which proved so effective during the last War, such as early closing and the prohibition of treating" may possibly cause some unfortunate misunderstanding among the many who do not study licensing problems. I know nothing of the Government's intentions, but I am sure that any restrictions proved to be necessary for the successful prosecution of the war would be accepted as they always have been.

The crux in this matter is reasonable proof of necessity. The Council of the T.C.C.C. might be taken to imply—though I am certain that they did not mean this—that after the last War the country reverted to the position as it had been before, and that now we ought to start again building up restrictions. A comparison between 1914 and 1939 shows a reduction of 50 per cent. in the hours of sale, a reduction of nearly 75 per cent. in the convictions for drunkenness, an increase of 1,200 per cent. in the duty on beer, and an increase of 450 per cent. in the duty on spirits. The consumption of beer and spirits is about half what it was in 1914.

The last War was a time of revolutionary and successful experiment in licensing reform. The results of the remarkable work of the Central Control Board under the sagacious chairmanship of Lord D'Abernon were gathered up and embodied in the Licensing Act of 1921. We are now enjoying the benefits. The danger lies in any unreflecting departure from the principles which the Central Control Board by trial and error found to be essential. The Board never persisted in a plan which was shown to be unnecessary or which outran popular consent. At the beginning of the last War there was too much beer; towards the end there was too little; and the Ministry of Munitions had to beg the tribunals to release labour for the brewing industry.

This letter is only a word of caution which may fairly be directed to both the Trade and Temperance reformers. If either side should use the war as an opportunity for achieving its particular desires without regard to the principles safely established a great national good might be undone. Anyone who cares to study what is commonly shunned as a dull subject but may be made fascinating by a master of statistical investigation should read "Drink in 1914–1922" (Longmans), by the late Dr. Arthur Shadwell, whose work in *The Times*, though anonymous, could always be recognized from internal evidence.

I am, Sir, your obedient servant, J. B. ATKINS

The Wisp, Woodgreen, Fordingbridge, Hants

Sir,—Mr. J. B. Atkins's approval of the appeal made by the joint presidents of the Temperance Council of the Churches for self-restraint in the consumption of liquor during the war leads one to hope that he may modify his view concerning the necessity for further restriction of the sale and supply of intoxicants at this critical time. He would accept again the restrictions which formed part of what he describes as a "successful experiment in licensing reform" in the last War, if they can be shown to be necessary.

Will you permit me, as a member of the Government Liquor Control Board from 1916 onward—under Lord D'Abernon's distinguished chairmanship—to point to some considerations which explain the present concern that the Government should take early restrictive action on the drink issue? Your correspondent, like every social student, is impressed with the general improvement in sobriety which followed the restrictions of the last War. But he fails to recognize that this improvement suffered a rude check in 1933, since which date the figures for drinking and drunkenness show a continuous and alarming increase.

The restrictions at the beginning of this war are not, as Mr. Atkins seems to imply, those with which we ended the last War. Many of them have lapsed. For example, the prohibition of the week-end sale of spirits in certain areas has disappeared; the non-treating order has gone; the hours of sale have been lengthened in many districts; 10,000 additional registered clubs have appeared since the last War; night clubs in the West End are now reported as appointing touts to lure Service men on their way through London.

The black-out, which is perhaps the most striking of the differences between this and the last War, does not appear to have been noted by your correspondent. It enforces early closing on shops and institutions; interferes with effective police supervision of licensed premises; and makes any unsteadiness among the crowds that emerge from public houses at the present late closing hour a source of special danger amidst motor traffic in the darkened streets. The reports of observers in many parts of the country supply evidence for early restrictive action. The Dean of Manchester has recently stated that he has seen more drunkenness in that city during the last two months than in the previous eight years.

Mr. Atkins refers your readers to Dr. Arthur Shadwell's book "Drink in 1914–1922." In the final chapter of that careful review Dr. Shadwell states among his conclusions the following:—(1) The fact that the Government had to call into existence a special body armed with extraordinary powers to restrict alcoholic liquors during the last War is a tremendous indictment of the part drink plays in national life, and (2) appropriate measures of legislative restriction effectively check intemperance.

I am yours faithfully, HENRY CARTER

The Social Welfare Department of the Methodist Church, 1, Central Buildings, S.W.1

DEC. 28

Sir,—Brewing and distilling must be using up something like 17,000 tons of barley, 5,000 tons of other grains, and about the same tonnage of sugar, molasses, &c., weekly. Dare we any longer put off deciding (1) whether the nation can afford all this drain on feeding stuffs, and (2) whether (as you allowed me to inquire three months ago) it can permit all the attendant expenditure of not far short of £3,000,000 a week on materials and labour? The total expenditure on intoxicants is roughly £5,000,000 a week—the cost, possibly, of running the war for a day—of which perhaps two-fifths goes to the Revenue.—MR. J. W. ROBERTSON SCOTT, *Countryman* Office, Idbury, Kingham, Oxford

1940

THE ENGLISH ACCENT

As radio became the principal source of news and opinion, so listeners became critical of the way in which certain broadcasters spoke. Lord Haw-Haw's accent and Winston Churchill's sublime indifference to the pronunciation of foreign words were remarked upon.

JAN. 2

Sir,—Your correspondent Mr. Hobson repeats the curious popular legend about Lord Haw-Haw's voice being aristocratic, upper class, "haw-haw," and so forth. What is this based on? Lord Haw-Haw speaks excellent English, but surely not "Cholmondeley Plantagenet out of Christ Church." He seems to have a slight provincial accent (Manchester?) and to commit such solecisms as accenting the second syllable of "comment." I should not call it "public school" English. Do any listeners really think it is, or is the legend merely derived from music-hall parodies, composed and sung by those who are not experts in the niceties of accent themselves? It would be interesting to hear opinions, since this eloquent peer seems so much in the news just now.—MISS ROSE MACAULAY, London W.1

JAN. 29

Sir,—I listened carefully the other day to Mr. Churchill's pronunciation of "Nazi," and it was "Nahzi," not "Narzi." Now this is not an "honest English version," as your correspondent suggests, but a horrid mixture of the open German *a* with the English *a*. The English pronunciation would be "Nayzi," the *a* as in bake or cake, which are sounded "bayk" and "cayk": certainly not "bark" and "cark."—MR. T. STEPHENSON, 15, Priory Avenue, Kingskerswell, South Devon

SUGAR AND BUTTER

The sugar ration—¾lb per person per week—was generally felt inadequate and provoked considerable correspondence.

49

It soon became clear that the implications of rationing as a whole had not been fully worked out by the government.

JAN. 5

Sir,—The allotment of ¾lb. only of sugar to each person will create a distressing problem for families of small means, in which so large a part of the bill of fare consists of daily porridge, milk puddings, and other inexpensive but satisfying dishes impossible to make palatable without sweetening. Mothers are accustomed also to make little buns, &c., in the oven, being unable to afford the expensive cakes of the confectioner. Worry and under-nourishment will follow in these cases. The whole of their bacon and meat rations will not be sought for (too expensive), but sugar is most vitally necessary.—MR. A. R. OFFER, 83, Kimberley Road, West Croydon, Surrey

---

JAN. 10

Sir,—In the article on "Rationing" on page 10 of your issue of January 1 it is stated that "those women who wish to make jam or marmalade will be allowed extra sugar" on production of the receipt for the fruit. This is indeed very encouraging, but it entirely overlooks the position of the small private gardener who grows her own fruit. During last summer I made about 90lb. of jams, for which I bought only 16lb. of fruit—all the rest being picked from the garden. Shall I be able to obtain sugar for making my own fruit into jam this coming summer?—MRS. IRIS M. SAUNDERS, Glenwood, Meadow Way, Burgh Heath, Surrey

---

JAN. 12

Sir,—The allowance of ¾lb. of sugar per person can hardly be said to afford a "distressing problem," as Mr. Offer suggests, for "families of small means." Salt, not sugar, is the orthodox addition to porridge, and golden syrup is a most popular substitute for sugar with milk puddings. Moreover, the cost of sugar was not raised even by 1d. per lb.—MR. C. M. E. BELL, Elie, Fife

---

JAN. 12

Sir,—I think your correspondent Mr. Offer is unduly pessimistic about the sugar ration. In the last War I had five young children, all of whom drank milk, so no sugar was required for their tea. We used no sugar in cooking, and all sugar was added when the dishes came to table, which is a perfectly satisfactory way of doing things.—MRS. M. M. PEARSON, Ashley House, Ratho, Midlothian

---

FEB. 19

Sir,—We have two large medlar trees in our garden and each year our cook makes medlar jelly. The trees have been full of fruit and I have applied for sugar, but was told that nothing could be done about it; that I could have sugar for preserving oranges from abroad, but not for medlars grown at home. If you or any of your readers could tell me any logical reason for discriminating between home-grown and imported fruit, in favour of the latter, I should be satisfied.—BRIGADIER-GENERAL L. C. KOE, Uplands, East Grinstead, Sussex

---

MARCH 4

Sir,—My wife has just received a letter from the farm which has supplied us with butter for years. It says:—"We have far more butter than we can sell and are not allowed to dispose of it; consequently it is useless to make it and the milk is given to the young pigs." Comment is unnecessary.—THE VEN. C. P. S. CLARKE, The Chantry, Chichester

---

MARCH 7

Sir,—I was interested by the complaint you received from Sussex. Surely it is only another confirmation of the lack of coordination between the Government Departments? The Ministry of Agriculture is urging increased production of food, while the Ministry of Food is discouraging home production of butter by unnecessary rationing and compelling us who prefer farmer's butter to increase the consumption of the imported article. This is my experience as regards my home in Devon. It is "pull devil, pull baker." Can we not have our own butter as well as our guns?—MR. E. C. W. OLDHAM, Terminus Chambers, 6, Holborn Viaduct, E.C.1

APRIL 1

Sir,—As British butter production is not likely to be increased greatly in the next few months, a doubling of the butter ration means more than doubling the cargo space for butter in our ships. Now we have passed through an unusually severe winter on ¼lb. per head per week apparently without harm. Grumbling has been conspicuous by its absence, as well it might be in view of the excellent taste and quality of the margarine available. Furthermore, we are approaching that half of the year when abundant fresh vegetables, increased daylight and probably sunshine, lessen our need for butter. I am naturally at a loss to explain this surrender of valuable cargo space at this juncture and apparently without good reason other than to pander to our palates, for as propaganda it must be almost negligible. On the other hand cargo space costs men's lives. But suppose extra cargoes of butter have been purchased by design or oversight, surely it would have been wiser to have this surplus preserved and stored against next winter, when the extra butter may well be needed.—MR. J. G. C. SPENCER, 22, St. John's Hill, Shrewsbury

STREET BEGGARS

———◆———

Street begging was a source of disquiet. Many letters came from gentlemen of the cloth—not always seemingly inspired by Christian charity.

APRIL 23

Sir,—In drawing attention to the practice of street begging *The Times* is doing a real public service. There was a time—and most of us have gone through it—when I gave to the blind, the maimed, and the singer. It was an easy form of charity and satisfied a latent instinct. One day I refused, and the man's opinion of me was devastating! Like your correspondent, I, too, have been asked again and again—and not only by foreigners—how such poverty can exist in a wealthy city such as London.

My reply has not been that the London County Council provides against such hardships by the giving of food, clothing, shelter, &c. And that for the sole reason that I knew nothing about it. I am certain there are many like me. Thanks to your correspondent we are now wiser. But I would suggest that the London County Council should go a step farther and help the charitable imbecile. Why not issue books of tickets, the value of a few shillings, such tickets to be given to the beggar, instead of money, which would entice him to assistance in the right quarter? But when all is said and done, it is well to remember that the hardened street beggar makes a better thing out of it than the hard worker! "And there's the rub."

I am, Sir, yours faithfully, T. COMYN-PLATT
The Carlton Club, S.W.1

———

APRIL 23

Sir,—A few years ago I saw an old man seated near St. James's Park Station selling matches. It was a bitterly cold day, and as I did not want matches and never give money in the street I went on to the Army and Navy Stores and bought a blanket, gave it to the old man, and saw it wrapped round him. Not very long after I was returning to the station and saw the old match seller still seated shivering, but the blanket had disappeared. It was suggested to me that the old man or his relations thought the appeal of a shivering beggar would be considerably diminished if he was seen to have a good warm blanket round him, and it had been or would be turned into cash at the nearest pawnshop.

Yours faithfully, VERONICA S. BATCHELOR
Hill Wootton House, near Warwick

Sir,—The recent letters of your correspondents have touched upon the main features as they present themselves to this society, with its 122 years' experience and records of street begging in London. The heart of the problem is found by Sir Thomas Comyn-Platt when he refers to a gift to a street beggar as satisfying a latent instinct of the giver by an easy form of charity. It is the view of this society that the present law as it stands is sufficient, if fully enforced by the London magistrates and the police, to clear the professional beggars off the streets—therefore it is in the full enforcement that the remedy must lie. Perhaps street beggars, however, are always likely to receive over-lenient treatment from authorities whose attention is mainly taken up by criminal as opposed to merely statutory offences. To some an alteration of tribunal seems the remedy.

It has been noticed that the war demands for man-power do not seem to have appealed with any great force as yet to the street beggar. And this society can vouch for the distress produced in the minds of foreign and provincial visitors to our city at the sight of them. Incidentally it would appear that no other city in Europe can vie with London in this respect.

Meantime, as a partial remedy, this society throughout its history has supplied to its members books of food tickets which can be handed to street beggars and presented at any coffee-house printed on the ticket, but as our esteemed ex-magistrate, Mr. Mead, points out they have this defect, that they are not negotiable for beer or tobacco, but it is unlikely that this defect will be remedied.

I am, Sir, your obedient servant, D. C. MEDLEY, Secretary, London Mendicity Society

45, Gower Street, W.C.1

Sir,—A slight experience of relief work in Central London led me to believe that food and lodging tickets, speaking generally, give more satisfaction to the donors than to the recipients. Among the reasons are: (1) The "old lag" wants money and he will either destroy the ticket or barter it (a very common occurrence); (2) the tickets, in certain cases, have conditions attached to them, including a mild form of discipline in the lodging houses, that is perhaps necessary but is generally unacceptable; (3) the tickets, in any case, are only a convenient way of handling the situation for, say, 24 hours. They do not get to the root of the matter where the man or woman has no desire to work but finds street begging more profitable, especially at week-ends.

It would be a pity if this Good Samaritan attempt at pouring in the oil and the wine side-tracked your correspondence from the major issue—*i.e.*, how to rid the road of the "robbers." May I add that, having left London for a rural area, I find there is seldom a week goes by in which several of the same fraternity do not call at the vicarage, with an effrontery that is often amazing. To give them money is to court disaster: they chalk the fence to advise others and exchange confidences along the road.

I am, Sir, your obedient servant, ARTHUR H. DOLPHIN

The Vicarage, New Romney, Kent

ALTERNATIVE FOOD

The acquisition of food, in addition to the ration, was a recurring theme. Traditional rural recipes for rook pie (and, elsewhere, squirrel pie) were aired, together with some more bizarre suggestions.

APRIL 8

Sir,—The time for rook-shooting is at hand. In my childhood days I remember rook pie was a spring season dish in many country houses, and was much enjoyed. I can find no recipe, but I believe only the breasts of the young birds were used. If any of your readers can give a recipe it would be greatly appreciated. The pie might be welcome in many homes as variety in these rationed menus.—MRS. JESSOP-HULTON, Mead-Way, Kingston Lane, Southwick, Sussex

---

APRIL 9

Sir,—May I answer Mrs. Jessop-Hulton? My mother used to make rook pie in the following manner, and it was very good:—Use only the breast and legs of the bird, as the other parts are very bitter and unsuitable for eating. Fill the piedish with layers of breast and legs with hard-boiled eggs and a little fat bacon. Well season with pepper and salt. Cover with a good crust of pastry, and cook well in a moderate oven.—MISS. H. BROWN, 27, Peppard Road, Caversham, Reading

---

APRIL 19

Sir,—As you have just published interesting correspondence concerning rooks I would like to stress their usefulness, which is so often overlooked. No bird is more active in destroying such harmful pests as grubs, wire-worms, leather-jackets, and other enemies of the farmer. For this reason the rook is well worthy of protection, especially at the present time, when so much depends on the nation's food resources.—MR. ROBERT H. MORGAN, M.P., House of Commons, S.W.1

JAN. 31

Sir,—It does not appear to be common knowledge that snow can be used as a substitute for eggs in certain forms of cookery. Snow pancakes are excellent, using about one large teacup of snow to replace two eggs. —CATHARINE LADY HEADLEY, 98, Portland Place, W.1

MAY 2

Sir,—In view of the publicity you have accorded to Mrs. Barrow's letter in your edition of to-day, I hope that you will spare me space to say, as an advocate for the consumption of grass-mowings, that I have eaten them regularly for over three years, and off many lawns. The sample I am eating at present comes off a golf green on Mitcham Common. I have never suffered from urticaria or any of the symptoms Mrs. Barrow mentions. Nor did any of the many of my horses to which I have fed grass-mowings, freshly cut, and cleaned from stones, &c. For my own consumption I also wash them well.
Yours faithfully, J. R. B. BRANSON
105, Westbury Court, South Clapham, S.W.4

The nature of the relationship between some newly-suggested foods and the humble English coney was also questioned.

APRIL 9

Sir,—A little while ago there was a good deal of correspondence in *The Times* about the growing of Jerusalem artichokes. I wonder if any of your readers can say whether they are interfered with by rabbits?—MR. ALAN R. WHITTINGTON, Little Boarzell, Hurst Green, Sussex

THE BLACK-OUT

Problems posed by the black-out continued to afflict the hapless traveller.

APRIL 2

Sir,—May I plead that after dark railway porters should be requested to call out the names of stations distinctly and intelligibly? At present, when the carriage lights go out as the train draws into the station, only the regular traveller knows where he is; the stranger is utterly bewildered; it may be the station he wishes to alight at, but to him the call of the porter, intoning his clipped and mutilated version of the station, is utterly incomprehensible. Indeed one might hazard the generalization that nowhere in England is the porter's pronunciation of his station immediately intelligible to the stranger.—MR. C. A. WHITTON, Fir Cottage, 17, College Street, Petersfield, Hants.

FEB. 7

Sir,—Is it not time that running in the black-out hours was made a punishable offence? Many cases of injuries being caused by heedless pedestrians rushing along in the darkness have already been reported, and two instances have recently come to my knowledge. In one case a man who has been a cripple since he was gravely wounded in the last War, was knocked down and rather badly hurt. In another case a man well over 70 years of age was crossing a City street when he was in collision with a younger man running in the opposite direction. The victim of this unfortunate accident is now in hospital with cuts on the head, a broken arm, and a fractured thigh.—MR. F. E. BELL, London, N.W.9

FEB. 13

Sir,—The black-out has made it extremely difficult to ascertain whether a taxi is or is not engaged. The only known methods are to shine a torch on the meter—and in all probability dazzle the driver—or to shout at anything which looks like a taxi and hope that it will stop. A small blue light attached to the meter, which would go out when the flag was pulled down, might solve the difficulty. Alternatively, create more ranks and make the taxis stand on them instead of roaming the streets.—MR. R. C. HUDSON, 27, Primrose Mansions, Prince of Wales Drive, S.W.11

A VOICE FROM EAST AFRICA

◆

Even in 1940, correspondents were looking to the future after Allied victory. That of the colonies was frequently mentioned, sometimes in patriotic but intemperate language.

FEB. 5

Sir,—As it now takes many weeks for us to receive our newspapers out here, I may be out of date with this letter, but there is a matter which is causing much despondency and alarm out here in East Africa. I refer to the suggestions put forward by certain theoretical armchair members of the *intelligentsia* that as a reward for the part which the inhabitants of our various Colonies are endeavouring to take to help win the war they should be driven out of the British Empire and put under the control of some vague international body, which presumably would include Huns, Bolshevists, and other similarly high-principled members of the human race.

How easy it is to find beautiful idealistic solutions of the world's troubles at other people's expense! These would-be world appeasers seem to look on Colonies as mere bits of land, possibly containing minerals or other commodities coveted by the various nations of Europe, and altogether ignore the human side of the problem. We, on the other hand, who live here look on the question very much from the human side, because our homes are here, homes which we intend to hand on to our children and their children in turn. We have no delusions as to why we are doing what we can in our small way to help win this war. We know we are fighting for the preservation of all decency in civilization, which means the preservation of the British Empire. We know that the preservation of the British Empire intact is the greatest safeguard the world can have against a third repetition of a world war caused by Germany and her greed for world domination. How fortunate it is for the world, and the trade of the world, that those shortsighted people who advocated the return of Colonies to Germany did not get their way! And yet now again we hear of proposals to disintegrate our wonderful Empire, of which every British national has such a right to be proud.

Out here we are accustomed to these defeatist ideas being put forward from time to time, but what has alarmed people is the absence of any authoritative statement from the Government to the effect that under no circumstances shall any British subject of whatever race be thrust out of the British Empire under any pretext whatever.

I should be very grateful if you would publish this letter so as to let the British public know that we in the Colonies of all races have no intention of being used as pawns in the peculiar games of these defeatist gentlemen. We are part of the British Empire and we intend to remain so at all costs.

Yours, &c., FRANCIS SCOTT

Deloraine, Rongai, Kenya

WASTE

◆

The waste of food and vital materials such as paper and re-cyclable metals caused outrage. The position became acute after the Nazi invasion of Denmark and Norway in spring, 1940. Many ingenious solutions were proffered.

FEB. 22

Sir,—The railways with little trouble could be of great assistance in this matter by providing at their stations bins "For your yesterday's newspaper, other clean paper or cardboard." The millions using the stations daily would surely respond to an invitation involving such a minimum of effort, and the paper would be on the spot for transport. Scrap metal might be collected similarly.—MR. H. F. SANDEMAN, 16, Nevern Square, London

---

MARCH 9

Sir,—My servants have been saving waste paper, according to instructions, for some months past. On Monday last my butler informed the dustman that he had several sackfuls and asked what arrangements had been made for collection. The reply was, "None, but we will take them on payment of 6d. a sack." Comment is unnecessary.—MR. R. BALL DODSON, 1, Vicarage Gardens (69, Montpelier Road), Brighton, 1

JUNE 5

Sir,—I have this morning received, gratis, from the Ministry of Information a handsomely finished printed pamphlet of 32 pages. It contains these sentences:—

Six months have passed without any serious fighting on land. The war so far has been a "war of nerves." Herr Hitler has been keeping us guessing. He has threatened every neutral nation in turn. We do not know where or when he may launch his attack. One week he seems to be menacing Holland and Belgium, another he is threatening Switzerland, another he seems to be about to attack Rumania.

In what way does it help the national cause that the Ministry should be circulating expensive material which is two months out of date? I enclose my name and address.

Sincerely yours, INDIGNANT

APRIL 22

Sir,—We are consistently begged not to waste paper and not to throw litter about. Walk along any country lane or road, and 75 per cent. of the litter is cigarette cartons. During the war could not cigarettes be sold without cartons? It certainly would not be a big matter to devise means of distributing without this big waste, and the saving of paper and litter would be astounding.—MR. H. BROOKS, Cotswold Gateway Hotel, Burford, Oxford

---

JUNE 8

Sir,—The length of the ordinary safety match is 1⅞in. Normally not over one-quarter of an inch is used of each match. If they were made not over 1in. long the shorter match would still be enough for all except pipe smokers, who are in a minority. Alternatively could not the collection of waste be extended to used matches and boxes; or both economies instituted?

In the aggregate the loss of wood must be enormous.—MR. K. T. PINKNEY, 56A, High Street, Uxbridge

---

MARCH 1

Sir,—Among the valuable suggestions for waste-saving I have read in your columns I have seen no mention of safety razor blades. These are thrown away in hundreds of thousands yearly. The collection thereof would be simple as they could be posted to a central collecting station.—BRIGADIER-GENERAL J. B. POLLOK McCALL., Kindeace, Delny, Ross and Cromarty

---

JULY 20

Sir,—May I bring to the notice of the general public that the present situation provides the answer to the question so often asked:—"What can be done with our old razor blades"? The reply is:—"Add them to our steel resources." At a very modest estimate, at least 250,000 razor blades are jettisoned every day throughout the country. The average razor blade weighs 1 gramme. 10,000 grammes = 26lb. Therefore:—10,000 blades = 26lb., and therefore:—250,000 blades = ¼ of a ton. At the above computation (250,000 blades per day) this means the acquisition of 1¾ tons of pure steel per week, or 91 tons per annum, which would otherwise be thrown away.

It may be objected that the difficulty will be collection, but where there is a will there is a way. If a scheme for collection be properly devised (and this might take the shape of a house-to-house collection once a month by a local body) it might yield a far greater amount than that suggested above. If this is adopted (and the matter is certainly worth treating seriously) perhaps the appropriate authority will say where the collected blades should be delivered. The Navy, Army, and Air Force are being approached with a view to a similar collective scheme.

I am, Sir, yours faithfully, H. FRANK T. FISHER
Gateway Chambers, Burford, Oxon

TREATMENT OF ALIENS

Among the many hurried measures introduced by the government in the first year of the war, the wholesale incarceration of many Europeans (after June 1940) who had sought refuge in Britain was the most notorious. Despite fears of a Nazi Fifth Column, most correspondents advocated the introduction of a less hysterical solution to the problem.

Sir,—On all sides one hears surprise expressed that all enemy aliens are not interned. The authorities for one reason and another apparently are still of the view that such a step, even in these times, is as yet unnecessary. There is, however, one aspect of this question which I beg leave through your columns to bring to the notice of all those concerned—namely, the employment of enemy aliens by members of the L.D.V., especially by those who hold the position of commanders, however junior, in that force.

It is unnecessary to expand on the subject of Fifth Column activities, but the presence of enemy aliens in such employment, if not dangerous, may become at least a nuisance, and, more important still, meantime raises disquiet in the minds of other L.D.V.s. I suggest all L.D.V.s should cease the employment of enemy aliens immediately, and that if this step is not carried out promptly they should be asked to resign from the force. Alternatively, the new Inspector-General of the L.D.V. might issue an appropriate general order.

I have the honour to be, Sir, your obedient servant, D. MATHIESON
7, Gracechurch Street, E.C.3

Sir,—The call has gone forth to all free men and women to unite against a common tyranny. The free men who have escaped from Czecho-Slovakia, Poland, Norway, Holland, Belgium, and France have been asked to rally to the common cause. But some free men have been ignored. For what has been the answer to the response of free men from Germany and Austria? —men and women who were the first to oppose the Nazi régime and to suffer its full menace—men and women who were eager to serve this country as doctors, scientists, engineers, toolmakers, nurses, and trade unionists—and who up till yesterday were filling useful posts, so far as they were permitted, to serve this cause. Our answer to these free men and women is wholesale internment, isolation from their homes and news, idleness, and demoralization, and the danger of a growing bitterness against this nation which has thus humiliated them.

England has been slow in recognizing her real enemies. Will she also be as slow in recognizing her real friends? These men and women could assist us in the right approach in propaganda: in knowledge of strategic points, and of the weaknesses of the enemy: could make contact with the underground forces for freedom in enemy countries: could help to stir up trouble there when the time is ripe. Surely the time has come for us to look at friendship and enmity not vertically in terms of nationality, but horizontally in terms of men either devoted to freedom or to tyranny.

The logical thing to do now is to permit a German National and an Austrian National Committee on the same lines as the Czech and French

National Committees to be formed, which could be instrumental (1) in forming a Foreign Legion, (2) in controlling and supervising the activities of its own compatriots free to work and serve this country to the best of their ability. The internment of refugees and those opposed to the Hitler regime is just what the Nazi Government would have desired, and has probably worked for, in devious ways. We have removed a potential danger to themselves and a potential asset to our cause. One more victory to Hitler!
Yours sincerely, M. I. ROGERS
The Rectory, Birmingham 15

JULY 16

Sir,—I am an alien and a refugee from Nazi oppression. Hitler has deprived me and others like me of our homes and of all we possessed. He has threatened to destroy us wherever he finds us. How can anyone believe that we should help him and his Gestapo to our own destruction? We refugees must be prepared to sacrifice everything, even life itself, when England and all it stands for, the freedom of the world, is at stake.

If the present wholesale internment of refugees were for England's sake I would accept it in silence. But is it of any use to England; is it not rather helping the enemy by enabling him to proclaim in his propaganda that England is no longer a sanctuary for the unprotected? And England and the cause stand to lose by depriving the country of the services of many willing helpers whose knowledge and skill would be of great assistance, but who are now to be interned.

In these difficult times it may be unwise to allow any refugee the benefit of the doubt, but the innocent man who can prove that he is trustworthy should be exempted from internment and given the opportunity to work for England and freedom. I would suggest that a tribunal should be set up to deal with doubtful cases, and that ex-German lawyers and judges of proved reliability should help to cross-examine refugees who claim exemption. With their knowledge of German conditions they would easily expose bogus claimants.
Yours, &c., FRITZ FRANK

JULY 17

Sir,—May I draw attention in your columns to cases which demonstrate the danger and absurdity of some of the present methods of handling the enemy aliens question? I need not say that I entirely agree that all possible measures should be taken to curb Fifth Column activities in this country, but I feel that mistakes are being made which may convert potentially valuable friends into enemies.

Dr. X., a German official of importance with Social Democratic views, left the service and came to this country shortly after Hitler attained power.

He sent his son to the Leys School, Cambridge. The father gave no occasion for suspicion. The son, who had only lived in Germany for 11 months since his birth, obtained a scholarship before he had turned 17 at Brasenose College, Oxford. The father was recently interned near Liverpool. The son, who was waiting to go up to Oxford, was first interned there, then sent to the Isle of Man. With him was another boy of 17 years of age from the same school. The headmaster, having known both for years, made application to the Home Office asking for reconsideration. He was informed that the facts which he had submitted were being reviewed. On July 4 both boys were shipped to Canada, the parents being informed by telegram after their departure. The father, now interned, asked if he might be sent to join his boy. He was told that his ultimate destination was not fixed. He might be sent to Australia. He is still in the camp.

The evacuation of these boys before they can complete their British education is an injustice. It also imposes financial burdens on the heavily taxed public which is called upon to pay for measures which are contrary to national interests. Can any arrangements be made that boys in such a case could continue their education in Canada? The present indiscriminate methods of dealing with the refugee question are likely to turn Socialists into Communists and refugees of the Right into Nazis or Fascists. Is that a British interest?

I am, Sir, &c., P. P. GRAVES

AUG. 24

Sir,—A study of Sir John Anderson's speech in your issue of to-day shows that the Government are moving, but moving slowly, in the right direction in this matter. There is, however, no evidence that they fully realize the real harm that is being done to our cause—essentially a moral cause—in America and in Europe by the continued imprisonment of political refugees who came to this country of recent years as to the land of liberty. Sir John Anderson, in an admirable statement about air raid warnings, laid it down that in war-time slight risks must be taken to avoid greater evils. The same principle applies to the release of friendly aliens, and the risks would be infinitesimal if the release of all political refugees were boldly adopted. I am sure the Prime Minister knows what a fatal injury would have been done to our war effort between 1689 and 1713, if when war broke out Huguenots who had come over since the revocation of the Edict of Nantes had been imprisoned for the duration, because one in a thousand might be a Jesuit in disguise!

One of my Italian anti-Fascist friends is at the bottom of the sea, having been sent in that ill-omened barque, in spite of clear proofs lodged with the authorities of his friendship to England and his hostility to Mussolini. Another family famous in the annals of Italian anti-Fascism is broken up, one of the boys in Canada, another with his father in detention over here. The Nazis keep their concentration camps for their enemies; we use them for our friends. How far the concessions announced yesterday by Sir John Anderson will in effect remedy this state of things remains to be seen. I live in hope, but not yet in confidence.

Yours, &c., G. M. TREVELYAN
Cambridge

NATIONAL DEFENCE

◀──────────▶

The German invasion of the Low Countries and France in May and June 1940 induced a new urgency to letters. The threat of cross-Channel invasion by hordes of paratroops provoked many suggestions for defence of the realm. The idea that German paratroops had landed near Rotterdam attired in Dutch uniforms was a source of particular disgust to Field Marshal Sir William Birdwood, who had planned and executed the Allied evacuation from Gallipoli in 1916.

MAY 13

Sir,—I see it is stated that German soldiers dressed in Dutch and British uniforms have been landed by parachute behind the lines in Holland. No mention is made of their disposal. They can of course only be regarded as spies and disposed of accordingly. It might perhaps be well that Germany should realize without delay that such will invariably be the procedure.

Yours faithfully, BIRDWOOD, F. M.
Deal Castle

─────────

MAY 16

Sir,—When considering the formation of a corps and the method to deal with the possible menace of parachute landings by the enemy in this country, would it not be wise to invite the leading road organizations to cooperate in formulating, and, if necessary, in carrying out a scheme?

For some considerable number of years past the R.A.C. and A.A. organizations have been giving assistance to road travellers in distress. Before the outbreak of war it was possible, without great difficulty, to locate a patrolman of one or the other of these organizations from practically any spot in the country, however remote. The system of patrol boxes and telephones has been on many occasions a boon to the motorist in trouble. Patrolmen are trained to know the different directions from place to place. The local patrolman would know the only routes of approach from place to place, and would therefore be in a position to set his men at the junction spots. There are, I believe, organizations which give similar facilities to cyclists.

Local knowledge is essential, and who could cooperate in such work better than the organizations who for years have made a study of routes by the roads of the country? The benefit of their joint experience should be of great value to those responsible for guarding against the dangers of this new method of warfare.

Yours faithfully, LEWIS CIVVAL

Ling House, Dominion Street, Moorgate, E.C.2

MAY 18

Sir,—May I suggest that anti-parachutists be armed with Winchester .44 repeating rifles and shotguns using solid "paradox" ball? By this means no extra demand would be made on service rifles and ammunition.

The Winchester is used by professional kangaroo hunters and is very effective at moderate range. Heavy stocks are probably held in America and Canada. As for shotguns, there must be tens of thousands available in this country, and a "paradox" ball will stop big game at short range.

Yours faithfully, ROY L. NAISH

11, King's Gardens, Hove

MAY 20

Sir,—During every day (except Sundays) a large number of ex-Service men are scattered all over the country carrying on their normal work as employers or employees (road making, farming, gardening, tradesmen, drivers of motor vehicles, builders, A.A. and R.A.C. patrols, &c., &c.). The large majority are thoroughly fit and reliable, and capable of using a rifle or machine-gun. We, in the British Legion, know these men and could carefully select those best fitted to deal with enemy parachutists or agents. We consider that these men should be armed forthwith, carry their arms and ammunition with them wherever they go, and be looked upon as scouts ready to act instantly.

Behind these we could organize groups of ex-Service men in every village and town ready to proceed at once (we will find the transport) to their help as soon as firing is heard or the alarm given (a rifle shot or two in our quiet countryside would act as an efficient alarm signal). Behind these again would be Army units; but ex-Service men (organized as suggested above) could deal effectively with small enemy numbers and pin down large numbers until regular troops arrived, when they could cooperate with them. At night the above groups of ex-Service men could be quickly assembled and act according to circumstances. Their local knowledge of ground, &c., would be an immense advantage.

The essence of the whole thing being immediate action these men must be armed, and old soldiers would be proud to wear any arm badge or uniform thought necessary and be responsible for arms and ammunition entrusted to them. They are willing and eager to serve. In Hampshire we have 114 branches of the British Legion covering the whole county, with a head-quarters in Winchester in close touch with them all. Whatever is asked of us we will do: our membership is well over 11,000, and we are willing and capable of organizing and acting under the orders of the three G.Os.C. in whose areas Hampshire is in such a way as to destroy any enemy activity in this county.

Yours, &c.,

THOMAS HOWARD, Brigadier-General, County President, B.L., Hampshire
Littlehayes, Itchen Abbas, Winchester

MAY 21

Sir,—I am venturing to draw attention to an important matter which appears to have been overlooked yet to merit the early consideration of the authorities.

Observer Corps throughout the country were established before the war and now consist of a highly trained personnel of 20,000 or more persons located at points specially selected for early audition and other observation purposes. At one time these corps did not appear to have much to do and they suffered uncomplainingly an arduous and trying winter perfecting their period of training. The Local Volunteer Defence Corps of armed and uniformed men has now suddenly been brought into being and meanwhile the Observer Corps remains unarmed and without uniforms, and its men can, it would seem, under International Law be shot at sight without being able or allowed to defend themselves or their records. Some of them are at present instructed, in the event of the imminent arrival of enemies, by parachute or otherwise, to leave their posts and destroy their records—and to do so just when the need for continuity and clarity of observation for which they have been specially trained is most needed.

Such instructions would appear to be ill-advised and are most distasteful to the men whose work and duties are officially recognized as indispensable; so they should therefore, it seems, be armed and equipped like members of the Local Defence Corps with uniforms as combatants. A further point is that their posts are known throughout the countryside and they are on duty continuously by day and night. These places would in many cases form most suitable rallying points for men of the newly formed Local Defence Corps. It is to be hoped that these points will receive the early consideration of all concerned with the question.

Yours, &c., ELTISLEY
Croxton Park, Cambs

Sir,—As an old soldier who has seen a good deal of guerrilla warfare, may I suggest that the only effective defence against parachute troops is to handle them as they land. Once let them get to ground and the job becomes immensely more difficult. Give them long enough to dig in and it may even call for mechanized troops and artillery. On the other hand, there are few more helpless objects than parachutists nearing the ground.

The method should be roughly as follows. Small sections of riflemen should be trained to proceed with all speed to predetermined positions on receipt of a warning. Each section would have a precisely defined area to protect. Once in position they should take cover from view and remain until the aircraft had released its parachutists. The section should then double to the indicated landfall and take them as they came. The warning to act would be given as soon as it was determined that hostile aircraft approaching our shores were accompanied by troop-carrying aeroplanes. To cover the country the organization would have to be vast, but any attempted air invasion of this country would also be immense, and vast indeed are the issues at stake. There is no lack of evidence in the columns of your journal alone that the necessary personnel would be forthcoming.

The simple arrangements I have outlined would, of course, be supplemented by observers and by mobile and more heavily armed columns. Then, even if a section found itself too late or hopelessly outnumbered, it could at least pin the enemy down until the arrival of reinforcements.
I have the honour to be, Sir, your obedient servant, W. J. BARR
Murree, Riverpark Avenue, Staines, Middlesex

Sir,—There seems to be a somewhat prevalent idea in rural areas that the primary function of the Local Defence Volunteers is the local defence of the village in which they are enrolled. I think the sooner it is generally realized that the primary role of these detachments is to provide the commander of the nearest military garrison with early and accurate information of the landing of hostile planes or parachutists the better it will be for harmonious collaboration between the different local defence organizations, A.R.P., &c.

To carry out their function of providing early information of hostile landings, and to harass the enemy when landed and to keep them under observation pending the arrival of the military, a proportion of the available Defence Volunteers must keep observation from fixed vantage points at or near telephonic communication with the police (for transmission to the military) while the remainder are held in readiness at a central spot to operate in the area in which the reported landing has occurred.
Yours, &c., R. H. MANGLES, Brigadier-General (retd.)
East House, Dedham, Essex

Sir,—Surely it would be better for those with good suggestions for the country's defence, like removing signposts, hiding away maps in unattended cars, &c., to make them privately to the War Office or authority concerned and not by letters to the Press. We know from the enemy's broadcasts that he notes all such information in our newspapers, and adjusts himself accordingly.

I am, Sir, yours faithfully, FRANCIS HOWARD
11, Carlton House Terrace, S.W.1

The realities of invasion did not, however, strike home with everyone.

JULY 6

Sir,—In this village yesterday a man remarked, "Oh, well, if the Germans win, at any rate I have my pension, and they can't touch that."

Can nothing be done by the Press, the B.B.C., or the Ministry of Information to bring home to people some of the implications of a German victory?

Yours obediently, H. A. SMITH
Broadwell Manor, Lechlade, Glos

By the late summer, the Home Guard appears to have settled down to its routine, notwithstanding some dissent among the ranks.

AUG. 21

Sir,—The proposed grant of 1s. 6d. per week to members of the Home Guard appears to be an absolute waste of Government funds, as not one man I have spoken to wants to accept it.

We are giving our services voluntarily and do not expect any remuneration. Taking the numbers at 1,500,000, the amount to be paid out is £5,850,000 per annum. Every one would appreciate the issue of denim overalls, which would do much to save and protect one's clothes. Many have to go on duty straight from their work or business, which does not allow of time in which to get into older clothes. A large number have been in the L.D.V. for over eight weeks, and there seems to be no prospect of receiving the uniform for a considerable time.

Why this delay? Why waste money and material on ties which no one wants?

Yours truly, ONE OF THE HOME GUARD

AUG. 23

Sir,—Your correspondent "One of the Home Guard" appears to be somewhat disgruntled because a subsistence allowance of 1s. 6d. for each period of five hours' duty has been made to Home Guards. If in stating that we do not expect remuneration he wishes to imply payments for services rendered, then he is correct, but to receive remuneration—*i.e.* repayment, for expenses incurred in the provision of such comforts as food, tea, and tobacco consumed while on duty, appears to me, and to others, to be a very different matter. In this locality the granting of a subsistence allowance has been appreciated by Home Guards, and their households, as a very just and reasonable measure.

Ties we certainly don't want, as we prefer trousers and other equipment of which we are a bit short at present, but matters are improving in this department, and meanwhile we carry on without grousing (except to the quartermaster). Cold, loss of sleep, and a few other discomforts incidental to the job of thwarting Hitler's plans by watching for his parachutists we don't worry about, and no grouse is heard except on the adjacent moor, and as above excepted.

F. R. POOLE, In/c. No. 4 Platoon, Grassington Company
Buckden, Skipton, Yorkshire

The prospect of a peace settlement with Hitler's Germany was treated with derision.

MAY 29

Sir,—Herr Hitler is said to have informed his party leaders that he will proclaim peace on August 15. There seems to be a special appropriateness in the date selected.

(1) It is the Feast of the Assumption. The word has more than one meaning, and he is making a large assumption.

(2) It was the birthday of Napoleon. He may be intending to pay a tribute to another corporal who aimed at world domination, with what results we know.

(3) It was on the fifteenth day of the eighth month that Jeroboam, we are told in I Kings, xii, 32, ordained a feast, when he tried to substitute the worship of golden calves for the old religion of the children of Israel: but the old religion survived.

Yours, &c., A. S. OWEN
4, Bradmore Road, Oxford

ARE WE AT WAR?

By May 1940, with the British Expeditionary Force seeing action against German troops on the Continent, the question of

wasted manpower was raised again. Racing was a particular
target, but correspondents widened their range to include the
building industry and publishing. Predictably, such attacks were
stoutly rebuffed.

MAY 23

Sir,—On returning home from a war area I saw, among the many things to
be admired, certain others which are not admirable. I refer to the number of
men employed on work of no national importance or on work which could
be done by older men or women. In the present circumstances, is it really
necessary to employ able-bodied men to stand outside hotels with the sole
duty apparently of opening car-doors for guests? Is it right that so many
young men should still be employed as shop assistants and bus conductors?
If they cannot be at once enlisted in one of the Fighting Services they can at
least be trained as munition workers, placed in labour corps, turned into
dockers, or placed in home defence units. And one hears women on all sides
begging to be allowed to do something useful.

It is strange, too, at such an hour to see shops selling quite useless
luxuries. These things make our Allies think that many people in this
country have not yet realized that a supreme effort is necessary. They are
right. Unselfish service and hard work devoted directly to the war effort is
now the duty of every citizen. All our citizens are loyal and it is only
necessary to explain to the slower thinkers what to do and they will do
it.

I am, Sir, your obedient servant, "X. Y. Z."

MAY 23

Sir,—It is heartening to hear from the Prime Minister that this country
after nine months of war is at last to take its coat off. Even if the large
number of unemployed were absorbed it would not necessarily mean the
country's full effort was being put forth. How many are employed on work
necessary for the prosecution of the war and how many on work entirely
unnecessary for that purpose only the Government knows. But when one
sees Tubes being built, Underground stations enlarged, B.B.C. house
increased and such work going on, presumably all over the country, it is
evident this country is not organized for war. It is extraordinary that a
nation of 45 millions should so lightly undertake the task of fighting for its
life against a nation double its size, organized to the last detail and having
an enormous number of subject people working for it.

The French are giving up their amusements while we continue our
racing, our dogs, our day-long cinemas. Are we being fair to our Allies?

Yours truly, JOHN W. PILE

34, Great St. Helens', E.C.

Sir,—A large majority of letters on this subject which have been published by you have contained requests that horse racing should be stopped. It may well be that all outdoor and indoor forms of amusement and entertainment should, for the time being, be shut down. If it is necessary to close down horse racing then greyhound racing, pony racing, theatres, and cinemas, cricket matches open to the public, and any other form of public entertainment should also go. As outdoor relaxation and entertainment must be better for everyone during the spring and summer months, surely the indoor entertainments should go first.

Of the outdoor forms of entertainment the only one which is of any real value financially to the nation is horse racing. Since the war began certainly more than £100,000 worth of bloodstock have been exported from this country, while there have been no imports. No men of military age are employed in racing. All jockeys of military age have registered, as have all trainers, if there have been any of that age. At Newmarket last week there were no men of military age. The trainers present were either too old for service in the last War or had served in it. Several of them had also served in the Boer War. The several thousands of "lads" employed in the stables of this country are either old men or young boys. They are not fit physically, nor in some cases mentally, to be employed in any other capacity. The bookmakers working at Newmarket last week either served in the last War and are now too old for calling to the Colours or are not yet of military age.

It is claimed in more than one of the letters published on this subject by you recently that too much space is given to sport. Outdoor amusements get less space in *The Times* in these days than do indoor amusements. It may well be that for the time being neither should get any space at all, but surely the open air is of the greater value. A race meeting lasts for 2½ hours. "Gone with the Wind" lasts for four hours.

Yours, &c., R. C. LYLE

Weston Grange, Weston Green, Surrey

Sir,—May I add my protest against the continuance of racing, especially of small meetings, which cannot be called of any great importance. These may be a considerable distance from a station and the only means of getting there, bar walking, is by petrol, many hundreds of gallons of which must have been used in this way.

I have the fortune to command a company of L.D.V. My district is largely open downs and therefore very vulnerable, and some of my posts are, of necessity, a long way from their bases and rallying points. The whole essence of our organization is speed of information, but the only petrol we have is an allowance for myself and my platoon commanders to get about.

Had I but a small fraction of the amount expended at one meeting our efficiency and ease of operation would be increased a hundredfold.

During the past four or five days a canteen has been in operation day and night at a certain station, supplying troop trains of evacuated men which have come through at frequent intervals. I am assured that the arrival of a racing crowd and of horse-boxes has in no way helped their work, and I only wish the crowd could have been forced to witness the arrival of one of these trains and contrast the condition of some of the men with their own.

Yours, &c., ESSEX

JUNE 1

Sir,—Your "Are We At War?" correspondence seems to be boiling down to: "Let's take away the other man's job."

As a frequent contributor to what Mr. F. R. R. Burford calls " 'female' magazines," may I remind him that these form part of the relaxation of the wives and sweethearts of serving officers and men? Also the very efficient departmental services of such magazines enable women to dress and cook more skilfully and economically than otherwise they might be able to. They are also a source of expert information on the care of children, which is fairly important just now.

Beautiful hands in war-time keep up a woman's moral, and if a girl can look like a glamour girl on £5 a week she certainly cheers up the troops.

Yours faithfully, F. E. BAILY

5, Pembroke Walk, London, W.8

THE STILETTO

———◆———

Italy, traditionally an ally of Great Britain, entered the war at the instigation of Mussolini, 'the Italian miscalculator', in June 1940. This was treated with a suitably measured tone of abuse by Times *readers.*

JUNE 14

Sir,—In connexion with your article it is interesting to recall the picture which Macaulay, in his celebrated Essay on Machiavelli, drew of the typical Italian statesman in the sixteenth century. The passage is too long for quotation in your columns, but a few sentences may perhaps be given: "His whole soul," he says, "is occupied with vast and complicated schemes of ambition: yet his aspect and language exhibit nothing but philosophical moderation. Hatred and revenge cut into his heart: yet every look is a cordial smile, every gesture a familiar caress. His purpose is disclosed only when it is accomplished. His face is unruffled, his speech is courteous, till vigilance is laid asleep, till a vital point is exposed, till a sure aim is taken, and then he strikes for the first and last time. He cannot comprehend how a man should scruple to deceive those whom he does not scruple to destroy."

Macaulay argues that this "peculiar immorality" belonged rather to the age than to the man; but unfortunately the type apparently persists.
Your obedient servant, WALTER CRICK
Eastbourne

Not long beforehand, the fate of the leading British fascist had caused amusement.

MAY 27

Sir,—It was with much pleasure and amusement that I observed this morning that you have seen fit to publish the news of Sir Oswald Mosley's arrest in the fifth column of to-day's issue.
Yours, &c., J. M. DARROCH
39, Cornhill, E.C.3

THE HOUSEHOLDER'S PIG

Supplying the beleaguered British Isles with adequate rations was a paramount problem. The rural population was exhorted to keep a pig, to be fed on domestic waste. As in so many areas, this laudable proposition was frustrated by the clammy hand of bureaucracy.

JUNE 1

Sir,—I am glad to see from Mr. Cedric Drewe's letter in your issue of May 27 that a campaign is to be launched for encouraging smallholders to keep pigs; but before the campaign is launched the regulations need alteration. May I narrate my experience? I bought a couple of slips and fed them until they were about 12 score each. I sold one in the market, the other I kept for myself. After obtaining permission I had it slaughtered. Now I am told that I must not eat more than the ration—but what am I to do with the rest? I may not sell it or give it away, and it will be a crime to let it go bad! Some mitigation of the law is clearly necessary, and concession should be made to the householder who grows and kills his pig.—THE REV. KENNETH W. P. TEALE, Stourton Rectory, Zeals, Wilts

Sir,—For some months the Government has been urging the public to "Keep a Pig." I kept a pig. In due course I arranged, subject to a permit to slaughter from the Ministry of Food, for a bacon factory to kill and cure the said pig. Having sent it to the factory with the permit to slaughter for our own consumption, I now receive from the local food office (from whom the permit was obtained) a letter in which they say that "in no circumstances" may the bacon factory cure the pig for me and that the carcass must be collected by me the day after it is killed.

In a household of two we could not possibly eat a whole pig, and we have no knowledge of or the necessary equipment for curing; we may not sell any part of the carcass, and if we were to allow it to waste through being unable to eat it before it went bad we should, I have no doubt, be liable. What does "A" do with the pig? Is this sensible in a time of food shortage or is it crass idiocy?

Yours truly, H. ASHTON-HOPPER
Tytherington, Warminster

BUDGET SUGGESTIONS

The British affection for animals, and consideration for their welfare in wartime, elicited many letters. However, they were expected, like everyone else, to play a suitably patriotic and productive role in the war effort.

Sir,—Cannot something be done to persuade the responsible Ministries to take a more active part in the encouragement and organization of rabbit keeping? As a consumer of vegetable waste the domesticated rabbit is to be preferred either to the fowl or the pig, both of which require considerable quantities of cereals if they are to thrive. This superiority is due to the much more accommodating digestive tract of the rabbit. But, as many discovered to their sorrow in the last War, even rabbits cannot be fed and kept just anyhow; and properly organized education on the subject is badly needed if past errors are to be avoided.—MR. E. C. RICHARDSON, Ecclesbourne, West Byfleet

Sir,—Would a tax on cats be worth while? At the most it would not yield much revenue, and if it had the effect of reducing the number of half-wild cats it would be positively mischievous. These homeless animals have to get a living somehow, and in my opinion the community is much indebted to them for the large numbers of rats and mice killed. The ordinary domestic cat that is well housed and fed is nothing more than a pet. If we want a good mouser and ratter pussy should live outside and receive no more than a drink of milk once or twice a day.

Cats, I know, may be a nuisance in preserves, but I fancy they destroy far more rabbits than game. Unfortunately, many of them kill song birds, not being able to distinguish between a sparrow and thrush, but on the whole the good they do outweighs the evil. Rats are such a serious menace that any means of compassing their destruction should be encouraged.

Yours, &c., A. CROXTON SMITH

Kennel Club, 84, Piccadilly, W.

APRIL 12

Sir,—May I be permitted through your columns to reply to Mr. A. Croxton Smith's letter, published on April 8, on the question of cats? I imagine, from the address, that Mr. Croxton Smith knows more of dogs than he does of cats. The majority of cats are not good ratters, although there are, of course, exceptions. A hungry cat is not considered a good mouser, he is far too concerned with finding food for himself to spend the time looking for prey. Had Mr. Croxton Smith seen the terrible condition to which these strays have been reduced, I imagine that he would alter his opinion. Were his suggestion to be carried out, there is no doubt that this country would be overrun with cats to a greater extent than it is at present with vermin, and that there would be in that case a serious outbreak of disease among the population. It has happened before. As a member of the Kennel Club, I should think that Mr. Croxton Smith would know that the terrier is a far better ratter than the cat, and if cats were all he suggests, surely, then, the obvious answer would be that professional rat-catchers would have used them for this purpose long ago.—MR. E. KEITH ROBINSON, secretary, Our Dumb Friends' League, Grosvenor Gardens House, Victoria, S.W.1

APRIL 13

Sir,—In a brief letter protesting against any measures that would bring about a considerable destruction of cats, it was not possible for me to amplify too much. I have no desire to see the country overrun with cats, and I agree that it is kinder to put out of the way those that are starving or diseased, but there is reason in all things. Many cats that have no interest in domestic life are to be found in warehouses and other buildings where they gratify their sporting instincts in killing rats and mice, thereby performing excellent service to the community. Though, as Mr. E. Keith Robinson says, many cats are not good ratters, I have known numbers that were. I have even been told that in some parts of the country men who go round with threshing machines take cats with them for the purpose of killing rats. That terriers are better auxiliaries in the work of extermination under certain aspects is obvious. They will destroy rats that are bolted by ferrets, that leave stacks that are being threshed, or beat hedgerows in the summer, but they cannot hunt about nocturnally as cats do.—MR. A. CROXTON SMITH, the Kennel Club, Piccadilly

NEWS BROADCASTS

◆

The BBC was often criticised for its presentation of news. An early example was its treatment of an air fight over the Straits of Dover.

JULY 17

Sir,—As a pilot in the last War, will you allow me to record my protest against the eye-witness account of the air fight over the Straits of Dover given by the B.B.C. in the News on Sunday evening, July 14? Some of the details were bad enough; but far more revolting was the spirit in which these details were given to the public. Where men's lives are concerned, must we be treated to a running commentary on a level with an account of the Grand National or a cup-tie final?

Does the B.B.C. imagine that the spirit of the nation is to be fortified by gloating over the grimmer details of fighting?

Yours faithfully, R. H. HAWKINS

Dalston Vicarage, Carlisle

JULY 19

Sir,—Thank you for printing Mr. Hawkins's protest against the latest deplorable manifestation by the B.B.C. in their eye-witness account of the air fight in the Straits. The B.B.C. standard of taste, feeling, understanding, and imagination is surely revolting to all decent citizens.

I am, sir, your obedient servant, GUY P. DAWNAY

15, Moorgate, E.C.2

JULY 19

Sir,—I also listened-in to the B.B.C. broadcast of an air fight on July 14, but my reactions were very different from those of the Rev. R. H. Hawkins, whose letter of protest you print to-day. It was something quite different from "an account of the Grand National or a Cup Final"; to me it was inspiring, for I almost felt that I was sharing in it, and I rejoiced unfeignedly that so many of the enemy were shot down, and that the rest were put to ignominious flight. My uplift of heart was due to a better understanding, which the B.B.C. enabled me to get, of the courage and daring of our pilots, and of the reality and nature of the victory they are achieving for us. We are proud of their feats, and such a description as Mr. Gardiner gave made it possible for us to rejoice with them. I fancy that his commentary caught something of the spirit of the pilots themselves. If our cause is a just and worthy one, then to rejoice in its success is the obvious thing.

Yours, &c., C. FISHER

30, Glenhurst Avenue, N.W.5

JULY 22

Sir,—Major-General Guy Dawnay protests in your columns this morning against "the latest deplorable manifestation" of the B.B.C.'s "standard of taste, feeling, understanding, and imagination" being "surely revolting to all decent citizens." These are grave words, which Major-General Dawnay no doubt weighed very carefully before he felt justified in using them. May I, for the B.B.C., which, subject to the necessary Government sanctions, was responsible for this broadcast, explain that it, too, was earnestly considered before it was included in the news?

This broadcast gave an eye-witness account of an air action, successful without loss of British aircraft, against enemy attack on a convoy. The business of news broadcasting is to bring home to the whole public what is happening in the world and, at a grim time like this, to play some part in maintaining civilian moral. British fighting men do not wage war with long faces. The high gravity of German troops is alien to them. Theirs is a spirit of cheerful realism, and, in a total war, is it not also the spirit of the British people as a whole? That young men, on a fine July Sunday afternoon, fight to the death over the Channel instead of bathing in it is horrible. But it is, alas, through no fault of our country, a fact. The young men face this fact without loss of their native high spirits. Do civilians want it presented to them in any other way?

People in all walks of life have assured us since this broadcast that they found it heartening and a tonic. One group of 15 listeners voted it "the finest thing the B.B.C. has ever done." Many have suggested that the record should be sold for the Red Cross. Others hoped that it would be relayed to America (as in fact it was), to show the British spirit at this moment. These comments came from all parts of the island. On the other side there were objectors, though not many who thought as ill of us as does Major-General Dawnay.

Broadcasting must face the war, as do individuals in and out of uniform. There is a debatable borderline between gaiety and levity, between cheapness and the cheerfulness that springs from a stout heart. Evidently I shall not persuade some of our critics that we were not guilty of crossing to the wrong side. Other critics, no less detached and reputable, believe us to have been right. Listeners as a body will, we hope and believe, give us the credit for being aware of that borderline, and, equally, of having no intention of being brow-beaten into a retreat to the safe regions of the colourless. Cheerfulness, even in time of battle, will keep breaking in on the ordinary men and women who, after all, have to win this war, and we mean to keep it in our programmes too. It would be a bad day for listeners—that is, for the great mass of ordinary people in this country, faced at the moment with all the monotony and anxiety of waiting—if the B.B.C. stood, out of deference to the gravity of the situation, with bowed head and arms reversed.

Yours very truly, F. W. OGILVIE
Broadcasting House, W.1

JULY 23

Sir,—Mr. Ogilvie has every right to the last word; but he rebukes me so courteously that I feel bound in courtesy to offer a word in amplification of my protest. I agree with almost all that Mr. Ogilvie writes in your issue of to-day. But it is no question of gravity or gaiety. There may be high and noble jest in tragedy. Taste and feeling are as much a question of method as of matter. I believe that the football match technique is inappropriate.

I did weigh my words most carefully. For this was not the first unfortunate manifestation; the action of Narvik Fjord is remembered among others. If, however, not I—for I am of no importance—but the very many who felt as I did induce in the B.B.C. a finer sensitiveness in dealing with these superb transactions, our views will not have been expressed in vain.

I am, Sir, your obedient servant, GUY P. DAWNAY
15, Mooorgate, E.C.2

Similar problems for the B.B.C. appeared later in the year . . .

NOV. 19

Sir,—Will you allow me to protest against the matter and manner of the news broadcasts on many occasions? I take as an example the announcement of the bombing of Berlin during the visit of M. Molotoff. There was an element of vulgar jeering in the matter and of sneering in the manner of delivery which struck me as being in the worst possible taste. This is not the opinion of a single individual; it has been remarked on to me by business people, working men, and domestics. It strikes one person at least as an insult to the splendid young fellows who took part in the raid and a slur on us all. The German broadcast in reply for once justified the pot calling the kettle black.

Your obedient servant, A. SLADE BAKER
Peans Wood, Robertsbridge

NOV. 22

Sir,—May I endorse the letter of Brigadier-General A. S. Baker in to-day's issue? The B.B.C. announcers' witticisms and sarcasms are extremely hard to bear. Can they not realize that they are acting as a mouthpiece for the dissemination of news, not as individuals?

Yours faithfully, MILLICENT FERGUSON

East Worldham House, Alton, Hants

NOV. 26

Sir,—Letters of complaint to the Press frequently, if not generally, represent the views of a vocal minority. The contented majority have nothing to write about. I think that this is so in the case of your letters condemning the B.B.C. news, and that it is time someone put in a word on the other side.

To me, and I believe to most people, the B.B.C. announcers seem to be extremely efficient and admirably chosen for their work. Their voices are good, their knowledge of foreign languages exceptional, and their method of presentation free from any objection except of a carping kind. If they occasionally allow a human touch of exultation to colour good news, surely it helps to raise our spirits and should be encouraged. After all, what could be more jubilant in tone than the records of their exploits of our modest young airmen, yet nobody complains of them. To cavil at the way in which air raid casualties are announced is probably to put the blame on the wrong people.

I am, Sir, yours faithfully, H. C. MARILLIER

The Garth, Haslemere

NOV. 26

Sir,—Tastes differ. I enjoy the witticisms and sarcasms of the B.B.C., and I can see no reasons for sparing the finer feelings of Hitler and Mussolini if they have any. And surely these witticisms and sarcasms are the responsibility of the B.B.C. and not of the announcer who, I imagine, merely reads them?

Your obedient servant, R. HENVEY

Croydon

NOV. 26

Sir,—To take a particular instance: Who allowed at the time of the Taranto raid, the jocose reference to the Italian fleet as "residential property"? What profit to what kind of people is supposed to accrue from this facetiousness?

Yours truly, GEORGE SAMPSON

33, Walsingham Road, Hove 3, Sussex

Sir,—In its untiring search for fresh illiteracy the B.B.C. spoke of "Guardists" in the broadcast news last night. Unless this horror is curbed, men of the most famous units in the British Army will soon hear themselves described as Grenadier Guardists, 12th Lancerists, Sapperists, and Gunnists (or perhaps Lancists, Sappists, and Gunnists). And then, I hope, there will be a row, and the B.B.C. will be taught to use the King's English.
I am, Sir, your obedient servant, HENRY STRAUSS
House of Commons

DEC. 4

Sir,—Mr. Henry Strauss fears that because the B.B.C. said "Guardist" the other day, "men of the most famous units in the British Army will soon hear themselves described as Grenadier Guardists, 12th Lancists," and so on.

As a purist, Mr. Strauss has caught us out. The stockists already have on their shelves too large a supply of pacifists, militarists, and Leftists. Our attempt to deal clearly with the rival factions in Rumania led us off the rails. But we promise not to tamper with the Army List. Indeed, "Guardist" was, we suspect, born (not in the B.B.C.) out of the feeling that, if there was no word to distinguish between a British Grenadier and a Rumanian Iron Guard, one ought to be invented. Your own use of "Guardsmen" in this same confusing Balkan context is unlikely to call up "Sapmen," or to enlist "Gunmen" in the Royal Regiment. Mr. Strauss would probably pass "Guardee" as a colloquialism, without expecting to hear next of "Lancees."
Yours, &c., A. P. RYAN
The British Broadcasting Corporation, Broadcasting House, W.1

TOBACCO FOR SOLDIERS

Tobacco was considered a necessity, rather than a danger, to a serviceman's life, while snuff was held by some to be especially efficacious in warding off colds.

JULY 26

Sir,—Now that the price of tobacco and cigarettes has been increased again, is it impossible to arrange for the troops to be supplied at a lower rate? The Naval forces are able to buy tobacco and cigarettes duty free, but the Army and the Air Force have no such privilege.

I understand from some chaplains that many of the men have come to the end of their tobacco or cigarettes on a Wednesday and have no money to

buy more until the weekly pay day, and that a considerable amount of depression and dissatisfaction arises in consequence. It is useless to treat smoking for men on active service as a mere luxury, and one may hope that the authorities will give the matter reasonable consideration.
I am, Sir, yours faithfully, GEOFFREY WARWICK
The Rectory, Bloomsbury, W.C.1

JULY 30

Sir,—Could not the problem of cheaper tobacco for the Forces be solved by utilizing the method adopted in the last War? Every soldier on active service was given a weekly issue of tobacco; what more he wanted he could afford to buy.
Yours faithfully, N. A. DUDMAN
The Three Candovers, Inglis Road, Ealing

DEC. 10

Sir,—Your suggestive leading article on "Masks" revives interest in correspondence you published some years ago on the common cold and snuff. Experience has amply proved that those who take a daily pinch of snuff rarely, if ever, suffer from a cold in the head. Snuff stimulates the flow of nasal mucus, which is naturally antiseptic, and poisonous bacteria and viruses are washed away before they have time to establish themselves. All children as well as adults, would do well after exposure to danger of infection in shelters or any indoor assembly to take a liberal pinch of snuff.

Snuff is handy and agreeable to most people. Some of the most dangerous viruses, such as that of the dread disease infantile paralysis, will pass unchanged through any filtering material and prompt removal is absolutely necessary.
Yours &c., BUCKSTON BROWNE, F.R.C.S.
Wimpole Street

CAMOUFLAGE OF CARS

Cars, among much else, had to be camouflaged. One correspondent had repeatedly to repaint his to conform with changing government directives.

SEPT. 6

Sir,—I see that, for the third time, the Ministry of Transport have changed their minds with regard to the method to be adopted by private owners for the purpose of camouflaging their cars.

They first issued an intimation that all cars would have to be camouflaged. I therefore immediately had mine painted in black and yellow stripes. They then said that Army colours were not allowed. I therefore changed mine to black, maroon, and blue, neat but not gaudy. Now it says that cars are not to be painted with what is generally known as disruptive camouflage or with a jazz pattern. Is it not time that the Ministry issued definite orders instead of these, which, for want of a better phrase, may be termed negative orders?

I am, Sir, your obedient servant, SELWYN W. HUMPHERY, Mayor
Town Hall, Lowestoft

THE BRITISH SPIRIT

There was a general, indestructible conviction that, despite their parlous situation, the British would win through with their 'national spirit'.

SEPT. 10

Sir,—At dawn, September 8, I happened to stand close to a statue of George Livesey, around him some of his work damaged. As the light got better I examined him. There he stood as in life, quite unmoved, quite undismayed. This is no cheap advertisement for gas or copartnership, his great ideal, but, I think, a good lesson to many.

Some others who were with me showed signs of tiredness, but the same undaunted expression. There is no fear for our future so long as Liveseys and their successors in all walks of life look as they looked to me this morning. I speak not only of those in the gas industry, but I visited in darkness and light many incidents. Can anyone say more than I do: I am proud to be British?

Yours faithfully, FRANK H. JONES
Housham Tye, Harlow, Essex

P.S.—The fire services in many parts of London as I saw them this morning are wonderful.

SEPT. 19

Sir,—Perhaps the following may serve to illustrate the spirit in which those who have so terribly suffered in recent air raids take their sufferings. A few days ago I was visiting a large hospital in which many air raid casualties from South-East London have been received. I was with a father, a man about 40, whose child had just died. Another, seriously injured, was also in the hospital. While I was with him he received the news that his wife and remaining three children were also dead. When, a little later, before I left him, I asked what he was going to do, this was his reply—"Do? Why, join up to-morrow"—and he meant it.

I do not think, Sir, that this is an isolated case, but is, rather, typical of the spirit which the German brutalities are arousing, increasingly, in all classes of the community. This the German mind cannot understand. It is the lack of understanding which will contribute to Germany's ultimate destruction.

Yours, &c., CYRIL H. GOLDING-BIRD, Bishop
Tiltmead, Cobham, Surrey

SEPT. 28

Sir,—We have just returned from a small country town where a parachute-mine exploded on reaching the ground at 9.10 p.m. on September 23, causing indescribable devastation. A row of small houses was completely demolished, and about 80 houses rendered uninhabitable. The heroism and cheerfulness and extraordinary good humour were beyond belief, but this is of course universal throughout England.

The point I wish to make is that only three people were killed and there were few major casualties, and that this is attributed by the inhabitants to the fact that they were one and all, old and young, downstairs at the time listening to a broadcast recording of the message from his Majesty the King. There had been an air raid warning in their district at 6 o'clock that day, and the speech could only be heard then with great difficulty.

I am, Sir, yours faithfully, ETHEL DESBOROUGH

SEPT. 28

Sir,—There is a typical example of the unconquered, the unconquerable Cockney spirit—the spirit of old London. A famous City tavern, windows shattered, has the following notice posted up where the windows once stood:—

OPEN AS USUAL

The little tea and coffee shop next door, windows also shattered, has gone one better and announces cheerily:—

MORE OPEN THAN USUAL

I am, Sir, your obedient servant, SAMUEL WELLER
The White Hart, Borough

OCT. 21

Sir,—The tributes to the spirit of Londoners are numerous and impressive, but perhaps the most impressive example of it is to be found in a part of *The Times* where few people would think of looking for it: the column entitled

Domestic Situations Required. While looking through the advertisements contained in this column recently, I found four in which the advertisers expressed their wish for work in "Town or country," "Town" meaning in these advertisements, London. In one advertisement a cook "wants" a job in "London"; in another a cook-general and house-parlourmaid are free to take employment in "Town or near"; and in a third a cook-general wants work in "Town only." These advertisements, if they could be brought to Herr Hitler's attention, would, I think, puzzle and, perhaps, appal him.
Yours faithfully, LEONORA M. ERVINE
Honey Ditches, Seaton, Devon

DEC. 11

Sir,—Not far from a well-known London street which suffered in a recent air raid there is a little book shop. This had suffered damage in company with its neighbours, but the owner showed that he "could take it," for he posted up a notice which reads:—

VERY WIDE OPEN
PLENTY OF BLASTED BOOKS

One felt like saluting this demonstration of the spirit of London.
Yours, &c., A PASSER-BY

AIR-RAID STORIES

The Blitz—German strategic bombing of London and other industrial cities—began in strength during the autumn of 1940. The British 'spirit' was finally being put to the test.

SEPT. 11

Sir,—Recently several bombs were dropped in my neighbourhood, incendiary and high explosive, and not for the first time. It is a purely residential district in an essentially residential area, and even Goebbels could not claim that anything of importance, such as food stores, could possibly be destroyed there. Later, when efforts were being made to put out fires started by incendiary bombs, the fire parties were heavily machine-gunned by Göring's "knights of the air." He is full of threats as to what will happen if his parachute troops are not treated with all chivalry according to his conception of the rules of war, in spite of the fact that experience shows that one of their main purposes is the murder and terrorization of the civilian population. Are we to accept tamely this typical German attempt to have it both ways?
I am, Sir, &c., R. J. DRAKE, Lieutenant-Colonel

Sir,—The official approval which has now been given to the system of roof watchers is admirable so far as it goes, but I question whether it goes far enough. A considerable amount of information concerning the movements of enemy aircraft is available by various means to the fighting Services and is, indeed, the basis for the issue of public warnings. The red warning is an alert signal and means that enemy aircraft are in the vicinity. This does not tell the factory manager anything not known to every one else with ears in the head. Yet it is the manager, acting in cooperation with representatives of the workers, who then has to make the difficult decision whether or not to stop production.

I submit that we must regard our important war factories as the equivalent of battleships in a fleet or divisions in the field, and that in each of such factories there must be a war-room in charge of a duty officer, and that this war-room must be in direct communication with its local look-out and an area intelligence centre. In the latter position should be a staff of people having at their disposal, in plotted forms, all the available enemy intelligence which will assist them to appreciate the situation and issue guidance to the duty officers in the war-rooms of the individual factories. Mistakes are bound to occur, but in order that workers shall have confidence in the decisions of their managers as to when to hold on and when to take cover it is desirable that the workers should know that the decisions are based on the best available information, collected both by the roof-watcher and by those better situated to make a comprehensive picture of the situation. Another important point is that there should be a first-class internal communications system between the war-room of each factory and the individual worker, either by loud-speakers, flashing lamps, or gongs.

The proposals suggested in this letter might be tried in an experimental way with, say, 250 key factories in half a dozen areas, and the system developed in the light of experience.

I am, Sir, your obedient servant, STEPHEN KING-HALL
House of Commons

Sir,—As the object of the night bombing is to break the spirit of the civilian population, may I draw attention to the universal delight of the victims when they heard our own guns give tongue? For four nights we had hardly heard them; and we read the German boasts that their airmen cruised undisturbed over London. It was like being bombarded in the trenches when unable to fire back.

The military effect of last night's change of tactics appears to have been a greatly diminished visitation of bombs; but the moral effect is reflected in every face this morning; satisfaction that the enemy is getting a little of his own medicine. Even unaimed shells must disconcert airmen, especially if they are of inferior training: the noise disguises the explosions of such hostile bombs as do fall and heartens the listeners as well. "Hard pounding this, gentlemen," said Wellington at Waterloo; "let us try who can pound the longest!"

Yours faithfully, MAURICE HEALY

72, Courtfield Gardens, S.W.5

SEPT. 13

Sir,—After the "All clear" sounded this morning I thought of the words of a devout Englishwoman, Julian of Norwich:—". . . He said not: 'Thou shalt not be tempested, thou shalt not be travailed, thou shalt not be distressed'; but He said: 'Thou shalt not be overcome.'"

Therefore, in this hour of trial, let us pray not that we be spared suffering but that we be given the strength to bear it. This is a prayer that God, faithful to His promise, must answer. Thus we shall not be overcome and England will live.

Faithfully yours, GEORGE P. VANIER

Office of the High Commissioner for Canada, Canada House, S.W.1

SEPT. 14

Sir,—At a time when everyone seems to be complaining about the wailing of the air raid sirens, it may interest your readers to know the name given to it by the 25 small children under five, belonging to a day nursery that we are housing for the "duration." They call it "The King's Whistle."

To them it is a signal from the King that he wishes them all to get to their nursery as quickly as possible and fetch their gas masks, and the "wail" does not seem to worry them in the least. The other day I met some of the children out for their walk when I was hurrying home through the village, and they called out to me:—"Has the King blown his whistle?"

Yours truly, MONICA C. BANCROFT

Elibank House, Taplow, Bucks

SEPT. 14

Sir,—The wardens in one small post in South-West London were magnificent. Although their district was purely residential, they were called out nearly 20 times during a series of attacks that went on throughout the night.

After one particularly loud crash, a warden dashed out into the darkness and, skirting a crater in the road, came to a pile of bricks which had recently been a house. Climbing over some of these, he called, "Is anybody there?" From the depths a male voice replied, "Yes. An old lady and myself." "Is she all right?" called the warden. "No," said the voice, "she's a little bothered to know where she is going to spend the rest of the night."

Yours, &c., O. BEAUMONT

SEPT. 17

Sir,—May I be allowed to add a word to your notice this morning of the successful removal of the delayed-action bomb from outside St. Paul's? I was fortunate enough to be on the spot, not indeed in time to witness the actual removal, but in time to be able to express to the majority of the men concerned the profound gratitude of the Cathedral authorities for the devotion and skill which had succeeded in averting what might have been a major disaster.

After an adjournment for suitable refreshment to celebrate the successful conclusion of their labours, I had the privilege of showing some of the men round the Cathedral in order that they might see some of the things which they had saved, particularly the Geometrical Staircase which must undoubtedly have been destroyed if the bomb had exploded. I was also fortunate enough to be able to secure the signatures of the entire party, which will be preserved as a greatly prized possession by the Cathedral.

Their attitude to the whole episode was what one has come to expect of members both of the military and civil defence forces. One of the men, surveying the burrow which they had had to dig to extricate the bomb, remarked, "I think when this war's over I shall retire and keep rabbits." May I add that the Dean and Chapter are taking steps to express their appreciation in suitable form?

I am, Sir, yours, &c., F. A. COCKIN
1, Amen Court, St. Paul's, E.C.4

SEPT. 18

Sir,—If Marshal Göring's young men go on bombing Buckingham Palace they will make it unfit for occupation by Herr Hitler during his triumphal visit to our shores. Happily, two previous invaders of England have left another royal residence, the Tower of London, where he could be housed as he deserves. His acceptance of a suite of apartments in the Bloody Tower would give widespread satisfaction.

I am, Sir, yours, C. H. H.

REPRISALS

The indiscriminate bombing of British cities led to calls for retaliation in kind; others advocated civilised restraint. The question of strategic bombing of non-military targets was to become one of the outstanding ethical debates of the war.

Sir,—There may have been many good reasons why we did not bomb Germany during the first nine months of the war, and equally convincing ones why we have up to date confined our attentions to what are known as military objectives and vital areas. I suggest these reasons are now out of date.

The Germans have decided to employ indiscriminate bombing with the definite object of "getting down" the moral of the civil population. Both in the country and in London there is ample evidence of this. It does not, and never will, get the people in this country down. It would nevertheless be foolish to underestimate the effect of this bombing. If continued it must have a very disturbing effect on the life of the whole country, quite apart from the material damage done. People are up all night in town and country. Loss of sleep takes its toll on work done during the day. If continued over a long period of time, it becomes a weapon of real value. The attack on the civil population is a military weapon. Can we possibly afford to give Germany a monopoly of this weapon?

Morally we need have no further qualms. We must utilize the same weapon, and I am convinced it will have a most striking and speedy effect upon the German population, fed and maintained as they are on propaganda based on military success and the belief of certain victory. Widespread bombing will quickly disillusion them.

We should, I suggest, designate some 12 German towns, and openly declare that unless this indiscriminate bombing ceases we intend to wipe out each night one of these German cities. Let each of the towns selected anticipate when their turn may be coming. If they evacuate them all—we will choose 12 others. One lesson we have learnt from the Germans —namely, that there is no law which they will not contravene, no crime which they will not excuse and no depths of infamy which they will not fathom in order to conquer the British Empire. Can we allow the enemy the choice or monopoly of any one weapon in his efforts to achieve this end?

I have, Sir, the honour to be your obedient servant, V. A. CAZALET
House of Commons

Sir,—As this bombing of London appears to have come to stay and we cannot stop it and don't want to retaliate by killing German women and children, I suggest we should adopt the system used on the N.W. Frontier of India—namely, warn the German Government of our intention to bomb Berlin as long as they continue to bomb London, giving them 48 hours' notice to evacuate their women and children and saying that after that period, at our selected time, we shall bomb Berlin. Then, if women and children suffer, it will be the fault of the Germans themselves, as they will not have availed themselves of our warning and the necessary time to remove them.

Yours faithfully, C. W. R. HOOPER, Captain, R.I.N.

2, Pittville Lodge, Cheltenham

Sir,—May I endorse every word of Major V. A. Cazalet's letter of this morning?

I also entirely agree with the sentence in your leading article of to-day: "To reply to the indiscriminate attack upon civilian London by diverting the whole force of British bombers to Berlin" is an obvious temptation. I do not suggest, neither does Major Cazalet, that Berlin should necessarily be chosen. I only desire to make two comments upon his letter: (1) An indiscriminate attack upon 12 cities is the kindest thing in the long run to the German people, because it will shorten the war and curtail their losses; it need not divert anything like the whole force. (2) Why choose only 12 German cities? Why not six German cities and six Italian cities?

I am, Sir, yours faithfully, CLAUDE H. HORNBY

39, Great Marlborough Street, W.1

Sir,—There are good reasons, both practical and ethical, for objecting to the policy of deliberate terrorization of civilians through bombardment, advocated in recent letters to *The Times*.

Practical.—(1) Ruthless bombardment of civilians is uncertain in its effect. It may cow some; in others, and probably the majority, it rouses hatred and determination and stiffens resistance. This effect was apparent in the Spanish civil war. (2) The Germans could, and would, retort by intensified bombing of civilians here. At present, from fear of retaliation, they have not openly adopted the policy of deliberate wholesale slaughter of civilians. (3) If this policy is openly adopted by both sides the suffering caused by the war will be enormously augmented. I am inclined to think that at the moment the Germans could inflict more suffering on us than we on them, though later no doubt the scales would tip the other way. (4) If we adopted the proposed policy of wholesale murder we should rightly forfeit the sympathy of neutrals, and of decent men the world over.

Ethical.—(1) If we deliberately set ourselves the task of slaughtering the greatest possible number of civilians we reduce ourselves to the moral level of Nazi Germany, and our greatest asset in this war is lost. We can at present reasonably believe that we deserve to win because we are upholding a higher standard of truth and justice. Murderers of women and children have renounced that standard. (2) At present our airmen have the right to regard themselves as clean and honourable fighters. If they are made the instruments of a policy of terrorization they will have been deprived of that right. (3) To put such a policy into effect would stain our honour ineffaceably. It would poison our minds with shame, and the minds of our enemies with inextinguishable hatred; and would go far to stultify the efforts of good men to create a saner world after the war.

Yours faithfully, F. W. STOKOE

The Manor of Comberton Green, Comberton, Cambs

SEPT. 18

Sir,—It is difficult not to feel sympathy with Major Cazalet and Mr. Hornby pleading that we must fight Hitler with his own weapons. But bombing of civilians knowingly is murder though warning is given. The effect on the Germans will be to rouse them to believe what they are told about our hypocrisy. For—I quote from the current number of the *Christian News Letter* dealing with another more urgent subject—"if we are not standing for ideals of humanity and justice which our enemies have repudiated what grounds are there for expecting world opinion to rally to our cause?"

Yours faithfully, EDWARD LYTTELTON

SEPT. 18

Sir,—Except as a means of shattering enemy moral retaliation is futile. Our primary object should always be to destroy the enemy's air power. Every other objective is of secondary importance. Once the enemy's air power is broken its army is useless and its industrial organization at our mercy.

Retaliation is a temptation to diffuse our energy when it should be concentrated on the single object of destroying the means by which the enemy is interfering with our own war production. All our force should be directed towards destroying enemy aircraft, aerodromes, and aircraft factories. After that the rest is simple.

Yours, &c., A. NELSON HEAVER, late R.N.A.S. and R.A.F.

6, Buckingham Gate, S.W.1

SEPT. 18

Sir,—Major Victor Cazalet and others have written expressing their conviction that the R.A.F. should at once proceed to the deliberate bombing of civilians in Germany, and their contention is no doubt shared by many people.

This is no time for controversy, but in all fairness it may be stated that there exists a large body of opinion in the country which takes the opposite point of view. It may be summed up as follows:—Britain must keep her hands clean if she is to experience the blessing of Almighty God, and His deliverance in the hour of danger. To all who think in this way, the recent official announcement that the R.A.F. intends to continue its policy of confining its attentions to military objectives will have brought great relief and thankfulness.

I am, Sir, yours, &c., R. E. A. LLOYD
Kinson Vicarage, Bournemouth

SEPT. 18

Sir,—We all agree that only military objectives should be attacked; but now that Germany has bombed the oil tanks near Buckingham Palace is it not time that we bombed the submarine base at Berchtesgaden?

Yours faithfully, C. PALEY SCOTT
19, Rotherwick Road, N.W.11

SEPT. 20

Sir,—We owe you sincere thanks for selecting Mr. Stokoe's admirably clear letter explaining the unwisdom of mere reprisals. I hope it will convince my friend Major Cazalet, whose proved humanity and political good sense make me reluctant to differ from him.

There is a tendency among both the advocates and opponents of reprisals to confuse the argument with the analogy of blockade. The analogy is a false one for various reasons; but a sufficient reason is that blockade is one of the most effective weapons of war, whereas reprisals on any feasible scale would be of negligible military value and politically detrimental to ourselves.

I am, Sir, your obedient servant, NOWELL SMITH

SEPT. 20

Sir,—We English are very slow to appreciate the true significance of certain modern acts of war, and when we talk of "barbarism," "brutality," &c., in connexion with recent events we are apt to overlook the fact that a systematic battering of the civilian population by promiscuous bombing from the air is in accordance with a definite war policy on the part of the enemy. The Germans do not think it "barbarous" or "brutal": they look upon it as a perfectly legitimate act to bring us to our knees just as we look upon the blockade as a job to be done. If indiscriminate bombing on our part is a necessary act to win the war then it should be done without any talk of "reprisals."

It is quite evident that the German tactics and strategy are fully up to date, and it is not the first time in this war that the civilian population has been used and made to suffer to attain a military gain. Without considering any question of "ruthlessness" we have confidence that our war officers will not shrink from taking the initiative in doing anything that may be necessary to win this war. We are up against a strong and determined foe and nothing will stand in his way of getting us down, and we must expect even more effective weapons to be used against us.

Yours obediently, H. A. WILSON

Brackendale, Rugeley, Staffordshire

SEPT. 24

Sir,—As I read your correspondent, Mr. H. A. Wilson's "up-to-date" explanation of "certain modern acts of war," and his remark that "it is not the first time in this war that the civil population has been used and made to suffer to attain a military gain," I was reminded of a quotation from Goethe's "Faust." When Faust voices his rage and passionate indignation at the terrible fate which had overtaken Gretchen, he is met by Mephistopheles with the cool comment, "She is not the first." To this Faust promptly responds, "Dog! Ineffable monster! . . . Thou art grinning calmly over the fate of thousands!"

I do not wish to hint that Mr. Wilson is smiling up his sleeve at the death of hundreds of his fellow-countrymen, nor that he takes a Mephistophelian pleasure in the present difficulties of our commonwealth, but I am sure that he does the English people less than justice when he accuses them of slowness "to appreciate the true significance" of recent events. The English people, as a historical entity, have had a centuries-long experience of the ups and downs of human life, and, to adapt a remark of Sairey Gamp's, it may be said that the wickedness of the world is print to them. They are quite aware that it is (not a modern, but) a very ancient device of the worshippers of power to represent that inhumanity is not a sin when it is practised with the excuse of a cold-blooded policy. They have suffered from that doctrine before, and, as their undertaking of this war proves, they are prepared to suffer that way again, in their determination that the modern exponents of the hoary fallacy of brute force shall be brought to a well-deserved reckoning.

Mr. Wilson's warning that "we are up against a strong and determined foe and nothing will stand in his way of getting us down," is, no doubt, well meant, but it contains a serious *petitio principii*. Something will stand in the way of our foes getting us down. It is the spirit of a nation strong in its resolution to defend the liberties which it is quite willing to preserve, as it gained them, by fighting and suffering. The Germans are not the first people who have deemed it "up to date" and "legitimate" to lend themselves to be the tools of tyranny. We have dealt with such before, and, God willing, we can do it again.

Yours, &c., R. A. WILLIAMS

St. Catharine's College, Cambridge

JERVIS BAY

Particular heroic exploits, on occasion, provoked weighty correspondence. The action of the armed merchant cruiser Jervis Bay, in protecting a convoy by attacking a German pocket battleship (5/6 Nov. 1940), was only one such instance.

NOV. 18

Sir,—I do not think that the British public realize the great gallantry displayed by Captain Fegen, R.N., commanding the armed merchant cruiser Jervis Bay, when he headed her for the German pocket battleship in defence of his convoy.

The enemy was a powerful fighting craft heavily armed with six 11in. guns and eight 5.9in. guns. Her vitals were mostly below the water-line, and where not so protected were behind heavy armour. The Jervis Bay was only a passenger ship armed with 6in. guns temporarily placed upon her decks! Her vitals were above the water-line and she was entirely unarmoured. Her guns were quite incapable of doing any vital injury to the enemy. One well-directed shot from the enemy's guns was sufficient to put the Jervis Bay out of action.

The gallant officers and ship's company of the Jervis Bay knew full well that the great majority of them were going to certain death when Captain Fegen placed his ship between the enemy and the convoy he had to defend and proceeded to attack the pocket battleship. That so many of the convoy managed to escape was a glorious justification of the sacrifice of the Jervis Bay and her captain, officers, and men.

I am, Sir, your obedient servant,

H. MEADE FETHERSTONHAUGH, Admiral, Retired

Uppark, Petersfield

NOV. 18

Sir,—It is of some interest to quote in juxtaposition the following extracts from Admiralty *communiqués* appearing in *The Times* of November 14:—

(1) "Of the [four] enemy supply ships, one was sunk outright, two were set seriously on fire and almost certainly sunk, a fourth was damaged but succeeded in escaping under cover of a smoke screen. Both the escorting [Italian] destroyers escaped at high speed under cover of smoke."

(2) "Further details have now been received of the gallant action of H.M.S. Jervis Bay, which enabled such a large proportion of a convoy to escape when attacked by a powerful enemy raider. As soon as the [British] convoy was attacked by the raider, H.M.S. Jervis Bay steered for the

enemy. . . . Although partly out of control and seriously on fire she continued to hold the enemy fire while ships of the convoy were making good their escape. . . . She subsequently sank."

Comment is unnecessary, but these two extracts must make Hitler and his friends think, and their thoughts cannot be happy ones.

Yours faithfully, LUXMOORE NEWCOMBE

Bourne Lodge, Hemel Hempstead, Herts

NOV. 20

Sir,—It is to be hoped that some memorial to the officers and ship's company of H.M.S. Jervis Bay will be erected somewhere—perhaps in Liverpool Cathedral.

The inscription might appropriately include the reply of Judas Maccabaeus when confronted with the army of Bacchides:—"God forbid that I should do this thing and flee away from them; if our time be come let us die manfully for our brethren and let us not stain our honour" (I Maccabees ix, 10, A.V.).

Yours very faithfully, R. H. MALDEN

The Deanery, Wells, Somerset

DEC. 2

Sir,—I avail myself of this opportunity to write to you after safe arrival in this country on behalf of myself and the crew of the Polish steamer Puck, the smallest of all which took part in a recent convoy from Canada which was shelled by a German raider of the Graf Spee class on November 5, to express our grateful thanks through the columns of *The Times* for the way in which the Jervis Bay defended us to the last. The fine example set by the British crew of this ship, who through their sacrifice saved a lot of valuable tonnage and very valuable cargo, filled us all with deep admiration and made us their spiritual debtors. This fresh example of British valour on the high seas is sufficient to give renewed confidence in the British Navy and in British victory.

On behalf of my crew and myself I should like to say how much we commiserate with the relatives and friends of the courageous crew of the Jervis Bay who lost their lives in this historic action, but who may be proud for the role they have played in their fight for freedom.

I am, Sir, your obedient servant, J. PIEKARSKI

London

DEC. 6

Sir,—The Royal Navy has just written another brilliant page of its history. I suggest that it would be a fitting tribute to two gallant ships to name two of the battleships now building the Rawalpindi and the Jervis Bay. Those

names must not fade into obscurity, but must be placed where no member of
the Navy can ever forget them.
Very truly yours, GEOFFREY BOLTON
27, Main Street, Ayer, Massachusetts

BINOCULARS

*The Government issued an urgent request to the public for
binoculars. But were they to be donated as a gift or as a loan?*

NOV. 29

Sir,—May I, as Commodore of the Royal Thames Yacht Club, to the
members of which I am making a personal appeal, heartily endorse the
appeal of Lord Derby to the public for binoculars for the fighting Services?

I am quite sure that my fellow-yachtsmen will not hesitate to give for this
very practical use binoculars which they no longer urgently require for their
own purposes. One hundred and twenty-five thousand pairs of prismatic
binoculars of 6, 7, or 8 magnification are needed, and I am confident the
general public will promptly respond to this appeal.
Yours truly, QUEENBOROUGH
60, Knightsbridge, S.W.

DEC. 6

Sir,—As one responsible for the present campaign in which owners of
prismatic binoculars are asked either to give or to sell them to the
Government, I wish to thank Professor Louis Arnaud Reid for his suggestion that glasses should be accepted on loan and returned after the war.

I can assure him that this method has been fully considered, and the main
reason for its non-adoption was that during the last War such loans of
binoculars were made, but the promises to return could not, in general, be
implemented. Questions of compensation in the event of loss naturally
arose. Many of us would like one day to recover our glasses to which so
many pleasant associations cling, but the immediate need to collect over
100,000 is so pressing that we are bound to adopt the scheme which is the
simplest from the administrative point of view. I am glad to state that over
50 per cent. of the binoculars received in the past few days at one of our
depots have been unconditional gifts, and many of these donors have, I feel,
decided that the pleasantest association of all is for their binoculars to help
spot the enemy bomber.
Yours faithfully, F. E. SMITH, Director of Instrument Production, Ministry
of Supply
Great Westminster House, Horseferry Road, S.W.1

Sir,—There are many like myself who will respond unconditionally to the appeal for binoculars but who will regret the rather blunt refusal of the Ministry of Supply even to consider their possible return to the owner when the war is over—as suggested by Professor Reid.

Obviously no definite promise of such return, involving liability to compensation for loss, can be asked for or made, but the appeal might be much more successful if a rather more sympathetic reply could be given than that of the Director of Instrument Production in your columns on December 6. Meanwhile I suggest that any owner who would hope to see his old friends and companions back should have his name and address clearly stamped on them. Possibly after the war some rather less wooden attitude may be adopted by the Ministry where previous ownership can be identified and no payment has been asked for.

Yours faithfully, BINGLEY

Bramham Park, Boston Spa, Yorks

1941

MAN MANAGEMENT

---◆---

The management and care of troops was largely the responsibility of junior officers. Many were by now being commissioned from educational establishments other than the public schools. A lieutenant-colonel started a vast correspondence by deploring this.

JAN. 15

Sir,—The authorities who govern the Army and, indeed, all senior officers, are rightly and justly worried about one of the aspects of life in our new armies. That aspect is known as man management, and man management is chiefly the responsibility of the junior officers—the company and platoon commanders. The subject embraces not only the physical but the mental and moral welfare of the soldier—and the word moral is not used here in the customary "goodie-goodie" sense.

Two or three weeks ago a Sunday newspaper published an address by the Prime Minister given to Harrow School on the subject of the character training acquired by the boys at the older public schools and completely justifying the human product which cheap music-hall artists have jeered at and labelled the old school tie. Never was the old school tie and the best that it stands for more justified than it is today. Our new armies are being officered by classes of society who are new to the job. The middle, lower middle, and working classes are now receiving the King's commission. These classes, unlike the old aristocratic and feudal (almost) classes who led the old Army, have never had "their people" to consider. They have never had anyone to think of but themselves. This aspect of life is completely new to them, and they have very largely fallen down on it in their capacity as Army officers.

It is not that they do not wish to carry out this part of their duties properly, but rather that they do not know how to begin. Man management is not a subject which can be "taught"; it is an attitude of mind, and with the old school tie men this was instinctive and part of the philosophy of life. These new young officers will be just as brave and technically efficient, but they have been reared in an atmosphere in which the State spoon feeds everybody from cradle to grave, and no one feels any responsibility for his fellow men. This, Sir, is a sad reflection on our educational system.

I am, Sir, your obedient servant,

R. C. BINGHAM, Lieutenant-Colonel, 168 O.C.T.U.

Sir,—Colonel R. C. Bingham, in his letter on junior officers of the new armies, has opened a vast subject. The difficulties which he has mentioned became apparent towards the end of the last War. The traditions of the public schools have been largely imitated by Government schools, and have gathered an added impetus from the work of the founder of the scout movement. In actual teaching secondary schools, as is shown by university scholarship and other results, can rival and surpass public schools, but they cannot yet produce to the full their qualities of leadership in peace and war. In public schools such qualities, often innate and the product of generations of service, are developed by responsibility given to individuals in the organization of a house, of games of every kind, and more especially by scouting and the Officers Training Corps.

The important point at this moment is that the developing fusion between the public schools and the Government secondary schools should be pushed on with the utmost speed. The public schools are already suffering gravely, and it is necessary to emphasize the fact that unless immediate Government action is taken a great opportunity will be lost with the passing of the public schools even before the end of the present war.

I am, Sir, your obedient servant, C. H. PIGG

Aberfoyle, Keynsham Road, Cheltenham

Sir,—Colonel R. C. Bingham's letter in your issue of the 15th cannot be allowed to pass unanswered. Is it not too early to draw conclusions about the modern army, when little or no fighting has yet been done?

Quite different conditions apply to an officer in and out of the field. In the one case, the qualities most called for are a capacity for self-sacrifice, a genuine concern for the welfare of those surrounding him, and a clear unruffled intelligence in face of danger. Are these the attributes of education or are they the properties of the "man," which it is in the power of an educational system to develop but not endow? In the other, the quality chiefly required is the ability to command and in this, of course, the public school boy excels. Is he not brought up to command and to expect obedience? And as we cannot all be masters the place of the day school boy is to serve: need we be surprised therefore if in any other position he goes to excesses and generally displays the worst characteristics of self-consciousness?

The ability to command is one thing, but quite another is the view that the middle classes, lower middle classes, and working classes have never anyone to think of but themselves. It is convenient for some people perhaps to think of classes as if they were individuals, but I wonder whether the brilliant boy of 15 obliged to leave school to support younger brothers and sisters is as conscious of his lack of sacrifice on others' behalf? I cannot help feeling that Colonel Bingham would have had fewer complaints about recent promotions from the ranks if they had been based less on the superficial capacity to imitate the manners of the public school boy and more on an absence of affectations and a capacity for intelligent work. But the preference of senior officers for men of their own class or affecting the manners of their own class is human and therefore understandable enough.
Yours sincerely, W. L. FAIRWEATHER
30, Cornhill, E.C.3

JAN. 21
Sir,—When Colonel Bingham speaks of a certain inferiority in those officers who have not been educated at the public schools I think he leaves out of count a fact of great and far-reaching importance. I mean the remarkable improvement in the quality of the men whom they are required to discipline and lead.

Speaking generally, it may be said that the recruit for the Army is no longer the undeveloped and socially dependent person he very often was in the past. The old "feudal" conception of society—which still lingers, unfortunately, in the public schools, and raises much popular prejudice against them—no longer affects him, and he does not need now, and may even be disposed to resent, the meticulous direction and quasi-paternal oversight which were once confessedly indispensable. The relation between the officer and the soldier whom he commands is rapidly becoming less paternal than fraternal, and in the case of the best officers—if I may employ a great word once honoured in my own profession—pastoral. Fifty years ago, as the vicar of a great industrial parish, I had frequent occasion to observe the moral and intellectual inferiority of the young men who joined the Army as compared with those who joined the Navy and the Police. To-day that difference has disappeared. The great improvement in physique, in temperance, and in education, which has marked the nation as a whole, has had its effect. The more intelligent and sympathetic administration of the Army, and recently the adoption of compulsory military service, have counted for much in bringing about this salutary change. It seems to me both inevitable and apparent that it must slowly but surely affect the temper of the Army, and specifically the mutual relations of officers and men.

One thing appears to a non-military onlooker to be unquestionable, and it is full of encouragement. The performance of the British Army in the present war, wherever it has been brought to the test, gives no countenance to the suggestion that either officers or men have fallen below the highest tradition of their glorious Service.

Your obedient servant, H. HENSLEY HENSON
Canon of Westminster

Sir,—Lieutenant-Colonel R. C. Bingham's letter to *The Times* has stirred up quite a storm, especially in the provincial Press. It looks almost like the beginning of a class war, and this is a pity, as class has very little to do with it. It is merely a matter of education, as the last sentence of the letter shows.

In order to prove that it is merely a matter of education, take two brothers from all or any of the three classes. Send one to a good public school and the other to a good council school. The council school boy will of course live at home, and be more or less attached to his mother's apron-strings. He will see little of his fellow scholars out of school hours, and have little opportunity of having his corners knocked off. The public school boy, on the other hand, will find himself far from home influences and among a lot of boys who do not care whether he is the son of a duke or the son of a dustman, but take him entirely on his merits. He has to find his own level, and learns that truthfulness, cleanliness, honesty, and unselfishness are of the first importance. Later on he may join the school O.T.C., and perhaps become captain of the rugger team.

Such a boy will make a natural manager of men. He knows instinctively that their care is his first consideration, just as a good sportsman sees to his horse after a day's hunting, before he has his own hot bath. The brother, on the other hand, may have a sounder education and make a success of life, but, with some exceptions, he will rarely make a manager of men.

Yours, &c., GERARD F. T. LEATHER, Colonel, retired
Middleton Hall, Belford, Northumberland

Sir,—Colonel Bingham's letter on man management, like so many sweeping generalities, contains only half the truth. A very large number of boys, at Eton for instance, have no aristocratic tradition; they are the sons of new men who have made money, who were not at Eton themselves. But the sons of these "new" men absorb at their public schools, and later in their regiments, the old great Army tradition which may be summed up in the words "See to the needs and comforts of your men before you see to your own."

There is, therefore, no reason, if O.C.T.U.s and regiments do their job properly, why the sons of working-class parents should not equally absorb this fine tradition. During the last war I had the privilege of commanding a squadron, and occasionally a regiment, of cavalry. At the beginning all the officers came from the most expensive schools. Towards the end about half the officers came from the ranks. With, of course, some exceptions on either side, the two fused excellently, and there was nothing to choose between them as good officers and good comrades. Anyone who wants to see a very high quality of leadership can look to the Scout Movement, where the officers come largely from the working classes.

I am, &c., A. A. H. BEAMAN, Lieutenant-Colonel
Kingscote Grange, Tetbury, Gloucestershire

BUCKETS

Once again, Whitehall bureaucracy seemed self-defeating.

JAN. 15

Sir,—The reply to Miss Nettlefold from the Public Relations Officer on the Limitation of Supplies Orders, Board of Trade (Phoebus, what a title!) is surely the least convincing *apologia* that ever emerged from the purlieus of Whitehall. If its purpose were to darken counsel, it could not have been better expressed. Miss Nettlefold alleged that people are prohibited by Government Order from buying that homely article, the bucket—necessary to every would-be fire-fighter, and we are all urged by the Government to become fire-fighters to-day. Mr. Davenport seems studiously to avoid denying that allegation—indeed, by implication, he confirms it, in a statement to the effect, so far as I can interpret it, that local authorities may buy buckets. He merely alleges that "no difficulties have been brought to notice." No doubt an ostrich, with its head firmly buried in the sand, could truthfully make the same allegation.—H. G. THURSFIELD, Farnham, Surrey.

HERMANN THE IRASCIBLE

Sniping at the enemy through the columns of The Times *was a seemingly inexhaustible pleasure.*

JAN. 21

Sir,—The news that Field-Marshal Göring is descended from King Henry II and is likely in future to be satisfied with no uniform less than that of royalty was forecast by Saki before the last War. He told how, a plague having wiped out all the nearer members of the Royal Family, the throne was occupied by Hermann the Irascible. Of this astonishing monarch it was said: "He was one of the unexpected things that happen in politics, and he happened with great thoroughness. . . . before people knew where they were, they were somewhere else." Surely this prophecy applies to the Four-Year Plan and the concentration camp. Moreover, Hermann's method of dictating legislation to keep women out of politics is fully in accordance with Nazi practice and theory.

As, however, we know from Saki that Hermann the Irascible was also nicknamed "The Wise," it seems probable that the prophecy breaks down. I am, Sir, your obedient servant, RONALD MORRISON
40, Porchester Terrace, London, W.2

FOOD FOR HENS

◆

The quantity of foodstuffs allocated for poultry was curtailed in January 1941, a policy deemed ridiculous and counter-productive by many poultry-keepers.

FEB. 1

Sir,—Is it not time that the Ministry of Food revised its attitude towards certain essential foods, instead of pursuing its present blind course? I refer especially to such an essential article of diet as the egg.

The general public are at a loss to understand why a food which has always been recognized as one of the essential "protective" human foods, right up to and including the early months of the present war, has suddenly been relegated to the limbo of the completely unimportant. The only clue is to be found in the peculiar views of certain academic gentlemen whose advice on nutrition in war-time has been sought by the Government. One of these gentlemen, Sir John Boyd Orr, in a recent publication has given expression to these views. He makes the extraordinary statement, of the animal feeding-stuffs available in the country to-day, that the dairy cow must have the first call on them, "as she only requires 5lb. of foodstuffs to produce 1lb. of human food." After mentioning several other animals, he finally places the domestic hen last, "as she requires 15lb. of foodstuffs to produce 1lb. of human food."

Now to the facts. Sir John Boyd Orr says the hen takes 15lb. of animal foodstuffs to produce 1lb. of human food. Any poultrykeeper can tell him that the average pullet of utility breed (non-pedigree) will in the first 18 months of its life (which is all that need concern us) eat about 130lb. of food. In the same period she will lay at least 168 eggs weighing 21lb. In addition, the bird's own flesh will weigh at least a further 5–6lb., a total of at least 27lb. for a consumption of 130lb., or 1lb. for 5lb. consumed. This places the hen on exactly the same level as the cow as a producer of human food, with this advantage: that the hen converts more quickly than does the cow. Therefore, of the foodstuffs available to-day, the hen and the cow should have allocations on a 50–50 basis, instead of a 22–90 basis, as at present. The present method of pampering the cow and starving the hen is neither fair to the public nor just to the poultrykeeper. It just does not provide the general public with the varied and balanced diet which they require in these days.

Should anyone doubt the veracity of this statement, let him eat two slices of bread and margarine and an egg for breakfast. He will, at least, have had a meal. But let him eat two slices of bread and margarine and drink half a pint of milk. He will not feel that he has had a meal. A simple test of this kind is worth all the academic research in the world. I appeal to the Government to revise its present shortsighted policy, based as it is, on insufficient evidence and adopted far too hastily.

Yours, &c., C. J. SHEPHERD

Thatcham, Berks

FEB. 6

Sir,—I hate criticizing the Ministry of Agriculture when goodness knows it has enough to do in these days, but feel I must express my dismay at this new order regarding the rationing of chicken-food for the small poultry-keepers.

I have six pedigree hens. These hens have kept four households in eggs for the last 17 months. Now, because I only keep six hens, instead of over 12, they must go without any corn at all. These birds have helped to feed the nation; they will not be able to do this in the same way without a food that is essential to them. I know this is true because I have kept laying hens for over 15 years now. It is as though soldiers in a platoon were to get less food a man than those in a battalion, and about as sensible. We are told to use house-scraps for our poultry, but what house-scraps can we find these days? I do beg the Ministry to reconsider their ignorant ruling in this matter, for in this way the food production of the British Isles will be lowered in a small, it is true, but harmful way. I hope you may be able to use your valuable influence to get this ruling altered.

Yours, &c., H. M. PYE

Stockland, Chelwood Gate, Sussex

FEB. 6

Sir,—In your issue of February 1 Mr. C. J. Shepherd argues that available feeding-stuffs should be allocated to the hen and the cow on a 50–50 basis instead of 22–90 as at present. He bases his argument on calculations which show that for 130lb. of feeding-stuffs the hen produces 21lb. of eggs and 5lb. of "the bird's own flesh." According to Mr. Shepherd the hen thus gives 1lb. of human food for 5lb. of feeding-stuffs, which, as he states, is about the ratio I calculated for the dairy cow. His calculations and mine are, however, made on a totally different basis. He takes total weights whereas my calculations are based on the caloric value of the "dry matter" for both feeding-stuffs and products.

The method of calculation makes a very big difference in the result. If milk production were calculated on Mr. Shepherd's basis of weight, a high yielding cow, giving 70–80lb. of milk, might have a ration of less than this weight and so be calculated to produce more than she consumes. Calculations based on weights may obviously give absurd results. In considering the efficiency of the hen one must take into account the fact that the edible part of the egg consists of water to the extent of about 74 per cent. and of the total weight of the hen not more than about a half is edible flesh which, again, consists largely of water.

Calculations of the efficiency of different farm animals, on a common basis of calories or dry matter, show that the order of efficiency is the cow, the pig, the hen, and finally the bullock. Personally I have the greatest sympathy with the poultry-keeper and would like to see the hen given preference over the bullock.

Yours faithfully, J. B. ORR

The Rowett Research Institute, Bucksburn, Aberdeen

FEB. 7

Sir,—In a letter you publish to-day Mrs. H. M. Pye expresses concern at not being allowed, under the domestic poultry keepers' rationing scheme which has just come into operation, to obtain any corn for the hens she keeps because they do not number more than 12; and she fears that the four households which she has been supplying with eggs from her six birds will go short in future.

Your leading article on the same page very rightly explained why the supply of feeding-stuffs to poultry keepers has to be reduced to one-third of their normal requirements, and stressed the importance of making the maximum use of kitchen scraps and other waste materials from gardens and allotments as food for poultry. Mrs. Pye asks what household scraps can be found these days. They still exist, even under rationing, and the four households which your correspondent says she supplies with eggs should make their scraps available in return, together with any garden waste they may have. It should not be difficult, with a little cooperation and ingenuity, for domestic poultry keepers to find two-thirds of the needs of a small number of birds in these ways, and large numbers of householders are in fact doing so with successful results.

It is true that poultry keepers with 12 birds or fewer are being supplied with a special "balancer meal" instead of corn or mash. This meal is being provided at the rate of about one pound per bird per week, and its composition has been so devised by scientific advisers well versed in the practical problems of the poultry industry as to be sufficient, when fed with about half a pound per day of household scraps or garden waste, to keep a bird in good health and production. In this way we can hope to provide a useful supply of eggs from hens kept in the back yard or the garden and reserve our corn to the fullest possible extent for the urgent needs of human beings.

Yours faithfully, T. WILLIAMS, Chairman, Domestic Poultry Keepers' Council

Ministry of Agriculture and Fisheries, 55, Whitehall, S.W.1

Needless to say, an obvious solution to this problem was soon suggested.

MAY 13

Sir,—As one of the reasons for the great scarcity of poultry and eggs is the shortage of foodstuffs, why do not people breed geese in large quantities all over Great Britain? These useful birds live only on grass and require the minimum of attention.

Yours faithfully, BRENDA WALMISLEY-DRESSER

Two Old Coastguard Cottages, Barton-on-Sea, Hants

SUMMER TIME

The advantages—and disadvantages—of British Summer Time were a yearly topic.

MARCH 5

Sir,—I hope you will protest as strongly as possible against the additional hour to summer time. This may be all right for town dwellers, but it will be disastrous for farmers. Legislation cannot alter nature.

Quite apart from the inadvisability of so disastrously altering the hours of milking and feeding of stock, what will happen in haymaking and harvest time? The dew will not be off before 9 a.m. sun time at the very earliest, meaning 11 o'clock summer time, and the legal time for stopping work will be 5 or 5.30 p.m., meaning really 3 or 3.30 p.m. So the best hours of the day for loading will all have to be paid for as overtime. How can any farmer stand that?

Yours faithfully, W. HIGSON

Burton Lazars Hall, Melton Mowbray

1941

Sir,—As a working farmer with a milking herd I should like to warn your readers not to take Captain Higson's words too seriously. Nothing deserving the word "disastrous" will happen to farming because of an additional hour's summer time. At the worst slight inconvenience may result. And when Captain Higson tells us that 5 or 5.30 p.m. (really 3 or 3.30) is "the legal time for stopping work," he seems to me to say something which is quite untrue. There is no legal time for stopping work. The Agricultural Wages Acts lay down how many hours are to be worked in a week and the minimum wage which must be paid. The hours of beginning and leaving off are at the farmer's discretion.

I asked my men if they would prefer to start work an hour later on May 3 and disregard the change of time. They refused because they said they would value the extra hour's daylight for work in their gardens. If that is so the change may well lead to an increased production of food. And that is all that matters.

I am, Sir, your obedient servant, CONRAD RUSSELL

Sir,—Besides the inconvenience to farmers which will be caused by the extra hour of summer time, there is another grave objection. Many children to-day cannot be made to go to bed in daylight; and in the summer they are out in the streets till nearly 10 p.m., when they should be having the sleep they need. What will happen when the clock is put forward? They will probably stay up till nearly 11 p.m., and so lose another hour of sleep. Many children cannot get to sleep in daylight; but sleep is of vital importance for them.

Yours faithfully, JOHN H. LORING
28, St. David's Road, Southsea

Sir,—Children well managed have always had to go to bed by daylight, as witness Stevenson's

> In winter I get up at night
> And dress by yellow candle-light.
> In summer, quite the other way—
> I have to go to bed by day.

And there was no summer time in those days.

Yours truly, A. MUSPRATT
Care of Mrs. Orlibar, Crawley Park, Bletchley

VERMIN

———◆———

The destruction of valuable standing crops by vermin became of particular concern.

MARCH 11

Sir,—The wild rabbit should be regarded as a pest to be humanely destroyed, not as stock to be exploited by inhumane methods. This is the policy which this federation has consistently advocated. It is now almost universally admitted that wild rabbits destroy far more food than they provide. It is not so generally realized that there is a close connexion between the superabundance of these destructive animals and their exploitation for profit by the trapping industry. In the counties where this industry is most firmly established there has recently been an intensification of trapping, but trappers are not aiming at the extermination of rabbits any more than butchers are aiming at the extermination of sheep.

The exploitation of rabbits for profit discourages the adoption of fumigation and other effective methods of rabbit destruction. May we once more urge agricultural authorities to encourage the elimination of rabbits by humane methods, and to discourage a barbarous industry whose livelihood depends on the preservation of a large breeding-stock of rabbits at the end of each trapping season? We shall be glad to send "Instructions for Dealing with Rabbits" on application.

Yours faithfully, P. CHALMERS MITCHELL, President, Universities Federation for Animal Welfare, Hall Place, Lyndhurst Terrace, London, N.W.3

———

RARE BIRDS AS FOOD

———◆———

By contrast to the apparent neglect of the largely untapped food stocks represented by wild pigeons and rabbits, one reader spotted some exotic fare available for consumption.

MARCH 11

Sir,—I understand on good authority that in certain poulterers' shops in the neighbourhood of London certain birds are being exhibited and sold, which should certainly not be permitted. The birds in question are the goosander, red-breasted merganser, and last, but by no means least, the great-crested grebe! Ironically enough the grebe is being sold as a "shuffleduck"!

One knows full well how difficult it is to obtain the necessaries of life, but for such birds as I have mentioned to be exposed for sale and human consumption is abominable, and I hope that this publicity will cause a stop to be put to this distressing practice.
Yours very sincerely, W. PERCIVAL WESTELL, Curator, Letchworth Urban District Council Museum
Broadway, Letchworth, Herts

WHY RACING?

Racing, which had earlier in the war been banned by government decree, was once more sanctioned in 1941. This seemed astonishingly frivolous to some, sensible to others.

MARCH 10
Sir,—Many of your readers must be sharing the feelings of bewilderment which I experienced on learning that a resumption of Flat racing had been sanctioned by the Government. Are there not several inconsistencies which need some explanation?

(1) Our supplies of milk and eggs are being jeopardized by the shortage of feeding-stuffs, and a farm horse has to work on a daily oats ration of 7lb. A racehorse, I learn, can obtain 16lb.

(2) We are urged to cut out unnecessary travel. We are told that local shortages of food and fuel are partly due to transport difficulties. Race-meetings, however, are to be permitted to add to the labours of already harassed railwaymen and police.

(3) A considerable amount of paid labour will be required and will be found for work in connexion with race-meetings, which would seem to have no conceivable value to our war effort. Yet thousands of working men and women are expected to devote large portions of their spare time to unpaid civil defence duties.

(4) L.P.T.B., we learn, is to save 600 tons of paper pulp annually by printing thinner and smaller bus tickets. Are we to assume that this is to facilitate the printing of race-cards and bookmakers' slips?
Yours, &c., O. MORDAUNT BURROWS
Epworth Rectory, Doncaster

MARCH 11
Sir,—A correspondent has put forward in your columns four arguments in favour of the cancellation of racing, but some of them are hardly convincing.

On the figures published racehorses are depriving the human population of approximately 4oz. to 5oz. of oats per head per annum, and it must be remembered that racing is an industry which brings money into the country and pays none out. And if the few horses left in training were turned out they would not, presumably, live entirely on air. Local shortages of food and fuel may indeed be due to congestion on the railways, but why blame racing? There are no special trains in these days, and anyway most of the visitors are stationed, or live, in the district. A large number are in uniform. With regard to the amount of labour needed, all men of military age have registered. Finally, it is surely rather absurd to suggest that racing should be banned because of the "waste" of paper used for race-cards. To be logical this would mean the end of football, cricket, theatres, music-halls, concerts, and everything else which involves the production of a programme.

If and when the Government feel that the time has come to put a stop to racing they will, one assumes, say so. And the racing authorities will, of course, immediately comply.

Yours, &c., OLIVER BEAUMONT
Chatsworth Court, W.8

MARCH 13

Sir,—The opponents and advocates of racing, whose letters you have published, in some cases overstate the arguments for continuing and for suppressing racing. The one general opinion I hear expressed on all sides is that every effort has got to be made to avoid waste, and that racing as at present conducted causes quite unjustifiable waste of valuable foodstuffs.

Bloodstock breeding is a very valuable asset for this country, but the number of horses kept in training during the last War sufficed to produce many distinguished thoroughbreds from 1918 onwards. In 1917 there were 1,200 horses in training, each receiving 15lb. of oats per diem. What justification can be given for having at this moment 2,300 horses in training, receiving a bigger ration than their successful predecessors? The answer must be none—except to provide means of betting. One thousand mares and entire horses would be more than ample to keep the bloodstock industry flourishing.

There were nearly 100 runners at Nottingham yesterday: every one of those could be got rid of without any loss to the country—in fact, with a distinct gain. Inevitably the demand to stop this luxurious and senseless waste will gather strength as additional hardships have to be borne by the whole population—who will not submit willingly to going without eggs in order to assist bookmakers to flourish.

Yours faithfully, GILBERT JOHNSTONE
Turf Club, Clarges Street

IN PLACE OF TOBACCO

◆

Tobacco was in short supply and many substitutes were suggested; in the meantime many correspondents deplored the growing habit of flouting the rule on non-smoking railway carriages and elsewhere.

SEPT. 1

Sir,—Pipe tobacco is none too plentiful nowadays and briars themselves are in short supply. Can I persuade your readers to pool any experience they may have of home-grown substitutes for either?

Coltsfoot, as the old botany books show, is the countryman's traditional substitute for tobacco. The French, I read, are being advised to smoke the leaves of lime, ash, or nut trees. I have lately come across memories of a clergyman who always smoked watercress and of a Scotsman who preferred lavender—whether flowers, stalks, or leaves is not clear. I have experimented with these last two herbs and with a few others primitively dried. My results so far are instructive rather than alluring either to the smoker or those about him; but I have hopes of devising before winter some more tolerable blend.

Of pipes I can write more confidently. I have lately made, out of both pear and medlar wood, pipes which, if they do not as yet colour or polish so handsomely, taste just as well as briar and better than cherry. But here, too, your readers may have wisdom to contribute.

Yours faithfully, STEPHEN TALLENTS
St. John's Jerusalem, Sutton-at-Hone, Dartford, Kent

SEPT. 3

Sir,—I have been smoking home-made pipes for over a year. Pipes made of *pådauk* (Pterocarpus macrocarpua, Kurz), holly, and yew all give a satisfying smoke. I have recently tried Burma teak, which promises to be equally good.—DR. J. A. STEWART, 17, Avenue Road, Bishop's Stortford, Herts

SEPT. 3

Sir,—The other day in one of our local almshouses an old man assured me that he always smoked the sun-dried leaves of the chrysanthemum: I tried it, but found it rather over-scented. I have since found that mixed in equal proportions with tobacco it makes a good smoke and reduces one's tobacco bill by 50 per cent.—MR. J. M. SYMNS, Pilgrims' Rest, St. Stephen's Hill, Canterbury.

Sir,—I wonder if Sir Stephen Tallents has tried a mixture of raspberry leaves with his tobacco. One can get them from the chemists at about 4d. per oz., and I have used them in the proportion of one to two of tobacco. . . . They are not bad. . . . My gardener always has a supply of coltsfoot drying off, and mixed with equal quantities of tobacco it smells very good.—CANON R. G. F. WYATT, The Vicarage, Ashton on Ribble, Preston

---

SEPT. 3
Sir,—As the countryman's substitute for tobacco, raspberry leaves run coltsfoot very close. They should be dried slowly, preferably in the sun, and in this state they will be found smokable and not unpleasant.—MR. R. G. PARKER, Top Green, Sibthorpe, Notts

---

SEPT. 3
Sir,—For the problems of tobacco addicts there is a simple and satisfactory solution—to give up smoking.—MR. E. P. HART, 66, Junction Road, Andover

---

MARCH 15
Sir,—It must be obvious to most people that in recent months there has been a growing tendency to ignore the comfort and convenience of those who prefer to travel in non-smoking compartments on trains. The tendency began with members of the armed Forces, with whom there is a perfectly natural and understandable reluctance on the part of the public to interfere. But the example is being imitated by that section of the public, to be found in other spheres, which is consistently indifferent to the comfort and convenience of others. In a non-smoking compartment on the Underground a night or so ago, of about 40 occupants 16 were smoking.

Apart from those who just prefer to travel non-smoker, there are many who do so for health reasons. May I appeal to the railway companies to enforce their by-laws in this respect, and to members of the public to assist in seeing that infringements are not permitted?
I am, Sir, your obedient servant, F. A. BLACK
108, Downhills Park Road, West Green, N.17

MARCH 24
Sir,—A possible answer to the complaint of non-smokers against the abuse of non-smoking railway compartments is suggested by the report current 70 years ago in Worcestershire of the method adopted by the Rev. Woodgate, father of the well-known oarsman. When asked by a stranger, "Do you mind, Sir, if I smoke?" he replied, "Not at all, Sir, if you don't mind my being sick." The same plea would be useful against a practice of smart

young females lighting up cigarettes in the middle of breakfast without any question being raised. This was complained of in *The Times* about two years ago.

Yours, &c., EDWARD LYTTELTON

MORE CASES OF WASTE

Of the many subjects that caused indignation, waste of any kind perhaps came foremost. Waste by government departments and civil servants was a particular source of outrage.

MAY 2

Sir,—I beg leave to quote a paragraph in *The Times* of April 25:—

When Alfred Poole, a farmer, of Thornicombe, near Blandford, was at Blandford yesterday fined £40 for unlawfully possessing regimental stores and property, it was stated that a pig swill which came from a billet contained 200 loaves, 30 to 40 legs of lamb, tinned salmon, corned beef, tinned jam, and spoons and plates.

In *The Times* of April 18 it was disclosed that the delivery by the Army of the sum of 6s. 11d. cost, in motor transport, £3. 8s. 3d.

While the Government fervently adjures others to save, they themselves apparently cannot save.

Yours, &c., HERBERT BRYAN
Highfield, Keevil, Trowbridge

MAY 7

Sir,—In *The Times* of yesterday Colonel Sir Herbert Bryan referred to the case of a farmer, recently fined, at Blandford, for "unlawfully possessing regimental stores," to wit, the contents of a pig-swill "which came from a billet." Sir Herbert makes no reference to the remarkable (though not uncommon) feature of this case—namely, that the chiefly guilty party remains unmentioned and unpunished. The farmer would never have "possessed" those 200 loaves, 40 legs of lamb, tins of foodstuffs, plates and spoons in the swill, had the officer commanding the unit in question done his duty. The fact that such duties are all too frequently neglected is the cause of widespread and disgraceful waste.

I am &c. J. O. P. BLAND
Brudenell House, Aldeburgh, Suffolk

MAY 13

Sir,—Is not this a fitting time for Whitehall—as well as the multiplicity of local authorities and organizations that follow its example—to get off the foolscap standard and adopt quarto size? The saving in paper would be considerable, and in time there would be an important consequential economy in the cost of filing equipment (including the floor space it occupies). I would suggest that as a start the war damage claim form could quite conveniently be reduced to 10in. by 8in.

All commercial firms are on the quarto standard, and even in peace-time the waste involved by the use of foolscap regardless of the length of letters, &c., seems horrifying to business men and others, who find that the smaller size meets all normal purposes. But there may, of course, be a case for the standardization of foolscap for official and legal purposes that is not apparent to the lay mind; it may not be simply a relic of more spacious days.
Yours, &c., HAROLD HERD
London, W.8

NOV. 8

Sir,—The Government attaches great importance to avoidance of paper wastage, yet seems so far to have no machinery for dealing effectively with one form of this—namely, sale catalogues of clothing, fancy articles, &c., which can have no purpose except to encourage unnecessary purchases or to divert the purchaser from one shop to another.

This is an expensive form of publication, of which retailers might be glad to be deprived, if certain that other retailers were equally deprived. Yet seemingly the Government at present can only stop it by rationing the paper supplied to printers and so affecting all their publications, useful and useless. Should not a remedy for this be found, and in time to prevent the production of such catalogues for the Christmas and January sales?
Yours faithfully, ELEANOR F. RATHBONE
House of Commons

NOV. 11

Sir,—With reference to the letter printed in *The Times* on Saturday from Miss Eleanor F. Rathbone, M.P., concerning the alleged useless dissemination of sales catalogues for Christmas and January sales, I would say that every effort will be made by this association to prevail upon advertisers to use as little paper as is possible.

Since the start of the present campaign of this association, formed for the purpose of assisting Lord Beaverbrook in his appeal for the 100,000 tons of waste paper, it has received many hundreds of letters; some critical of the misuse of paper, some critical of the collection of waste; others containing ideas and suggestions; still others drawing attention to instances of such things as the burning of waste paper, extravagant uses, &c. All of these claims will be investigated and efforts made to assist with advice on saving and collecting. Plans are made to give technical advice to manufacturers and others, showing where they may save paper; suggestions will be made to workers in offices and factories. The householders will not be neglected. We even may be bold enough to investigate allegations made against Government Departments.

Your obedient servant, S. T. GARLAND, General Manager, Waste Paper Recovery Association, Limited

Bouverie House, 154, Fleet Street, E.C.4

NOV. 17

Sir,—The "Official Report" of the House of Commons out this morning contains three entirely blank pages in addition to one half-page and one three-quarter page blank. There is no reason why four full pages should not have been saved simply by running the matter straight on instead of leaving (in the pre-war manner) a blank page between each section, and by very little closing up of the matter in the debate.

Yours faithfully, D. REEVE-FLAXMAN

5, Winchester Road, Swiss Cottage, N.W.3

CONSCIENTIOUS OBJECTORS ON THE LAND

There was respect but general distaste for conscientious objectors. They were tolerated if they laboured hard at their non-belligerent tasks—but did they?

MAY 3

Sir,—May I call your attention to the unsatisfactory conditions existing where the employment of conscientious objectors on agricultural work is concerned?

Early in February I sought to avail myself of the excellent drainage scheme instigated by the Government, and with that end in view I signed an agreement with the Surrey War Agricultural Committee for a small drainage scheme estimated to cost £80 and, according to their expert, requiring two weeks for completion. In due course 12 conscientious objectors arrived. They were all strong young men between the ages of 20 and 30. They had no idea how to work, and appeared to have no desire to learn. Furthermore there was no one to show them. Their foreman was chosen from among themselves, and beyond the fact that he received 10s. a week extra he had no qualifications for the job whatever. They were transported daily a distance of 50 miles by motor-bus. They came at 8 a.m., their dinner occupied a long hour, and they departed at 4 p.m. On Saturdays they left at

11 a.m. Their wages were the same as a skilled farm worker who works from 7 a.m. to 5 p.m., getting to and from his work in his own time.

At a very conservative estimate the work has cost the Government £40 a week. They have been here two months and they have not finished the job yet. A simple calculation will show that this small drainage scheme, estimated at £80, has already cost £320. The ditches have been incorrectly dug and are quite inadequate for their purpose, and a good deal of damage has been done to fences, gateways, &c.

Is drainage important? Is farming important? Is it desirable that conscientious objectors should play a part, consistent with their conscientious scruples, in the national effort? Surely the time has arrived when an attempt should be made to organize these schemes on a satisfactory basis and steps taken to ensure that conscientious objectors give an honest day's work for their wages.

I am, Sir, yours faithfully, C. L. CARLOS CLARKE, Major
Elletts, Rudgwick, Sussex

GAS MASKS

After 18 months of warfare, the British army, let alone the public, had still not fully grasped the correct use of the gas mask.

MAY 7

Sir,—A lorry-load of soldiers passed me to-day with their Service gas masks in the "alert" position. All were put on the wrong way round, showing the press fasteners of the flap outside, instead of inside against their chests. I am told by a gas identification officer that he saw a whole parade of an infantry company making the same mistake.

Did you observe, Sir, that "The Recruit" in the painting at the Royal Academy (of which you gave a photograph in your issue of Saturday, May 3) had fallen into the same error? Possibly because he was a recruit. The adjacent photograph of the smilingly competent policeman in "Deep Shelter" shows the gas mask in the correct position.

I urge that constant care by instructors and inspecting officers be exercised in this small but vital detail. Tragic consequences might otherwise result.

Yours faithfully, J. GORDON HASSELL
116, Chancery Lane, London, W.C.2

PETROL

—◆—

The meagre civilian petrol ration was based on the horse-power of the owner's car. This seemed to many illogical and its further reduction in May led to a heavy correspondence.

MAY 5

Sir,—There are reports that the petrol allowance is to be reduced, with consequent hardship to country dwellers and to those who need their cars in connexion with their work. Any sacrifice necessary to the effective prosecution of the war will be accepted; but can we first be assured that a serious attempt is being made to check wanton waste?

Yesterday there was a race meeting at Newmarket, and those of us who live in the district were edified by the spectacle of roads crowded by hundreds of motor-omnibuses and cars converging on Newmarket from a wide area. Many of the cars were of high power, and thousands of gallons of petrol must have been consumed. To what end?

Yours, &c., P. GARDENER-SMITH

Fen Ditton Hall

MAY 20

Sir,—Although the civil population of this country undoubtedly waste a certain amount of petrol owing to thoughtless extravagance, they are not the only culprits. Many people are not a little discouraged in their efforts at economy by the knowledge that the fighting Services use petrol with a generosity amounting to recklessness.

Not long ago an Army carrier-pigeon strayed into my loft, to be retrieved by a sergeant who had come 40 miles for that express purpose, in a troop carrier that used on the whole journey about eight gallons of petrol. The basket he had to bring for the pigeon measured approximately two cubic feet and could easily have been strapped on to the back of a motor-bicycle, as he freely admitted, wondering that "He hadn't thought of it." From all accounts this incident was typical.

I know that efforts are being made to prevent such waste, but they seem to be more well-intentioned than intelligent. For instance, a certain division has forbidden the use of four-wheeled vehicles on one day a week. The futility of this plan should be obvious. Would it not be possible to induce those in authority to use their common sense and to concentrate on the reasonable use of the vehicles at their disposal, instead of making handsome but ineffective gestures?

I am, Sir, yours faithfully, A. K. ATHILL

Ditchingham Hall Farm, Bungay, Suffolk

Sir,—I live in the depths of the country, six miles from shops and a railway station, and my wife is an invalid who is absolutely dependent on motoring for all domestic and social purposes.

Before the war I had three cars, but I now have only one. Recently I was informed that my supplementary allowance for this one car, already inadequate, had been reduced by one-half. By the same post I had a letter from a friend who lives 70 miles from the sea, in which he stated: "The war must be going well! The cook's young man, a private in the Army, was able to come up two days running from his seaside station in a little car he has bought and take her for a joy ride."

Again, a battalion near my home was giving a dance. A subaltern made a sketch for the menu, which took the colonel's fancy. He sent it by lorry a journey of 45 miles to have it reproduced on the menu; when the printing had been done, another lorry was sent to fetch the copies of the menu. So by making journeys of 180 miles—not in a little car but in a lorry, costly in petrol—the dance took place in accordance with peace-time routine!

I am warned that I must in future keep a record of all journeys by car. Does that regulation also apply to the Army?

Yours, &c., ARCHIBALD HURD

Sir,—It is my practice, when driving my own car, for which I have an allowance of five gallons a month, to give lifts to soldiers. One soldier, a Canadian, to whom I gave a lift, expressed surprise when I told him I was rationed for petrol, and added, "There is no shortage of petrol in the Canadian Army." The truth of this remark was borne out when a very large Army car, driven by a Canadian soldier, and carrying a sergeant, made a journey of 40 miles expressly for the purpose of delivering to me a very small key measuring 1¼in., which could have been posted to me for 2½d. and brought to the door by the postman on his bicycle in the course of his daily round.

As I myself had just returned from a five-mile bicycle ride in the pouring rain in order to carry home as much food for the household as the basket on my bicycle would hold, the dispatch of a miniature key in an outsize car, escorted by two soldiers, on a journey of 40 miles made me wonder whether it was for trips like these that the civilian is being so strictly rationed. When I expressed surprise that the key should have been returned to me in person, the sergeant charmingly expostulated that it had been "No trouble at all."

Yours faithfully, RUTH BARHAM
Brackenhill, Munstead Park, Godalming, Surrey

JUNE 14

Sir,—With reference to correspondence on waste, it is a little difficult for anyone limited to the basic petrol ration to appreciate any rational basis for a system by which a driver by the simple procedure of hiring a motor-car for a week immediately acquires coupons to cover several hundred miles' travelling.

Incidentally, in view of the paper shortage, is it really necessary nowadays for annual reports to run into 16 octavo pages and a stiffened binding cover? One leading company has just circulated such a document to its thousands of shareholders, accompanied by six pages of advertising matter.

Yours faithfully, R. GOODCHILD
35, Colcokes Road, Banstead, Surrey

THE HESS AFFAIR

◆

The flight to Scotland on 10 May of Rudolf Hess, Hitler's deputy, caused general astonishment. There was even greater astonishment at the manner in which his exploit was reported.

MAY 16

Sir,—I beg you to allow me a few lines to point out one or two things about Rudolf Hess which urgently need saying. In the first place, he is not a film star, as some of the publicity accorded him might suggest, but a man who has been deeply involved in the crimes and machinations of the Nazis. He should therefore be regarded by all just-minded people with extreme suspicion and distaste. Secondly, if he escaped from Germany to save his own skin, he would surely have done everything possible, for the sake of his wife and child, to conceal his identity: unless, of course, he came as an open rebel against Nazism, in which case he would hardly have left his wife and child to German vengeance. Pending further disclosures, it is surely to be assumed that he is a tool of Hitler, who, like most Germans, is profoundly convinced of the "gentlemanly folly" of the British.

Yours truly, OLWEN W. CAMPBELL
West Kirby

MAY 16

Sir,—From the tone of smug complacency in which the announcer of the B.B.C. gave out the news this morning, he must have thought it would bring infinite satisfaction to the suffering victims of the bloody savagery of the enemy, of which Rudolf Hess is one of the most guilty, to know that Rudolf Hess is "very comfortable." Shall we next have our day made sweeter by being assured that, in spite of the treachery of his friend, Hitler has passed a good night!

Yours faithfully, BEATRICE BROWNRIGG

MAY 16

Sir,—Three stories that come down from the classics warn us not to take too much for granted in regard to the curious arrival in this country of Hitler's *fidus Achates*. The best known is the episode of Sinon in Virgil's story of the fall of Troy (Aeneid, ii, 57–198); less familiar perhaps are Herodotus's account of the taking of Babylon by Cyrus (iii, 154–5) and Ovid's of the taking of Gabii by Tarquin (Fasti, ii, 687–710).

All the three have certain essential features in common, both with each other and with the coming of Rudolf Hess to Scotland last Saturday. In each there is the stubborn resistance to siege; in each the devoted servant of the besieging leader gets himself made prisoner (in order to betray the beleaguered city from within); in each the betrayer does violence to himself to lend colour to his story. Zopyrus goes farthest, cutting off his nose and ears; the young Tarquin has himself flogged; Sinon is merely shackled; Hess has his ankle damaged.

Yours faithfully, LIONEL JAMES
Moyses, Five Ashes, Sussex

MAY 23

Sir,—The English language seems to be having a rough time of it these days. There was that elementary "I will drown, no one shall save me" slip in that Commons resolution, and now there is an outcry about Hess being allowed "idealism," that quite overlooks the fact that ideals may be good or bad. One would have thought even an M.P. would have been able to deduce this from your comment that "Hess has always had a quite false and idealized view of Hitler."

No wonder Mr. Churchill considers it necessary to offer to translate his Latin tags in the Commons, even if he is polite enough to pretend it is only for the benefit of Etonians.

Yours faithfully, SELDEN PIERCY
53, Willow Road, Hampstead, N.W.3

BUREAUCRACY

◆

The annoyance of bureaucracy was a recurring theme. During 1941, irritation was caused by such diverse matters as the

household coal ration, employment of servicemen on leave and mindless censorship.

JULY 17

Sir,—In the second week of June I ordered from the Midlands a truck of coal for winter use. This was in accordance with my usual habit, and also it had been specially asked for by the Coal Control of those who possessed large cellars. The order was acknowledged together with the statement that it should be carried out as soon as possible. Unfortunately, owing to railway difficulties, the coal in question only arrived at Chelmsford on July 8, by which time a new decree had been issued that each house should be allowed only one ton a month. In consequence the whole truck has been confiscated and handed over to a local coal merchant.

If the coal merchant in question should supply me with my monthly ration of coal, it will, of course, mean extra labour and petrol, as we are between three and four miles from the station. This weathercock policy of the authorities is very puzzling for those who are most anxious to help in the present coal problem.

Truly yours, E. R. REDMAYNE
Great Baddow, Essex

JULY 25

Sir,—I am the headmaster of a boys' preparatory school, recognized as efficient by the Board of Education. My household consists of 70 persons, composed of boys, teaching staff, domestic staff, and my own family. The only concession granted by the local fuel overseer is that I may lay in a stock of three tons of fuel. Apart from this, I am allowed the standard one ton a month for cooking, hot water, and heating. There is no gas. A couple in a cottage may have the same amount. Apart from equity, is this sanity?
Yours, &c., F. H. M.

AUG. 11

Sir,—In April, believing I was doing the right thing, I ordered a truck of anthracite French nuts from a colliery. It arrived on July 5. The local fuel controller seized nearly all its contents, informing me that I was breaking an order dated July 3, which prohibited the delivery of more than one ton of "coal" to any house in July.

In your issue of to-day is a paragraph headed, "More Coal for the Home," and stating that *inter alia* anthracite French nuts may now be supplied to premises of a non-industrial character "in any quantity." This is the sort of thing which increases our admiring devotion to Whitehall.
Your obedient servant, F. D. MAC KINNON

NOV. 7

Sir,—A short time ago a question was put to the Secretary of State for War as to whether the beating for game by soldiers on leave was authorized. The Minister replied in the negative, deprecating such employment. The sequel is that an order has now been issued to commanding officers prohibiting this.

Game is food and is largely distributed to hospitals and others who need it; in any case it is food and saves consumption of rationed food, and game cannot be rounded up and shot without beaters. Soldiers on leave have been glad to do this, and have received whatever emolument a beater would receive. It amounts to this, that a soldier on leave is restricted in his pursuits, even if his father be a farmer, and asks him to come out and help him to round up some rabbits. When I told the keeper of the restriction his language lost nothing from the vehemence of its expression, but he ended by saying, "I suppose they would rather the soldiers hung about the pubs instead of getting a little healthy exercise."

Yours obediently, CYRIL A. DRUMMOND
Cadland Cottage, Fawley, Southampton

NOV. 15

Sir,—The letter on the above subject which appeared in your issue of November 7 raises a point of further interest. What is the position of a keeper home on leave? Does the Order to which your correspondent refers apply equally to such a case? Recently, in the south, I was invited to shoot on a day on which my host knew that his young keeper would be on leave and thereby available to take charge of the day's proceedings. This he did to the complete satisfaction of all concerned, and doubtless also to his own enjoyment. If, in future, such employment is to be debarred (and this appears to be the logical conclusion to be drawn from this latest Order) the food supply of the country is likely to suffer and the individual to be deprived of an added interest to his eagerly anticipated leave.

Yours faithfully, W. H. P. LAW, Colonel (Retd.)
Fearn Lodge, Ardgay, N.B.

NOV. 19

Sir,—The following extract is taken at random from a Government Order, in this case the Limitation of Supplies (Cloth and Apparel) Order:—
"Where goods are or were invoiced by a registered person to another registered person who in relation to the supply of these goods is or was the agent either of the supplier or of the person to whom or to whose order they are or were to be supplied, the supplier shall be deemed to supply or to have supplied these goods to the agent, and, when the goods are or were supplied to or to the order of the person to be supplied, the agent shall be deemed to

supply or to have supplied them." May one suggest that the elimination of this sort of rubbish would not only save paper, but would release the men who concoct it and the thousands employed in interpreting it for the Forces?

Your obedient servant, J. DOLBY
317, Andover Road, Newbury

DEC. 31

Sir,—A friend of mine in Eire recently sent her daughter in England some eggs. The latter in her letter of thanks, said: "I wish you would send me a cow." It was, however, returned to her by the English censor with the remark: "Import of cattle into England from Eire by private individuals is not permitted. This letter, therefore, which asks for a prohibited article, is returned to sender." After this who can maintain that the censors do not earn their pay?

I had written this much when it occurred to me that possibly they may prohibit the import of this letter also into England. Let us hope that its examination will fall to a censor with a sense of humour.

Yours, &c., C. A. H. TOWNSEND
Red House, Castle Townshend, Skibbereen, Co. Cork

"ESQUIRE"

◆

Many post-war reforms were suggested. One correspondent wished to suppress the term 'Esquire', which met with general if perverse approval.

NOV. 14

Sir,—Among the minor reforms that are coming, would not the suppression of "Esquire" in general and business correspondence be welcomed? It is a relic of mid-Victorian snobbery, and has little or nothing to commend it. I believe the United Kingdom is the only part of the Empire that uses it.

Yours truly, LOUGHLAN PENDRED
The Athenaeum

NOV. 15

Sir,—With reference to Mr. Pendred's letter, it is interesting to note that the use of this suffix is not so limited as he supposes. Here is a recently issued official direction in India: "Indian gentlemen holding the office of a

Justice of the Peace, or of a Judge, so styled, or who are barrister-at-law, are entitled to be addressed as 'Esquire' agreeably to the English usage."
Your obedient servant, W. REEVE WALLACE

Sir,—How right Mr. Loughnan Pendred is in denouncing the use of this word as "a relic of mid-Victorian snobbery" and in demanding its "suppression"! But why does he not go further? Is not our all too frequent utterance or inscription of the word "Mr." an equally gross survival from an era which men of good will can hardly mention without embarrassment and shame? I do hope Pendred *will* go further.
Your obedient servant, MAX BEERBOHM
Abinger Manor Cottage, Abinger Common

Sir,—In his letter of yesterday's date my friend Mr. Reeve Wallace shows that "Esquire" is still a title legally borne only by persons on whom it has been bestowed by the Crown or who have the right to it in virtue of their office or recognized status. In practice, however, it has long been extended by courtesy to a much wider circle.

In this it has but conformed to a general tendency, due not to the levelling down but to the levelling up of the different social strata. "Mister," which Mr. Pendred would like to substitute for it, as in the Dominions and the United States, was at one time a title confined to those who had the right to style themselves "gentlemen," just as Herr in Germany and Monsieur in France were once titles restricted to the nobility. In William Harrison's time the "citizen" had no more right to be called "Master" than the French bourgeois before the great Revolution had to be addressed as "Monsieur." It was the assimilation of the middle classes, in wealth and manners, to the old aristocracy, which led to the wider diffusion of these titles by an inevitable process. The process is likely to be accelerated after the war; but it is possible to imagine a time when by a converse process "Comrade," like its Latin equivalent *comes* (Count), will become a nobiliary title.
Your obedient servant, W. ALISON PHILLIPS
Savile Club

Sir,—Your correspondent who wishes to abolish the title of "Esquire" is mistaken when he says that it "has little or nothing to recommend it." Mr. Pendred forgets that by the use of this appellation married couples are insured against the inadvertent opening of one another's letters. I have heard Americans express their admiration for the ingenuity of the privileged few in this country who, by a method so simple, have attained a

desirable end. Rather than suppress the "Esquire," I suggest that it would be in accordance with the spirit of the age to extend the use of it to all.
Yours truly, CLAUD RUSSELL
The Athenaeum, Pall Mall, S.W.1

NOV. 18

Sir,—Mr. Loughnan Pendred rightly invites us to suppress the lowest rank "Esquire" in the order of snobbery. But why stop there? Why not go higher up the scale?
Yours truly, A. V. HILL
House of Commons

NOV. 18

Sir,—Surely Mr. Pendred is incorrect in ascribing the use of "Esquire" to mid-Victorian snobbery? Samuel Pepys, in 1660, expresses his delight at receiving a letter addressed "S.P., Esq.", of which he "was not a little proud."

Pepys may have been a snob, but he was certainly not mid-Victorian. I shall risk Mr. Pendred's disapprobation (and place myself among the snobs) by subscribing myself, in the old-fashioned manner, as,
Your most humble
Your most obedient servant, NORMAN DAVEY, Esquire
Boodle's

NOV. 18

Sir,—Matthew Arnold urged the disuse of "Esquire." I well remember hearing him, in a public lecture, scornfully describe the word as "a relic of the great frippery shop of the Middle Ages."
Yours faithfully, WALTER WOOD
Ravendale, Hartfield Road, Seaford

NOV. 21

Sir,—Beerbohm's suggestion that the prefix "Mr." should be abolished does not go far enough. We are still left with our surnames, and this is undemocratic. I demand that we should all be called by the same name, as plain a one as possible. If this should render difficult the filling up of forms, a number could be attached to each—or rather the same—name.
Yours faithfully, OSBERT SITWELL
Renishaw Hall, Renishaw, near Sheffield

"TAXI!"

*Identifying, let alone securing, a taxi in the London black-out
was invariably a source of frustration.*

DEC. 5

Sir,—It has become obvious to me that certain taxi-drivers do not work in black-out hours because it is their job to do so, or because they feel it their duty to help, but because they can get double fares and more on each ride, or at least if this is not given they become extremely rude and impertinent. I experienced a scene like this only the other night. On a three-shilling fare a taxi-driver demanded 10s., saying that he had no change for paper money and anyway it was in the black-out and he couldn't be expected to give change (it was then precisely 7 p.m.). He became extremely offensive indeed, and eventually got paid his fare only without a tip at all.

I might add that this is not the first time this sort of thing has happened in my presence, hence this letter. Something should be done to stop this very unpleasant and irritating situation getting worse.

Yours truly, VERA LUMLEY-KELLY
London, S.W.1

DEC. 17

Sir,—Those who need taxicabs in the black-out would greatly appreciate some visible indication if the vehicle we dimly discern is a cab, and, if so, whether it is engaged or free. The word "Taxi" in red or green, to show whether it is free or not, would relieve both him who yells and (if it is engaged) him who feels selfish to be in the cab when the other man is in the rain.

Yours, &c., C. S. KENT
Knightsbridge, S.W.

DEC. 23

Sir,—Your correspondent in *The Times* of December 17, who suggests that there should be some visible indication on a cab which is available for hire, will no doubt be interested to learn that over 90 per cent. of the cabs operating in London are in fact fitted with a special sign on the driver's canopy which, when the cab is unhired, and only then, shows in illuminated letters the word "Taxi."

Yours truly, H. ALKER TRIPP, Assistant Commissioner of Police,
New Scotland Yard, S.W.1

1941

Sir,—I am certainly interested to learn from the letter of the Assistant Commissioner of Police that over 90 per cent. of the taxi-cabs in London are fitted with a sign which indicates that they are for hire. I did not know it. Nor did many of my friends and acquaintances. Only two out of many were aware of the fact. Those who have shouted "Taxi!" at me as I have driven through Central and West London on my way homeward from my office must have been equally ignorant. They clearly should have waited till one of the "over 90 per cent." came along unhired. Unfortunately for them, however, not all of the signs seem to work. Yet the need for them is greater than ever.

I suggest that the Assistant Commissioner takes to searching for a taxi at midnight between (say) Ludgate Circus and Hyde Park Corner on wet nights. He may then be convinced of the inadequacy of the present sign. He may even join the ranks of those who shout "Taxi!" in sheer desperation at every cab or car that passes.

Yours, &c., C. S. KENT
Knightsbridge, S.W.1

Sir,—It is a fact that the "Taxi" sign is fitted to most London cabs, but your correspondent rightly complains that as an illuminated sign it serves no useful purpose in the black-out. It is not a compulsory fitment, but, if fitted, as it is on most cabs, it must be in working order when submitted for annual inspection by the police. Unfortunately for the travelling public the police have thought fit to enforce a reduction of the illumination to about one-fifth of its pre-war power. The resultant light is so dim that the sign cannot be seen from a sufficient distance to enable the prospective fare to identify an approaching cab.

Representations to the Police Commissioner might reasonably succeed in his permitting a small increase in the illumination so that the sign may serve the purpose for which it was intended, and which is now more than ever required.

Yours faithfully, H. ESPIR, Managing Director, Metropolitan Fare Register Company, Limited
9 Harmsworth Street, Kensington Park, S.E.17

1942

BBC BULLETINS

The beleaguered Britons relied on newspapers and, more immediately, BBC news bulletins, which were also listened to by the people of occupied Europe, for progress reports on the war. The BBC was often criticised for its sanguine accounts of Allied reverses and for the on-the-spot language of its reporters.

FEB. 18

Sir,—Millions of people in this country listened on Friday night to the B.B.C. news and heard the account of the passage through the Straits of Dover of German warships. It is not my purpose to discuss this event from the military point of view; but I am certain that a large proportion of the listeners must have shared my feelings that this is only the latest incident showing that the authorities responsible for the tone of the broadcasts can have no understanding of the present temper of this country. Doubtless the tributes to the gallantry of those who took part in the battle were more than justified, and every one would wish to share in paying them. But it is intolerable that the account of their deeds should be used as a device to soften the effect of the blow which this German success has dealt us. What is the use of pretending that it has not fallen at precisely the point where we had been led to believe it was least of all likely?

Before the war the British public may have had an unfortunate taste for pleasant soporifics, but the authorities responsible for official and semi-official news to-day seem to be ignorant of the fact that that taste has long been outgrown. An appeal to the fighting spirit of this country will never fail as long as there is confidence that it is based on facts; but half truths which seek to minimize the facts or gloss over defeat can result only in confusion, lack of effort, and even in exasperation. I hope many of your readers will help to persuade the persons responsible that a change of tone is essential if this country is to brace itself for the long effort necessary before victory is won.

I am yours, &c., GERALD PALMER

House of Commons

FEB. 18

Sir,—We are told that our worst enemy is complacency, but could anything be better calculated to induce complacency than the presentation of the news by the B.B.C.? Every one is familiar with such phrases as: "The R.A.F. successfully bombed . . . ," "among recent successes," "further successes were obtained," "the Germans unsuccessfully . . . ," &c. Recently the words "success" and "successfully" were used nine times in a single broadcast. Is it surprising that such a presentation of news should breed complacency?

Also, we read the speeches of Ministers urging greater effort, higher production, and so on, but nearly always the appeals are prefaced by some such statement as "while ultimate victory is certain," which stultifies the whole argument. It is as though we were living through the pages of a book in which Britain is the hero, who will infallibly triumph in the last chapter. But, alas! the present times are not fiction, they are grim reality and victory is not certain—it must be won.

Yours faithfully, H. B. TURLE
10, Old Broad Street, E.C.2

FEB. 21

Sir,—Psychological facts should be kept in mind before passing censure on the news bulletins of the B.B.C. Their exceedingly difficult task demands obvious need to hold the scales evenly between successes and setbacks, for baldly to announce items of utmost gravity and disappointment, and make no effort to gild the pill when it is reasonable to do so, would instantly arouse adverse criticism. Then your correspondents must complain that the silver lining of every cloud was consistently ignored by the B.B.C. and the worst possible interpretation set upon events. The Prime Minister himself has not failed to indicate how countervailing aspects of recent ill fortune must be taken into account, that just balance may be struck in the public mind, and none can accuse him of complacency.

Faithfully yours, EDEN PHILLPOTTS
Devon

FEB. 21

Sir,—I write in support of the views expressed in your issue of February 18 by Mr. Gerald Palmer and Mr. H. B. Turle on the unfortunate tone of the B.B.C. news bulletins. We are passing through a time of great strain when things which would normally arouse little comment act as an irritant and, if persisted in, destroy all confidence. I would like to cite one instance which provoked a number of people to exclamations of disgust at its futility:—In the 6 p.m. News on Monday, February 16, we were treated to a brief reference to the number of prisoners in Singapore, a briefer reference to Rommel's advance in Libya, and then, with great gusto, the announcer proceeded to relate the story of a Filipino truck driver who had succeeded in killing himself and 11 Japanese soldiers by accelerating when driving round a bend and throwing the passengers from the vehicle.

The B.B.C. are sadly miscalculating the feelings of the people of this country if they think that such futile methods will serve to distract public attention from the really vital issues.

Yours faithfully, E. A. HOLLOWAY, Honorary Secretary, Economic Reform Club and Institute

32, Queen's Avenue, N.10

FEB. 23

Sir,—I think your correspondents Mr. Palmer and Mr. Turle are a little unfair to the B.B.C. There is a very nice and very difficult balance to be kept by so presenting the news that, on the one hand, "complacency" is not fostered and, on the other hand, "doubt and despondency" are not engendered. Take as one instance the Straits of Dover broadcast. Even at the risk of "softening the blow" was it not essential that the gallantry of our heroic seamen and airmen should be placed beyond a peradventure?—that we should be assured that their willingness to make the rich sacrifice of their young years is as great as ever it was?—that whoever was at fault they were blameless? So far from softening the blow, the tale of their fruitless sacrifice gave rise to anguish far greater than that occasioned by the story of defeat. I doubt if any listener misunderstood the nature of the calamity recorded or was in any way consoled by the alleged malpresentation.

As to Mr. Turle's objection to the use of the word "success," would he tell us what word the B.B.C. should substitute when they have to record events which have turned out favourably? Is any listener really deceived into thinking that a "successful" bombing by the R.A.F. is any more than a small incident in the course of the war? Or, on occasions on which the Germans fail to perform their intention, would it be better for the B.B.C. kindly to spare the feelings of our enemies by discreet silence or a non-committal reference?

Lastly, would Ministers be able to stimulate the nation to greater efforts if, instead of prefacing their exhortations by "while ultimate victory is certain," they were to speak something like this: "While ultimate victory is uncertain, please do your darnedest as it will look so much better if we have to give in"? Repeated auto-suggestion that victory is certain, especially if this is reinforced from the outside, is a munition of war of incalculable value. The appeal is not stultified by the assumption of certain ultimate victory. The greater effort and higher production are urgently needed to bring that victory nearer and to save life. The argument is, indeed, fortified by the confident assumption that victory will not pass us by.

Yours faithfully, E. W. ADAMS

Grasmere, Westmorland

Sir,—The B.B.C. have an excellent corps of announcers with clear, resonant voices, but every now and then, when they have received an important dispatch from one of their war correspondents, the announcers are taken off and we are treated to the distorted voice of the correspondent himself in a "recorded" message.

In the nine o'clock news on June 24, for instance, a dispatch from the Libyan front reached us in this fashion. One listened to it with painful interest but with a growing feeling of exasperation. The spoken words had to fight their way through a barrage of extraneous noises, and one or two were lost altogether. It was like having to read an important letter so badly written that in trying to decipher the script one missed the meaning. What possible advantage is there in this method of broadcasting? It is the report we want to hear, not the necessarily distorted voice of the reporter.

Yours faithfully, E. J. PHILLIPS

18, Victoria Terrace, Beaumaris, Anglesey

Sir,—Mr. Phillips's complaint, in your issue of July 1, of inaudibility of the Libyan dispatches seems unjustified. In my experience, the dispatches come through clearly and audibly and are usually only broadcast from London when fit for that purpose.

A report of momentous and important events on the battle-front read by an announcer in the same tone, however clear and resonant, as, for example, an announcement of an increase in points rationing, cannot possibly stimulate the same interest as the voice of the reporter on the spot describing in his own words what he has actually seen. We can all read and listen *ad nauseam* to written reports, but seldom are we given the opportunity of hearing an actual eye-witness of a battle in progress.

Your obedient servant, L. I. M. THOMAS

Regis House, King William Street (Monument), E.C.4

Sir,—Is it impossible to prevail upon the B.B.C. to read us out the actual text of the Middle East *communiques*? They are at present surrounded and interlarded with so many explanations and glosses and jejune comments that those of us who live in the country must always wait for next morning's papers before we can discover what is what. G.H.Q. in Cairo takes, I suppose, very considerable pains over the precise wording of its reports. Who, one wonders, is the conceited individual in London who presumes to improve them and brighten them up? The wireless stations of every single other country to which I have listened invariably read out official military

communiques verbatim, and explicitly indicate the point at which they begin and end. The failure of the B.B.C. to do the same seems to me not only to be unfair to the Army Command but also to be evidence of an unjustified condescension towards the intelligence of listeners.
Your obedient servant, JAMES STRACHEY
Lord's Wood, Marlow, Bucks

WHEAT SHIPMENTS

The Battle of the Atlantic reached its climax in 1942, with heavy Allied merchant shipping losses until May. This situation produced an abundance of advice from correspondents, the more imaginative pointing to radical reductions in food requirements.

FEB. 21

Sir,—Shipments to this country of wheat, including flour in wheat equivalent, must at present approximate 7,000,000 tons a year. It is known that this could be cut by more than 1,000,000 tons without any reduction in the bread supply. (Compulsory wheatmeal, in the terms of recent controversy, is only one of the methods to hand.) Rationing, and banning the sale of fresh bread, could save at least another million and still leave us better off than any other country in Europe. We are eating more and better bread than before the war, while every enemy and neutral country in Europe is severely restricted in quantity and quality. What dispensation have we of Providence, what indulgence have we earned by our military prowess, to entitle us to standards fully 50 per cent. higher than those which evidently leave our enemies fit enough to inflict defeats upon us?

Sir, these potential wheat economies mean a great deal of ship-space, much greater than is offered by any other comparable belt-tightening. Even 1,000,000 tons is 20 times as much as the soap rationing is supposed to save, and 10 times as much as would be saved by halving the tea ration. It is almost certainly more than the amount of tonnage for lack of which, according to Mr. Churchill, we lost Malaya. We must choose between unpalatabilities. There are important qualifications to this argument, but the broad facts seem to override them.
Yours faithfully, SYDNEY S. GAMPELL
Chiswick House, Ditton Road, Surbiton, Surrey

GOOD FRIDAY

—◆—

*The Allies thought—rightly, in the event—that they were
fighting evil. But should Good Friday be given to prayer, thereby
losing valuable man hours in their righteous cause?*

MARCH 3

Sir,—I venture to think that many will share with me great regret that the
Government have decided that Good Friday shall again be treated as an
ordinary weekday. Surely at a time when we are being told we are fighting a
righteous war we could observe the most solemn and one of the most sacred
days of the year in reverence of our Lord.

Yours, &c., MAMHEAD
House of Lords

MARCH 5

Sir,—The somewhat astonishing attitude expressed in Lord Mamhead's
letter in *The Times* of to-day must have surprised many thousands who saw
it. Surely much of our misfortune can be attributed to this complete
misunderstanding of the tempo of total war, so unfortunately apparent in
some of those who should be leading us. I am in deepest sympathy with
Lord Mamhead's desire to observe one of the most sacred days of the year,
Good Friday, but not as a holiday. Every man and woman who so desires
can find a moment during the day for prayer.

Was it with the observance of holidays that the magnificent stand of the
Greeks was made against the Italians? The feast of Easter is of far greater
moment to the Orthodox Greek than to the majority of us, yet last year the
whole of that small and courageous nation worked throughout, sparing
only a few minutes at midnight service to proclaim χριστὸς 'Ανίοη.

Yours faithfully, ALURED DENNE
Naval and Military Club, 94, Piccadilly, W.1

MARCH 11

Sir,—I would support Lord Mamhead's appeal. On Good Friday Jesus
died. His crucifixion is the symbol of the age-long tragedy of humanity. He
leads "the loveliest and the best" now so widely mourned. If some of
Christ's followers wish for a short time next Good Friday to think of the
death of their Lord, surely the Government should not deny them their
desire.

Yours faithfully, E. W. BIRMINGHAM
Bishop's Croft, Harborne, Birmingham, 17

Sir,—Many of your readers will, I think, have felt sympathy with the motive which inspired Lord Mamhead's letter to you regarding the Government's decision as to the observance of Good Friday. I do not think the letter of the Bishop of Birmingham will have the same effect. It is surely a matter of common knowledge that Good Friday, in past years, to the vast majority of the population has meant a holiday and not a Holy Day. The Bishop pleads that the Government will allow "some of Christ's followers a short time to think of the death of their Lord." What is to prevent them from so doing even if for eight hours they are working in order to defeat a very evil thing?

What I would venture to plead for is that the factories entertainments given from 12.30 to 1 p.m. on Good Friday this year should be used by song and speech—even prayer—to remind workers of the objective of their labour which is to bring about the conquest of an evil force which if victorious would rob them of "the loveliest and the best," and by their splendid part in the war effort help to produce a world in which Christ the crucified King's teaching can be put into effect and so the only lasting peace be achieved.

Yours, &c., CYRIL H. GOLDING-BIRD, Bishop
Tiltmead, Cobham, Surrey

Sir,—In a letter published in *The Times* of to-day, the Bishop of Birmingham writes:—"If some of Christ's followers wish for a short time next Good Friday to think of the death of their Lord, surely the Government should not deny them their desire."

But, Sir, why should the Government be brought in? Our Lord's injunction runs:—"When thou prayest, enter into thy closet, and when thou hast shut thy door, pray to thy Father, which is in secret; and thy Father which seeth in secret shall reward thee openly." Surely a Christian, who so wishes, can—Government or no Government—find time on Good Friday to think of the death of Christ.

I am, Sir, your obedient servant, HERBERT BRYAN
Highfield, Keevil, Trowbridge

CATS AND MILK

The Ministry of Food allocated an allowance of dried milk to those cats kept for destroying vermin in warehouses. Was milk a necessity for cats?

Sir,—It is reported that the Ministry of Food has granted an allowance of dried milk to cats of national use in keeping down grain-eating vermin in warehouses. Of all accepted popular errors, surely one of the strangest is the belief that full-grown cats need milk. Admittedly they like it, but they need it no more than do dogs or sheep or rabbits. Water, not milk, is the natural drink of all wild animals, except very young mammals; and so far as appetite and nutrition are concerned our tame cats differ in no respect from their wild prototype. If the favoured cats that are "doing their bit" were not artificially fed, they would hunt and kill and eat the warehouse rats and mice with greater zest than ever.

Yours, &c., R. I. POCOCK

British Museum (Natural History)

Sir,—Practical farmers, in Scotland at any rate, will not support the view of Mr. R. I. Pocock, published in your issue of Saturday, March 7, that milk for cats is a superfluity. It has been proved over and over again that if a farmer wishes to keep down rats and mice he must provide a saucer of milk daily, accessible to his cats. Not only will this prevent their straying away, but a diet of the flesh of rats and mice must be accompanied by milk. Such a diet keeps cats active and keen after their prey.

Yours, &c., HUGH SHAW-STEWART, a former chairman of the Highland and Agricultural Society

---

Sir,—Your correspondent Mr. R. I. Pocock suggests that full-grown cats need water and not milk. While this may be largely true, is there any necessity to go so far as to say that cats doing work of national importance should not have any milk at all?

It has been stated that a Japanese soldier can live on two handfuls of rice a day. Possibly that would be sufficient to sustain life for all of us, but I have grave doubts as to what our efficiency would be if we were forced to have that only as a ration. Surely the Ministry of Food have acted with common sense in granting an allowance of dried milk, but has not Mr. Pocock missed the chief point that this allowance mostly consists of dried milk that is unfit for human food?

Yours faithfully, ROBERT H. MORGAN

House of Commons

Sir,—In reply to Mr. Shaw-Stewart's letter of March 11, I may point out that farm cats free to roam the countryside have access to the same prey as cats that have run wholly wild, and these get along very well without milk. With regard to home-feeding and vermin-killing, it must be remembered that comparatively few ordinary house cats have the pluck to tackle a full-grown rat. Also that in carnivorous animals, like cats, the goad of hunger is a powerful factor in suppressing caution and instilling courage. A hungry tiger, for instance, will attack a dangerous beast, like a wild boar, or face a porcupine's quills, if harmless prey is unobtainable.

Yours, &c., R. I. POCOCK

British Museum (Natural History), South Kensington, S.W.7

SIMPLER CLOTHES

Clothing coupons were severely restricted. How did this affect ladies conscious of fashion? And could not the male's utility suit be single-breasted and without the customary waistcoat? Apparently not. And what of the superfluous ribbons on men's hats?

MARCH 9

Sir,—I see with dismay in your article on "Simpler Clothes" in *The Times* of March 4 that "changes in fashion are likely." Surely it would be in the best interests of economy, of money, and material to allow them to remain as at present, with the few minor changes of trimming also suggested. Having good clothes to wear out, both for winter and summer, I have followed the wishes of the Ministry of Supply and have used few coupons and bought no clothes, and could carry on through the coming summer complying with the call to thrift if only the fashions could remain unchanged.

The moment fashions alter old clothes become dowdy—and must we add to the depressing mental strain which women are trying to bear cheerfully a new temptation to spend because those who urge us not to do so dangle a new incentive before our eyes? No woman can resist new clothes if fashion alters.

Yours obediently, D. ROWLAND

7, Park Avenue, Shrewsbury

MARCH 16

Sir,—I hope no Russian women—nor any other allied women—will read the letter of your correspondent Miss D. Rowland in your issue of March 9. I write as one who likes new and fashionable clothes very much, but if we Englishwomen cannot endure to wear our old clothes and last year's fashions, and wear them cheerfully, we are in that way "doing our bit" to lose the war.

Yours, &c., JESSICA BLUNDUN
Southport

MARCH 21

Sir,—May one who is neither a tailor nor a bureaucrat, but merely an ordinary wearer of clothes, and therefore interested chiefly in the comfort and convenience provided by the design of clothes he wears, venture to suggest modifications in the restrictions just announced, which seem to be aimed chiefly at us of maturer years. It is only we who preserve the fashions of the last century in wearing a watch with a chain slung across the "lower chest," for the safety of which our tailors have devised the "chain-hole," now banned; it is only we who, with the changes in profile which only too often appear with advancing years, rely on the strap across the back of the waistcoat to preserve at least an appearance of fit in that difficult garment. Surely these two concessions to the deterioration of later middle age are not the cause of so much waste of textile materials that they must necessarily be banned. Then there is the matter of pockets—though in this matter we shall doubtless receive the support of that part of the younger generation which is still of the preparatory school age. Why are they to be so severely rationed in number when there is no limitation in size? Surely it would be better to ban the waistcoat altogether now that it has been ruined as a garment, and devote the saving to abolishing the restriction on number of pockets in jacket and trousers. Then surely, too, it makes for economy if the latter garments can be self-supporting, so that the need for braces disappears; but all devices for making them so are now forbidden. Why is "leather on bottoms"—does this mean the lower extremities or the seat?—which is surely designed to save cloth by protecting it from heavy wear, no longer permissible?

I am, Sir, your obedient servant, H. G. T.

MARCH 26

Sir,—The limitations now prescribed upon the design of men's outerwear will no doubt achieve the desirable objective of economy in manufacture. But should they not be considered also from the angle of consumer economy? The following examples illustrate the point:—

(1) Double-breasted jackets are obviously more extravagant to manufacture than single-breasted; yet their elimination means that men who would otherwise buy a two-piece suit for summer wear will instead buy a single-breasted suit with a waistcoat. We might usefully consider the alternative United States proposal that double-breasted suits should not

have waistcoats. If additional warmth is required, an old pullover would not show with the jacket buttoned.

(2) On trousers, which in fact will probably be worn with braces, it is certainly extravagant also to provide self-supporting devices. Yet their complete elimination means that many men who customarily wear flannel trousers may now have to buy braces or belts, both of which are made of scarce materials. It might prove a greater net economy to permit flannel trousers to have whichever of these self-supporting devices is most economical to make.

(3) Permanent turn-ups were introduced largely as a consumer economy. In their absence the labour expended in repairing frayed trouser bottoms may well exceed that saved in manufacture.

Yours faithfully, DONALD BARBER, secretary, Retail Distributors' Association,

7, Park Lane, W.1

APRIL 25

Sir,—My tailor assures me that a utility suit consists of a jacket, a waistcoat, and a pair of trousers, and that he is not allowed to make a utility suit for me without a waistcoat. This seemed to me so incredible that I visited a large popular firm of men's outfitters, who told me exactly the same story—a three-piece suit or nothing. There must be many men in England who do not wear waistcoats, and it seems ridiculous that one is forced to have a waistcoat which will never be used and the material therefore wasted. Perhaps this is a minor point of "national importance."

Yours faithfully, HERMAN SCHRIJVER

11, Chelsea Park Gardens, S.W.3

APRIL 27

Sir,—Mr. Herman Schrijver has trailed his waistcoat to some purpose since his letter on April 25 produced your pleasant fourth leading article. It seems almost a pity to destroy the legend, but it must be done. There is no compulsion whatever on makers-up of utility suits to produce a waistcoat. Wherever a cloth may be used for a man's three-piece suit, it may also be used for a two-piece suit or trousers and jackets sold separately.

I am, &c., F. W. P. CARTER, Public Relations Officer, Board of Trade

Millbank, S.W.1

MAY 12

Sir,—Few people who have not rowed a small boat realize that the double-breasted coat is worn by seamen and watermen because the handle of the oar catches in the front of the single-breasted variety. To these men, who usually wear under it a jersey or a pullover, the double-breasted coat is essentially a utility garment and ought certainly to be obtainable where no waistcoat is required.

Yours truly, T. R. L. GREEN, Hon. Secretary, Ilfracombe Branch, Royal National Life-boat Institution,

Fendower, Chambercombe Park, Ilfracombe

MARCH 7

Sir,—For economic, hygienic, and aesthetic reasons the Government should abolish for the duration of war and peace the superfluous, dust-preserving, and ugly ribbons on men's hats.

For many years the writer tore the ribbons from his hats, to the admiration of his innumerable artistic friends, though, alas! none had the courage to emulate this bold action. Now the Government has, in the name of utility, an excellent opportunity to uphold.

Yours faithfully, MOSHEH OVED

26, Museum Street, W.C.1

STORE CUPBOARDS

◆

In times of food rationing and fear of further shortages, was a domestic store cupboard, crammed with non-perishable foods, a patriotic expedient in case of emergency or was it deemed 'hoarding'? Opinion was divided.

MARCH 14

Sir,—Some time before the declaration of war you published a letter from Sir Arthur Salter. In it he pointed out that anyone who purchased goods while we were at peace, and traders could still replenish their stocks, was performing a patriotic duty of great national importance, while if he waited until war actually happened he might be justly stigmatized as a hoarder. This seemed to me sound sense, and I at once purchased goods to the limit of my available storage capacity. I have only drawn sparingly upon this reserve and have regarded it as essentially an iron ration to be used only in an acute emergency. Was Sir Arthur Salter right or wrong? Was I a patriot or am I a hoarder?

Yours, &c., PUZZLED

OCT. 10

Sir,—Major Lloyd George's definition of what constitutes food hoarding will be awaited with great interest and anxiety by many who, like myself, obeyed the Parable of the Wise Virgins and the exhortations of the then Food Minister at the beginning of the war to fill our store cupboards.

Victorians like myself were brought up with the idea that a well-filled store cupboard was one of the essentials of a well-run house. I have always had one, and when the war started had a large house in the country, six servants, and two permanent guests. Owing to the war my house is sold, I have now only two servants, and no guests, but I still have the remains of my well-stocked store cupboard. To add to my conundrums, last summer I followed my invariable custom, and purchased during the sales a year's supply of soap. Am I to be commended for all this thrifty forethought, or go to gaol?

Yours, &c., PERPLEXED

DEC. 3

Sir,—Will the Minister of Food clarify the position with regard to hoarding? The Press recently recorded the imposition of a heavy fine for hoarding 3lb. of butter, when it was stated that "inspectors also found 56lb. sugar, 3lb. tea, 2½lb. margarine, 13lb. jam, 61 tins of fruit, milk, and vegetables." I do not know the rights or otherwise of this particular case, but if it is punishable to "hoard" out of our weekly rations, then I am afraid all the frugal housewives in the country are guilty.

Are we or are we not to be allowed to put by for a rainy day? In my household of six we manage, by denying ourselves, to save ¾lb. or more of sugar each week, with a view to preserving fruit later on. We also save some tea and tinned goods in order to have a small stock to fall back on when lean times come. Is this to be discouraged and even forbidden?

Yours, &c., A HOUSEHOLDER

WASTE OF PAPER

◆

Government decree made wasting paper an offence in 1942. Many correspondents still gleefully cited examples of ministerial offices, among others, squandering paper on a seemingly massive scale.

MARCH 11

Sir,—It will shortly be an offence to waste paper.

Recently to economize coal, I wished to put in a kitchen range. As the cost was rather more than one is permitted to spend in 12 months, I had to obtain permission from the Office of Works and Buildings. I received a *questionnaire* on six sheets of foolscap, 702 square inches in all.

A farm wanted drains cutting. To obtain the Government 50 per cent. grant, application had to be made to the West Riding Agricultural Committee. I received a *questionnaire* of nine sheets of foolscap and three smaller sheets. The total cost of the drainage was £10 15s. With two plans that had to be drawn, the answers occupied two hours of my estate office clerk's time.

Should anyone carelessly throw his bus ticket away in the street, he will be liable to prosecution.

I am, Sir, your obedient servant, WHARNCLIFFE

Wortley Hall, Sheffield

APRIL 6

Sir,—I recently sent to the Collector of Taxes at Bournemouth a cheque for four Schedule "A" demands all in one envelope. I received back four separate receipts each in a brand new foolscap envelope. On the same day five Schedule "A" demands were sent to the same collector by one cheque in one envelope from my office, and we received back five separate receipts each in a similar new foolscap envelope. Can you beat it?

Yours obediently, PHILIP H. JACKSON

Pittismoor, Fordingbridge, Hants

SEPT. 4

Sir,—Considerable economy in the use of paper could be made if commercial, philanthropic, and other organizations who seek publicity through the Press, showed more appreciation of the war-time restrictions under which the news service is maintained. It is still not unusual for two, three, and even more copies of the same matter to be sent to the same address. In only a few instances has a mild remonstrance, involving paper and postage, been effective. Some of these communications are still being addressed to newspapers which went out of existence 30 years ago, but which are preserved in ancient mailing lists.

Yours faithfully, H. GREGORY PEARCE

Dartford Chronicle and Kentish Times, Dartford

SEPT. 8

Sir,—Ancient mailing lists—as Mr. Gregory Pearce points out—are a prolific source of wasted paper. Mailing lists can be kept up to date by the simple method of marking each envelope addressed from these lists with the words: "Please return, if undelivered, to . . ." If the original postage were one penny the Post Office would charge a like amount for returning each "dead" letter—a prospective liability well worth incurring with a regularly used mailing list, as it should prevent the continued dispatch of undeliverable communications that are otherwise destroyed by the Post Office.

Your obedient servant, G. SHAW SCOTT, Secretary, the Institute of Metals

4, Grosvenor Gardens, S.W.1

SEPT. 21

Sir,—On May 15 I wrote the Divisional Petroleum Office, Manchester, a very detailed four-page letter setting forth, as requested, the various purposes for which petrol was required, together with full details of mileage per month. On making renewed application for the ensuing three months, and referring to my previous letter, I have received an official form in which is stated:—1. Reference to previous communications cannot be accepted. 2. The same detailed particulars must be supplied in full.

Translate this into thousands of similar applications to one divisional officer alone and the waste of time and paper represents just one more instance of the appalling disregard of that economy which we are being continually urged to observe. Are we to believe that previous files are destroyed every three months, or that reiteration of the same particulars is needed to convince the authorities of the veracity of our claim?

Yours faithfully, F. C. SCOTT

Sand Aire House, Kendal

OCT. 14

Sir,—It would be interesting to know what approximately was the quantity of petrol and fuel involved in the transport of 75,000 persons, including the Home Secretary, to Wembley on Saturday last, a journey which it must be assumed was "really necessary." It would also assist the public in the efforts now being made to effect economy in the use of paper if at the same time information were forthcoming as to the quantity of this commodity permitted in producing tickets and programmes for the 75,000 spectators.

I am, Sir, your obedient servant, SYDNEY TATCHELL

Clifford's Inn, Fleet Street, E.C.4

Note: The event at Wembley Stadium was an Association Football match between England and Scotland.

DEC. 9

Sir,—In these days of acute paper shortage is it not time that publishers ceased to issue their books with "dust covers"? Our forefathers, I believe, never had them, and it is time we gave up this luxury, at least for "the duration."

Some of us do conscientiously endeavour to remedy this waste by promptly stripping off our covers and sending them to the salvage depot, but we are hampered by the fact that some publishers have an irritating habit of printing on the dust cover a portrait in the case of biographies, or some illustration in other cases, which is omitted from the body of the book. This makes the paper cover an integral part of the volume and effectually prevents any attempt to nullify the extravagance.

Yours, &c., E. W. ADAMS

THE HEAD-LOUSE

————◆————

The head-louse was found to be prevalent, particularly among female factory workers. The then fashionable 'perm' hair style was largely held the culprit.

APRIL 15

Sir,—Medical inspections indicate that from 30 to 50 per cent. of young women in industrial areas are infected with the head-louse. Many refuse to have their heads deloused because of their "perms." In certain hostels in London full of refugees from a Mediterranean country mothers refuse to be touched and oppose the delousing of their children. The Department of Entomology in the London School of Hygiene and Tropical Medicine has evolved a simple and effective means of delousing by the rubbing with the fingers into the roots of the hair a suitably medicated cream, and not washing the hair for eight–nine days so as to allow time for the lice to be killed (*British Medical Journal*, April 11, 1942). One such cream contains derris, another consists of 25 per cent. of a substance called "technical" laurel thiocyanate in white oil. These creams are not injurious so far as tests on many subjects have shown, and they do not make the hair unsightly.

The new fashion of a return to the shingle will be advantageous in the cleansing of the head, and it would be wise if the "perm" were prohibited. Much useless labour and electricity is wasted thereby. It is imperative that the louse be got rid of when there is a danger of typhus reaching this country.

I am yours, &c., LEONARD HILL
The St. John Clinic, Ranelagh Road, S.W.1

————————————

APRIL 20

Sir,—Sir Leonard Hill states that "In certain hostels in London full of refugees from a Mediterranean country mothers refuse to be touched and oppose the delousing of their children." Under the Scabies Order of 1941, "where a medical officer of health is satisfied, upon information given by a registered medical practitioner or otherwise, that a person is in a verminous condition, he may by notice in writing require the occupier of any premises in which that person is or has recently been accommodated to permit the inspection of the premises by the medical officer of health or by a person duly authorized by him in that behalf in writing." And, further, where the medical officer of health is satisfied after examination of any person that that person is verminous and requires cleansing or treatment he can "by notice in writing require that person to present himself, within the period specified in the notice, at a place specified in the notice at which suitable arrangements for the cleansing or treatment of verminous persons are available, and to submit himself to such cleansing or treatment."

The order is not confined to scabies but includes persons in a verminous condition, and local authorities have powers under this order to bring about the examination of persons even in hostels and, where necessary, to cleanse them of their vermin.

I am, Sir, your obedient servant, P. H. J. TURTON

Public Health Department, Heanor Urban District Council, Notts

---

APRIL 24

Sir,—Sir Leonard Hill's letter on the head-louse brings to the high light of *The Times* a misapprehension that has been skirmishing in the shadows ever since the Ministries of Labour and Health first became alarmed about the prevalence of head-lice and the danger of typhus. It is the belief that permanent waving is a handicap to hair hygiene. The truth is the reverse.

The best preventive of head-lice is thorough and regular brushing of the hair. This fact is well known to the Ministries concerned and is the basis of all their propaganda. Hair that is well permanently waved can be brushed and brushed until the arm muscles give in and the wave will only be enhanced. Since nothing in history has stopped women from waving and curling their hair, the woman whose hair is not permanently waved makes her waves and curls by hand by means of pins, clips, or bits of rag or paper. She sleeps with her hair uncomfortably and unhygienically screwed up in these all night. Hand-made curls come out if they are brushed. Therefore, the young woman with hand-made curls is not going to brush her hair. Even a comb will be used with the most delicate touch.

Incidentally, most of the high officers of the women's services, who try intelligently to set a good example, have their hair permanently waved regularly. They are too busy and too fastidious to adopt the alternative. Perhaps authority, which is masculine, could learn more from their experience and judgment than from young women who are so ignorant and stupid that they refuse to be deloused.

I am yours faithfully, W. NEVILLE, Managing Director, Eugene, Limited

Edgware Road, Welsh Harp, N.W.9

MAY 5

Sir,—The managing director of Eugene, Limited, suggests that permanent waving, contrary to common belief, is conducive to hair hygiene and to the elimination of the head-louse. In a recent report, written as the result of an investigation into the incidence of head-lice, made on behalf of the Board of Education and the Ministry of Health, I stated:—"Modern styles of hairdressing are, unfortunately, likely to favour an increase in the number of head-lice. I have heard of frequent cases of young women with long, permanently waved hair, which is apparently never disturbed for weeks and which forms an ideal breeding ground for the parasites."

I now learn that the reason these women do not comb their hair is not the permanent wave. Two processes are involved in the production of an elaborate coiffure. First, if the hair is straight its structure is deformed to produce a result alleged to resemble naturally wavy hair. This change is permanent and will withstand brushing and washing. The second process consists of "setting" the hair, which may be arranged in any type of bizarre confection. This "set" is a delicate structure, easily disturbed, and its production requires time, patience, and skill. In practice a non-permanent set is given at the same visit to the hairdresser as the permanent wave, which accounts for the confusion of the two processes.

The hairdressing profession will do much to reduce the incidence of the head-louse if it can persuade women to avoid elaborate "sets," which, because of the difficulty in replacing, are often left uncombed and un-washed for very long periods. Furthermore, the shorter the hair the less liable it will be to louse infestation.

Yours, &c., KENNETH MELLANBY
The University, Sheffield

FLOWERS OR FOOD?

◄►

One correspondent abhorred the practice of growing flowers rather than vegetables. He instigated a considerable, and hos-tile, response.

APRIL 29

Sir,—At a time when all are being urged to assist in every way towards the war effort it is very disconcerting to notice how this is ignored by some. Flower growers still continue to devote all their time and their land to the growing of flowers, a non-essential occupation and a non-essential com-modity. We are asked to "Dig for Victory" and "Grow More Food." It would be better if the flower growers answered these calls.

Thousands of boxes of blooms are sent in from the country districts to the railway stations by public service passenger vehicles, greatly to the incon-venience of the passengers who are already crowded out owing to restricted services. On some routes in this district as many as 80 to 100 and more boxes are on the bus at one time. We are asked to restrict our travel by rail so that the railways can carry munitions and essential supplies, yet special facili-ties are made by the railway company at Penzance and other stations to transport these flowers to London, Glasgow, Sheffield, &c. Extra staff are employed to deal with this traffic and special vans are attached to trains. A steamer makes special trips from the Scilly Isles, bringing over 35 tons and more of flowers at a time. We have to ship potatoes to the islands, whereas the islanders ought to grow their own instead of flowers.

I think the Government should prohibit the growing of flowers and the resultant wastage of man-power and transport.

I am, Sir, yours faithfully, ALEC. B. RICHARDSON
The Haven, Bay View Terrace, Porthleven, Cornwall

MAY 2

Sir,—May I put the case for the flower grower? Mr. A. B. Richardson appears to be referring to market-gardeners who still grow flowers exclusively. The war agricultural committees already have power to order these to grow whatever food they consider necessary. There are other market-gardens which grow exclusively fruit and vegetables and which, owing to the high rate fixed for wages and other production costs and to the low controlled market price, have been forced to reduce the labour employed and thereby to restrict production, and even in some cases to go out of business altogether, leaving their gardens unproductive.

According to my experience I have found that a solution to this artificial problem is to grow and sell flowers, the price of which is not controlled, in order to pay the labour to grow the vegetables for market. The flowers also enable me to keep bees and thus to produce honey.

Yours truly, J. V. E. LEES

MAY 2

Sir,—Your correspondent Mr. Alec. B. Richardson falls into the usual error of those who make sweeping generalizations, when he states that "flower-growers still continue to devote all their time and their land to the growing of flowers." My firm, without Government instructions, put the plough through 100,000 rose trees and stripped the greenhouses in order to grow food for the nation. Our action was not exceptional among nurserymen.

With regard to conditions in his locality, if his accusations have any foundation in fact, the remedy is not to write letters to the Press but to report the matter to the local war agricultural committee, who now have powers to enforce all flower-growers to devote the major part of their land, time, and labour to the production of essential foodstuffs.

I am, Sir, yours truly, HARRY WHEATCROFT
The Paddock, Edwalton Hill, West Bridgford, Notts

MAY 6

Sir,—Your correspondent who desires the Scilly Islanders to produce potatoes instead of flowers clearly does not know the Scillies. For over a century, ever since the coming of iron ruined their shipyards, and seaweed ash for the making of glass ceased to be a commercial proposition, these sturdy islanders have built up a wonderful industry in flowers and early vegetables. They have already restricted the former and expanded the latter and the revenue which they used to derive from the islands as a delightful holiday resort has ceased. To kill—or restrict any further—the flower industry would complete the ruin of the islands and leave the islanders dependent on the charity of the Exchequer for subsistence. The fact that the islands are agriculturally quite unsuitable for growing potatoes on any large scale for export is an economic fact which should not be ignored. The islands are doing their best and your correspondent ignores the fact that their young men are serving in the Royal Navy and Mercantile Marine and their old men are risking their lives as fishermen.

Yours, &c., E. A. BELCHER

Oxford and Cambridge Club, S.W.1

MAY 9

Sir,—From the letter published in your issue of April 29 the public would be disposed to think that flower-growers throughout the country were carrying on their businesses exactly as in pre-war days, were making no attempt whatever to help in the war effort to grow more food, and that the Government were permitting such a state of affairs. This is, however, very far from the truth, for the flower industry of the whole country has been controlled; and rightly so, since the outbreak of war by horticultural cropping orders which have successively increased each year the restrictions placed on flower-growers: their employees are reserved at the age of 30 only if they are occupied on food production.

The present cropping order limits the area on each nursery devoted to outdoor flowers to 50 per cent. of the pre-war area: under glass permanent flower crops, mainly carnations and roses, are reduced to 25 per cent.—all other glasshouses not planted with a permanent crop must be devoted wholly to the production of tomatoes. My own land, whose output in 1939 was entirely cut flowers, last year produced from under glass 950 tons of tomatoes and 125,000 lettuce, and from outdoors 320 tons of sugar beet, 100 tons of onions, and 75 tons of carrots, all from glasshouses and land previously planted with flower crops. This year 82 per cent. of our total glass is planted with tomatoes and 80 per cent. of our outdoor ground is growing food crops. This example is only typical of the war effort that is being made by all flower-growers, who it is estimated will this season produce 50,000 tons of tomatoes from under glass besides great quantities of outdoor food crops.

I am, Sir, yours faithfully, P. C. KAY, Director, Lowe and Shawyer, Limited The Nurseries, Uxbridge

DOGS AND THE WAR

———◆———

*Dogs, however, posed different problems. Were they an asset or
an extravagant indulgence?*

JUNE 20

Sir,—The question of the usefulness of dogs kept in towns merits a little
more thought than Mr. G. Wren Howard appears to have given it.
Undoubtedly a large proportion of these animals afford protection, companionship, and entertainment not only to many family units but to people
forced by present circumstances to live alone.

The dog's value as a vermin killer, too, should be borne in mind. The
Ministry of Agriculture, in its "Bulletin on Rats and their Extermination,"
gives the dog pride of place as a lethal agent. Last year this league organized
a rat-killing contest open to domestic dogs and excluding those belonging to
professional rat-catchers. The chief winner—a dog living in a large town
—scored 960 authenticated kills in five months. The leading 24 (mostly
town-dwelling) competitors between them killed 6,210 rats, while the
aggregate for all competitors multiplied this figure many times over. It is
obvious that these dogs must have saved from destruction an enormous
quantity of human food. As for the food consumed by dogs, the giving of
foodstuffs fit for human consumption is prohibited by law, and the supply
of recognized dog-foods is but a small fraction of what it was in peace-time.
The majority live on household scraps, and so the expenditure of money,
time, labour, and transport would be just the same whether these scraps
were eaten by dogs or not.
Yours faithfully, CHARLES R. JOHNS, Secretary, National Canine Defence
League, Victoria Station House, S.W.1

————————

JUNE 20

Sir,—I hope you will nip this campaign for canine austerity in the bud. My
dog furthers the war effort by keeping up the moral of myself and my
family, by providing companionship and much else which only a dog-lover
could appraise. As for feeding, it can be said with safety that if the sources
now available—no shipping space required—were reduced still further
owners would go without to feed their animals.
Yours faithfully, J. ALDRIDGE
Constitutional Club, W.C.2

————————

JUNE 23

Sir,—My dog is completely useless and I intend to keep him. He slept on
my bed all through the blitz. Tons of shipping are wasted on tobacco, and

tons of coal on cinemas. People are very keen on other people making sacrifices I notice!

Yours, &c., R. KENT WRIGHT
52, Clissold Court, N.4

POULTRY RATIONS

<hr>

The 'shell-egg' as opposed to the 'dried egg' ration amounted to one egg per person per week only. Those who could were enjoined to keep 'backyard' poultry; a morass of conflicting orders by bureaucrats ensued.

JULY 4

Sir,—May one who has recently started (on June 3) a back-yard poultry run—getting house, wire netting, and pullets at considerable expense, hoping in this way to help a national effort of great food value—make a protest about the reduction of the balancer meal ration allowance? True, our neighbours are very kind and generous in giving us their potato peelings, &c., and they are glad to see them put to good use and not wasted. But am I to kill my pullets, for which I have paid 22s. each, while people are allowed to keep five cats in one household, and dogs and old horses in great numbers?

Yours, &c., MARGARET GEDEN
2, Stourcliffe Avenue, Bournemouth

JUNE 7

Sir,—May I through your columns ask for a clarification of the position of the domestic poultry keeper with children under five? Under the new scheme for obtaining poultry meal the domestic poultry keeper is asked not to register for shell eggs, and I understand will be required to render one registration to obtain meal for one hen. Therefore, I presume one hen is roughly regarded as the equivalent of one registration.

Children receiving half the adult meat ration have had four shell-eggs to every adult allocation of one egg. It seems fair then to presume that a child's registration should be the equivalent of four hens. Registrations are already asked for in our district, and details on the plans for children's registrations would be welcome to enable us to do this.

Yours faithfully, M. C. DILL-RUSSELL
Cherry Tree Cottage, Bisley, Surrey

Sir,—With regard to the proposed new restriction on foodstuffs for small poultry keepers, the Ministry does not mention, or apparently allow for, a moving population. Say I have four children at school. Am I allowed to include them as living in my house all the year, or am I to go entirely without eggs myself during their holidays?
Yours, &c., J. H. ELVERSON
10, The Green, Marlborough, Wilts

Sir,—Miss Geden, of Bournemouth, who complains of the cut in the balancer meal ration for pullets, deserves the sympathy extended to the million small poultrykeepers. But her case is unnecessarily hard because her local authority is the only one in the country—with the exception of Manchester—to refuse the request of the Waste Food Board to collect house scraps and convert them into a palatable, non-rationed, poultry pudding.
Yours, &c., ALAN THOMPSON, Editor, *Poultry Farmer*
93, Long Acre, W.C.2

Sir,—Last February an official from the Ministry told our club, at a meeting held for him to speak at, that there was no shortage of balancer for the domestic poultry keeper, and that because we were going to have national bread it made no difference to the meal supply. He said he was certain that there would be no "cuts." He also said that my idea of growing the club's own food was ridiculous. It now seems that the idea was a good one, because our club will not feel the cut. Why did he not tell other clubs to do the same thing?
Yours faithfully, WILLIAM THOMSON, Secretary, Conway Poultry Club
Elbridge Lodge, Windlesham, Surrey

Sir,—Domestic poultry keepers need not slaughter any of their expensive young pullets because of the new method of rationing poultry food. Here is a simple scheme which has been readily appreciated by my neighbours: its motto is, "Help yourself by helping your neighbours."

The owner of the pullets undertakes to supply his neighbours with fresh eggs at the controlled price in exchange for their household scraps and their egg coupons; the latter can be used to obtain a balancer meal after October 1. An egg ration of one each week is not always obtainable from the shops,

whereas the pullet may reasonably be expected to lay more than one egg each week on the average. The mutual advantage is therefore obvious.
Yours faithfully, D. B. EPERSON
Charminster Vicarage, Dorchester

Sir,—Possibly Mr. Harrod's problems will be solved by the domestic hen. We are now allowed food for only as many hens as there are members of the family, and it will be a nice question for the egg-minded whether to reduce the hens or to increase the family. Let us hope that public-spirited persons will choose the latter alternative.
Yours faithfully, C. K. ALLEN
Rhodes House, Oxford

Sir,—The printing of Mr. T. L. Ward's letter is the first encouragement from the Press the poultry farmers have had. I am sure the public has never understood the injustice suffered by the egg producers of the country. May I be permitted to make a few points? I am not asking for more feeding-stuffs to be imported—that is probably impossible. I am asking for the sensible distribution of available feeding-stuffs. It is well known that in all industries there is a shortage of raw materials, and the Board of Trade has decreed the closing down of the smaller and inefficient factories, so that the available raw materials may be concentrated in the larger and more efficient. The Minister of Agriculture decrees precisely the opposite, closes down large numbers of efficient egg farmers and distributes their raw material feeding-stuffs—to millions of "backyarders," spending tens of thousands of pounds on staff and paper in his deplorable effort.

I am sorry for Lord Woolton—but why does he stand for it? He issues an egg-rationing order—states in effect:—"You will have one egg a fortnight." The Ministry of Agriculture counters with the following:—"You go and buy yourself some pullets. I will supply the feeding-stuffs, and you can put your fingers to your nose to Lord Woolton and his egg ration." Now this is only truth put rather bluntly, but would anyone have thought the absurdity possible? Now may I state something that is really undermining the war effort? Mr. Hudson's army of "domestics," having suffered some slight setback, are now ravaging the country's food supply to a greater extent than previously. In other words, sooner than give up their hens, people are feeding them on bread, porridge oats, potatoes, &c. I maintain that thousands of tons of food is being thus illicitly used, constituting a definite menace.
Yours faithfully, WILL C. MALLETT

"YOU'VE HAD IT"

◆

*The war years saw many strange expressions come into vogue.
One was this ironic form of refusal from those who were asked
for something which they could not reasonably give or supply.
Its possible origin was thus explained.*

AUG. 21

Sir,—Was not this the reply of the maiden to the very indifferent ballroom
performer who asked: "Can I have the last dance with you?"
Yours faithfully, JOHN R. JAMIESON
Edinburgh

THE FIVE-INCH BATH

◆

*King George VI ordered a line to be painted on his bath so that
he should not, as an economy measure, fill it with more than five
inches of water. But was this patriotic restraint emulated in
domestic and hotel bathrooms?*

OCT. 3

Sir,—I am reminded by your recent leading article on economy in the use of
water that there are certain devices on the market for automatically
regulating the quantity of hot water for a bath. The plimsoll-mark on the
inside of the bath is a great test of character and the temptation to exceed
the ration is great.

One such simple device, installed in a large Midland hospital some years
ago, has proved successful in effecting appreciable economy in hot water. It
consists of a small cylinder containing a float which turns off the supply
when a predetermined quantity of hot water has been delivered. No more
hot water is obtainable until the bath is emptied and the operation repeated.
Your obedient servant, WILLIAM KEAY
Leicestershire County Council, 6, Millstone Lane, Leicester

OCT. 10

Sir,—What is being done in the great hotels (and small) of London and the
rest of the kingdom to save fuel by the curtailment of hot water (and cold) in
the luxury baths to whose seductions so many of us are exposed? Are
warning notices posted conspicuously in every bathroom and bedroom? Is

the volume of bath fuelling being substantially reduced? Are the hours when hot water is freely available being restricted? Would not the "mark on the bath" adopted in the Royal household have a real psychological effect, like the admittedly successful, but at first despised, white line on the road?

And what of all the other buildings where men and women live in numbers, including barracks—and gaols?

Yours, &c., RODERICK JONES
29, Hyde Park Gate, S.W.7

OCT. 12

Sir,—Sir Roderick Jones asks what is being done in the great hotels (and small) to save fuel. It seems desirable to state that since the commencement of the campaign the hotel and restaurant industry has been working in full cooperation with the Ministry of Fuel and Power with a view to securing the utmost economy in all fuels.

As regards a notice in bathrooms, the Ministry has arranged through this association for such a notice to be made available to hotels, and copies of this notice, which is at present being printed, will be dispatched shortly to establishments throughout the country. I give below, as being of interest, the wording of the notice:—

THE BATTLE FOR FUEL

1. As part of your personal share in the Battle for Fuel you are asked NOT to exceed 5in. of water in this bath.

2. Make it a point of honour not to fill the bath above this level, and also to avoid wastage of water generally.

Also, attention has been drawn to the importance of marking all baths showing the 5in. level. In addition, the association has issued to its members what is known as "Fuel Battle Order No. II," which draws the attention of managers and staffs to the vital need of effecting all possible economy in the use of hot water and lighting. It has been further suggested that a suitable member of the staff should be instructed to act as "Fuel Watcher," to see that proper economy in all directions is carried out.

Yours faithfully, H. C. CLARKE, Acting Secretary, Hotels and Restaurants Association of Great Britain
11, Southampton Row, W.C.1

THE BIRTH-RATE AND REGULATION 33B

The birth-rate in Great Britain was less for its nubile population than in Germany. A correspondent argued that married service-

men should be granted additional leave for the purpose of reproducing themselves—once every 18 months was deemed sufficient. One problem, however, was the prevalence of venereal disease among servicemen. Defence Regulation 33B was introduced to halt its spread. The regulation's provisions produced an acerbic response from correspondents.

OCT. 7

Sir,—I fear that your Correspondent's very interesting article on the German birth-rate may create an unfortunate impression. We read that "every conceivable weapon was brought into play" to encourage population, but that the campaign met with a "signal defeat." This might seem to point the defeatist moral that it would be in vain to have a policy for promoting an increase in the birth-rate here.

But did the Nazis really do very much? Of course there was plenty of propaganda. They relied chiefly in the first instance on a marriage loan rising to a maximum of £50, of which one quarter would be remitted on the birth of each child. This means that the financial advantage of having a child amounted to a single lump sum of £12. 10s. Not much, in all conscience! Contrast this with the proposal to have a universal family allowance of 5s., which would mean £13 a year for each child, a very different matter, or with the more effective and economical plan, which I prefer, to give 10s. a week each for the third and fourth children only. It is true that the Nazis offered tax rebates and other miscellaneous advantages, but one needs a detailed estimate of what they all added up to in pounds, shillings, and pence. My impression is that the whole Nazi campaign, measured in deeds, not words, was extremely meagre. This may well have been due to the fact that there were other well-known claims upon their available resources to which they assigned higher immediate priority. The moral of the "defeat," if it was a defeat, is that uplift is not a substitute for generous practical measures to relieve the harassed mother and housewife.

Was it, however, a defeat? There was a very remarkable rise in the birth-rate, not matched here. To explain away this *prima facie* evidence of success, your Correspondent adduces certain special causes. He may be right. But the fact is that the peace-time period of experiment was too short to justify any firm conclusion from the statistics. There is nothing in the German evidence which should cast doubt on the idea that a bold plan of assistance would remove the danger of race extinction with which we are now faced. This assistance should cover the whole additional financial burden (including the provision of domestic help) due to the arrival of the third and fourth children.

I am, yours, &c., R. F. HARROD
Christ Church, Oxford

Sir,—With reference to your articles "Population in the Reich" and "The German Birth-rate" on October 5, I would like to ask, What are we doing about our own birth-rate, the increase of which must be considerably curtailed by the fact that innumerable husbands serving in the forces have been sent oversea for the duration of the war? Ought not these men to be given leave at least every 18 months, otherwise their wives are given no chance of fulfilling their natural function, and increasing Britain's birth-rate? There are any amount of young wives childless or with only one child who are denied any possibility of producing another till the end of the war—which may last another five or ten years, for all one knows.

The question of giving these men oversea leave periodically should be seriously considered for this reason alone, quite apart from the anguish and loneliness which an indefinite separation entails on the young wife.

Yours faithfully, HEATHER M. TOPPIN

16, Tekels Park, Camberley, Surrey

Sir,—I should like to make it quite clear why I have tabled a prayer against Regulation 33B, as there appears to be some confusion in the minds of your correspondents. My concern with the Regulation is chiefly on medical grounds. I regard this attempt to deal with a disease which is becoming a menace to our public health as of such a limited character that it will be quite ineffective.

Under 33B only those contacts who are informed upon by two infected patients will be obliged to submit to treatment. What of the others? There are a large number of innocent women infected by their husbands who will transmit venereal disease to their children but who will remain untreated because no informer will be forthcoming. I think the nation and the Government must face up to the gravity of the problem and treat syphilis and gonorrhoea as they would other complaints which are a danger to the public. I want compulsory notification and for the transmission of the disease to be made a penal offence. Only in this way can we hope to deal adequately with this scourge, for it is essential that patients receiving treatment should not be allowed to default. In this respect we can profit by the experience of Sweden, where compulsory notification was introduced some years ago. In 1935 in England the defaulter rate was 82.5 per cent., compared with 2.5 per cent. for Sweden. An argument is advanced that compulsory notification will drive the disease underground because those who are infected will fear public exposure. I take the view that it is because we have not had notification and ventilated the question that the victim whether innocent or guilty tries to hide the disease.

My other objection to 33B is based on the fear that some unfortunate woman may be wrongfully informed against by a man anxious not to reveal the name of the contact. It is conceivable that a young silly girl may have become infected, but if her name is given by a second informer she is labelled not as just young and stupid needing advice and protection but belonging to the prostitute class. This danger is a real one, and the Regulation must be amended in order to remove any possibility of abuse.

Yours faithfully, EDITH SUMMERSKILL

House of Commons

DEC. 9

Sir,—During our occupation of Cologne after the last war the figures of venereal disease among our troops rose to an alarming height. German authorities had a complete system of licensed brothels, with compulsory examination and imprisonment for failure to undergo treatment. Our Army medical officers exercised the most drastic control over the bodies of German girls as well as over our men, and they failed completely to check the rising rate. The War Office sent me out to report and suggest remedies.

The following recommendations proved effective because they were social and therefore preventive, and not merely medical and curative:—1. The appointment of an adequate number of women police to warn and help girls and their parents. To the surprise of the military authorities, the soldiers welcomed them warmly. 2. The relatively high pay of our soldiers was banked. (This would help our Canadian and United States friends here.) 3. The chaplains gave the necessary moral appeal to self-respect and discipline at special church parades.

The figures of venereal disease fell immediately and progressively. Adequate numbers of women police to patrol round camps and factories are the key to the problem, which is a moral and social one: doctors only tackle it when society has failed.

Yours faithfully, MARGERY I. CORBETT ASHBY

33, Upper Richmond Road, S.W.15

WAR FILMS

The realities of warfare were sometimes thought too harsh for home consumption. The point was strongly argued.

NOV. 23

Sir,—Will people with human feelings please support this, my protest, against the showing of dead soldiers on war films? Young and sensitive people are not protected from the sight of these films, and if humanity, culture, morality, and other of the finer attributes are to survive, these displays of the final result of violence and brutality are not the way to help it.

Yours faithfully, H. PRITCHARD
Five Ways, Merry Hill, Wolverhampton

NOV. 23

Sir,—There has lately been a strong tendency on the part of news-reel editors to include in their films of battle scenes close-up "shots" of dead and mutilated bodies of enemy soldiers. These scenes are not infrequently accompanied by a remark from the commentator pregnant with hatred and the lust for blood. We are all fully aware that war exacts this terrible price, but I feel that our already vivid imaginations do not require the camera's assistance to enhance them.

It is all too easy to substitute mentally the bodies of our own countrymen for those of the enemy, boldly, nay vengefully, shown to an audience which almost certainly contains wives and parents whose loved ones have given, or yet, may give, their lives in such grim circumstances.

Yours faithfully, P. R. AMES
153, College Road, Norwich

BLACK-OUT AGAIN

◆

Despite three years of black-out, basic problems persisted.

NOV. 26

Sir,—May I, through your columns, suggest that all military vehicles be fitted with rear reflectors so that when standing stationary without a rear light (apparently a military necessity) there would be a greater chance of their existence being indicated to other drivers? I write as one who has recently hit such a stationary vehicle with no visible rear light, narrowly escaping a serious accident, and am convinced that my misfortune, and many other similar ones, would not occur if the military vehicles were fitted with large reflectors such as are used on telegraph poles, and the like, on bends.

Yours faithfully, WILLIAM M. GODFREY
Brenchley, Kent

DEC. 9

Sir,—Five times recently I have been present, or near, when railway passengers have alighted in the black-out before the train has come to a complete standstill. On at least four of the five occasions the alighting passenger was under the impression that the train had come to a standstill. Trains, on the line in question, appear of late to come to a stop in a much more dilatory way than usual. This may quite well be one of the results of efforts on the part of the railway company to save wear and tear on brakes, &c., but, taken in conjunction with black-out conditions, it introduces a very real danger, because it is difficult for passengers to know when the train has stopped.

The accident which I saw last night might have been a very serious one, as the victim was a lady with a baby in arms, and, while she was able to push the baby clear, she herself went partly down between the platform and the train. I am moved to suggest that the railway companies might introduce a signal of some sort, *e.g.*, a distinctive whistle blast, to indicate to passengers when it is safe to alight.

Yours, &c., J. McALLISTER

162, Forest Drive, Theydon Bois, Essex

1943

DRAINS AND BRAINS

————◆————

To be interested in one's work, for other than purely financial return, seemed to Malcolm Sargent a self-evident blessing. But was it more rewarding to work as a musical conductor or in a sewer?

MARCH 3

Sir,—During a broadcast discussion by the Brains Trust on February 23 it was generally agreed that it was fundamentally necessary to have a definite interest in one's work apart from the profit motive. Dr. Malcolm Sargent said that he was one of those people fortunate enough to be absorbed in his own work, but he could not imagine, for instance, that a man working in a sewer could have any real interest in his job, but merely worked for money.

He was quite wrong. I have daily contact with sewermen on a very large main drainage system in the Greater London area, and I can assure Dr. Sargent that these men not only have a genuine interest in their work but consider themselves of a higher grade than their fellow workmen in the sense that they have special training and knowledge not normally possessed. They realize that on their skill and ability may depend the lives of their fellows, and the feeling of responsibility arising from this is a very real thing. In fact, I think it is highly probable that, rightly or wrongly, these men would consider Dr. Sargent's work as being of secondary importance in the national scheme of things compared with their own. I am glad to be able to enlighten Dr. Sargent in this matter, and to assure him that sewermen do not work merely for money.

Yours faithfully, M. W. SUMMERS
Arran, Broom Way, Oatlands Park, Weybridge, Surrey

————

MARCH 5

Sir,—While speaking extempore on the Brains Trust last week, on the profit motive, I evidently gave Mr. Summers the impression that I was sure that men employed on the drainage system worked "merely for money." This was not my intention.

I had hoped to make it clear that I believed that we should all work for the public good, but that as I was employed in a pleasant job, I had a greater and unfair advantage over those doing an unpleasant one. I stated that even if they work solely for their wages, and if it were wrong for them to do so, "Then," I said, "may God forgive them—I would." (My forgiveness was not given so readily to the speculator in stocks and shares.)

Mr. Summers states that these men "would consider Dr. Sargent's work as being of secondary importance in the national scheme of things compared with their own." Perhaps most people will agree with them, but I shall continue to work hoping that eventually we shall all consider national culture and national health to be of equal importance. In any case, it is a far nobler thing for a man to work in a sewer for the public good, than it is for him to conduct on a concert platform. I feel sure that even in the excitement of a Brains Trust reply, I could not suggest the opposite.

I envy Mr. Summers his friendship with these fine fellows, and thank him for having publicly corrected a false impression I may have made.
Yours faithfully, MALCOLM SARGENT
20, Chesham Place, London, S.W.1

THE ARCH-FIEND

◆

Hitler's personality and mental state continued to perplex readers. Finding an historical or literary stereotype to which to relate the man's behaviour became a popular pursuit.

MARCH 3

Sir,—The latest reports of Hitler's vapourings and violences recall the famous picture of the Arch-fiend in "Paradise Lost" (book I, 209–220):—

> So stretched out huge in length the arch-fiend lay,
> Chain'd on the burning lake: nor ever thence
> Had risen or heaved his head, but that the will
> And high permission of all-ruling Heaven
> Left him at large to his own dark designs:
> That with reiterated crimes he might
> Heap on himself damnation, while he sought
> Evil to others; and enraged might see
> How all his malice served but to bring forth
> Infinite goodness, grace, and mercy shown
> On man by him seduced: but on himself
> Treble confusion, wrath, and vengeance pour'd.

And, perhaps, the torturing paradox of the world's limitless misery is in some measure interpreted and even rationalized by the poet's courageous faith.
I am, Sir, obediently yours, H. HENSLEY HENSON, Bishop
Hyntle Place, Hintlesham, Ipswich

THE PRICE OF VEGETABLES

The price of vegetables was often thought exorbitant. That of cauliflowers provoked particular indignation.

MARCH 15

Sir,—Since the price of cauliflowers has been controlled, greengrocers in this area are selling cauliflowers with as many leaves and as much stalk as possible. As a result this vegetable now costs more than before the price was controlled. I hope the authorities will see a way to put a stop to this ramp.

Yours faithfully, F. DOBSON

Bhamnipal, Buxted, Sussex

MARCH 18

Sir,—Surely your correspondent Mr. F. Dobson is maligning the green-grocer? Our local greengrocer assures me that he has to buy cauliflowers with leaf and stalk, also leeks with leaf, root, and dirt attached, from his wholesaler, and to pay for them by weight. It appears to me that the ramp, if any, starts with the wholesaler and the producer. Meanwhile the public has to pay for a lot of inedible matter.

Yours, &c., A. C. LAMPSON

The Red House, Court Hill, Chipstead, Surrey

MARCH 18

Sir,—On Friday last I bought a cauliflower, price 1s. 2d. When I got home I weighed it. The flower with a good frill of small leaves weighed 15oz.—the stalk with the rest of the practically leafless mid ribs weighed 1lb. 7oz. Up till recently I should have paid about 9d. for it.

Yours, &c., MABEL F. WOOLLEY

34, Framlingham Road, Manchester

MARCH 22

Sir,—The vegetables which your correspondents have been eating recently are broccoli, not cauliflowers. They won't get cauliflowers till July: B comes before C.

As for the leaves, they should have no objection to that. A paper read recently by Dr. Magnus Pyke shows that broccoli leaves are the richest vegetable source of vitamin C.

Yours truly, H. W. ARMSTRONG

11, Richmond Avenue, E.4

MARCH 23
Sir,—In your issue of March 18 is a letter stating that a buyer had been charged 1s. 2d. for a cauliflower. Just previously, as a member of our local war agricultural committee, I had been asked by the chairman to inspect seven acres of savoys which had been offered by the grower first to the Ministry, and then to private buyers, and in every case refused on the ground that there was no demand, so permission was sought to plough them in for manure. This was given, but it is quite incomprehensible how a cauliflower can be sold for 1s. 2d. and at the same time a savoy has no value whatever. Moreover, it is very discouraging to the growers after all the urge for production.
Yours faithfully, T. J. WARD
Carrington Grange, Boston, Lincolnshire

ECONOMY IN INK

One correspondent, seeking to help the war effort, suggested ways of saving ink. This well-meaning but hapless gentleman was subjected to much pompous ridicule.

MARCH 26
Sir,—There is a well-known story to the effect that the Great Western Railway saved a large tonnage of paint by simply painting "G.W." on their locomotives and rolling-stock instead of "G.W.R." Is it not rather unnecessary for us solemnly to write "Messrs." in front of the name of even the most impersonal firm when addressing an envelope? Business practice has many cases of this kind, but tons of ink would surely be saved by omitting this one little (alien) word.
Yours faithfully, ERIC PERRIN
8, Den Bank Avenue, Sheffield 10

MARCH 30
Sir,—Your correspondent suggests that we should save "tons of ink" by omitting the word "Messrs." when addressing an envelope to a firm.

A simple little experiment shows that one can write the word 34 times with a single dip into the inkpot, and that an inkpot containing about ¼-pint would provide 5,642 dips, weighing altogether about 2oz. avoirdupois. From this it may readily be calculated that the useless word would have to be written 3,437,557,760 times before one ton of ink was saved.

In these days it should be a simple matter to launch a nation-wide campaign with posters, supervisors, district officers, inspectors, and the rest—for without something of the kind the effort would surely fail—the only difficulty being that such a campaign would undoubtedly involve the use of a much greater tonnage of ink.

Yours, &c., ERNEST BLAIKLEY

2, Bigwood Court, N.W.11

APRIL 1

Sir,—If Mr. Perrin wishes to save "tons of ink" in war-time let him and others (1) refrain from writing letters to *The Times*; (2) stir up in half a pint of boiling water a tablespoonful of soot from the chimney (especially if wood be burned in the fire as well as coal), and add a small teaspoonful of gum from an ordinary gum-bottle. The result is an ink which was good enough for Gainsborough and other artists of the eighteenth century to use for their drawings. One of Horace Walpole's proudest possessions was a set of seven illustrations "in Sut-water" made by Lady Diana Beauclerk for his tragedy *The Mysterious Mother*, 1768. They hung at Strawberry Hill in ebony and gold frames in a chamber lined with Indian blue damask.

To show that there is no deception, this letter is written in some hastily made soot-water. "Messrs." and other flourishes need not be omitted at any rate for the sake of economy in ink.

Yours faithfully, MARTIN HARDIE

Rodbourne, Tonbridge

APRIL 1

Sir,—Mr. Perrin's letter in your issue of March 26 about economy in ink suggests the suppression of "Dear" before "Sir" in business letters. This, unlike "Messrs.," has no tradition behind it, and involves an even greater waste of ink.

Yours faithfully, G. R. WARNER

Sutton Courtenay House, near Abingdon, Berks

MR. CHURCHILL'S BROADCAST

On 21 March, Churchill made one of his periodic broadcasts to the nation—and, in effect, the world. A lady approaching 90 wrote of her appreciation.

MARCH 29

Sir,—May an old woman of 89 years occupy a few lines in your valued paper to add her grateful thanks for that most wonderful broadcast from the Prime Minister on Sunday, March 21? I was born and brought up in the days of Palmerston and Disraeli, and was encouraged to read and enjoy their writings and the speeches of the latter, but what we heard, thanks to the B.B.C., is far above anything that these two leaders of public opinion ever taught us. The simplicity, the stout-hearted John Bullism, and the liberal recognition of the sufferings of nearly all Europe teach us how grateful we ought to be to God for being led in the present day by such a single-hearted, true Briton. Of course, we cannot expect one-half of the plans to be carried out in his lifetime, by such a mass of races, religions, and political views, but I am sure that God will lead our people and our great American allies in the task of unifying the nations and bringing the masses of varying tribes in China and in Russia into one brotherly willingness to cooperate for the peace of the world.

Yours faithfully, ONE BORN IN 1854

TRYING IT ON THE DOG

Bureaucracy intruded on the lives of dog-owners—and even those who supposedly owned them but did not.

APRIL 9

Sir,—I have just received from the London County Council, Room 49, the County Hall, a *questionnaire*—on the left the query, on the right, my reply. It says: "I am unable to trace any record of local taxation licence duty having been paid by you this year in respect of your dog."

It seems incredible that, when every man and woman is wanted to carry on the war, there are still some who have time to send out these ridiculous notices. The answer, of course, is that I have never had a dog in my life. Room 49 also asks me to put a penny stamp on my reply.

Yours faithfully, JOHN SAINSBURY
52, Welbeck Street, W.1

THE CRAWLING BUS

Among the many frustrations of travelling within a city was, as now, the 'crawling bus'. There were two sides to the argument, however.

APRIL 10

Sir,—The crawling bus is an increasingly frequent sight and experience in London these days. Crammed with warworkers eager to reach offices and factories, or rest and relaxation after a tiring day, it creeps along, courting traffic lights and every conceivable obstacle to delay progress. Meanwhile buses rush past, sometimes half empty. Nothing could be more exasperating or more calculated to undermine public confidence in the war effort.

There can be no sound reason for such a freak in war-time. Tyre economy, time schedules, and bureaucratic excuses are fatuous in the circumstances. The evil—for it is nothing less—points clearly to an organizing mentality working on a lower potential than the rest of a nation keyed up for peak effort. The crawling bus represents an onerous and unnecessary addition to the black-out and other necessary restrictions under which the nation is patiently labouring: accordingly it is inexcusable. And it is intolerable in any progressive country, particularly when striving to win a war.

Yours faithfully, THORBURN MUIRHEAD
33, Cornhill, E.C.3

APRIL 15

Sir,—Mr. Thorburn Muirhead has drawn attention to what appears as one of the really unnecessary restrictions. With half-empty streets the fare-payer may be forgiven for thinking that rigid time schedules should be relaxed, or, if this be impracticable, for asking the reason why.

We all wait resignedly in the queue, but having waited we are not resigned to our bus deliberately crawling for what seems in these days an arbitrary and unconvincing reason. Many bus conductors with whom I have talked about this have said, "I'm sick and tired of answering complaints from fares. It's all that red tape at the top."

Yours faithfully, JOHN STEEGMAN
Reform Club, Pall Mall, S.W.1

APRIL 17

Sir,—Surely this is an illusion; what matters is that the bus travels from "A" to "B" in, and arrives at, its scheduled time. Should the driver have to stop many times, he will therefore go more quickly between the stops, thus appearing to lessen the over-all time. If the bus did, in fact, ignore its schedule, Mr. "B." would no doubt be quite annoyed to arrive at the bus stop, ready to catch his train, only to find that his bus had gone five minutes early to satisfy impatient Mr. "A" on board.

Yours faithfully, A. W. HILLYARD
Send Fields, Send, near Woking, Surrey

WASTE OF EFFORT

Government ministers were assiduous in visiting factories and other places of work. One correspondent questioned whether their journeys were 'really necessary'.

JUNE 28

Sir,—As Parliament is showing a disposition to examine the procedure of legislation by order, might I advocate a general overhaul of the waste of time and effort by Ministers themselves? We are exhorted in these days to avoid travel, not to interfere with the movements of war workers, to economize, and to concentrate solely on the war effort. The new procedure of issuing ration books means a lot of unnecessary travel, the waste of at least several hours of working time each day, the clogging of public accommodation in vehicles, and the expenditure of money which could be saved and better used.

Here is another instance. Ministers are now touring the country on factory inspection. I make no objection to the practice—it is, in fact, desirable—but let them not make it a farce. When Sir Stafford Cripps a few days ago "secretly" visited a Lancashire factory, everyone in the town knew of it a fortnight ahead. The factory closed on the Friday at 4.40 p.m. for clearing and did not reopen till Sunday morning at 8.30. Seven hundred and fifty workers were told to report, though normally only a percentage of men work on a Sunday, but on this occasion all worked all day at double rates. The Cripps visit lasted just 16 minutes.

Ministers, too, are "spell binding" in the provinces just now—are all their journeys really necessary? And are we satisfied that the services avoid unnecessary travel? I notice a police court case at York in which it was stated an officer was travelling to London by car.

Yours faithfully, J. H. WOOTTON-DAVIES
House of Commons

THE BOMBING OF ROME

Only 19 July, 700 US aircraft dropped 800 tons of bombs on the marshalling yards south-west of Rome to disrupt German re-inforcements moving south. Strategic bombing of the Eternal City seemed to some brutally reminiscent of earlier Axis

attacks on civilian centres. Perhaps surprisingly, however, most
correspondents welcomed the raid.

JULY 22

Sir,—In your article of July 20 on the bombing of Rome the military principle behind it was clearly expressed:—"Unconditional concentration upon the ruin of the armed forces and war potential of the enemy"; and the significance of "unconditional" was revealed in the last sentence: "It must not be diverted by fear of the unintended damage incidental to the main necessity."

An important part of every country's war potential, especially when threatened with invasion, is its morale: and that, apart from individual courage, depends upon the conviction that one's own country stands for the right, for desirable life, for civilization, which is enormously intensified by evidence that the enemy, on the contrary, cares for none of these things. In the worst days nothing steeled us more than proofs, at home and abroad, that the strategy of the Nazis was "unconditional." It is possible, then, that bombing Rome has been good for Italian morale and bad for ours.

This possibility should be weighed against any temporary military advantage of dislocating railway traffic. How many times have the marshalling yards of Hamm been bombed? True, the war is going so well that we hardly feel for the moment the need of morale; but the war is not yet over.
Yours, &c., DESMOND MacCARTHY
Garrick's Villa, Hampton

JULY 23

Sir,—In reply to Mr. Desmond MacCarthy's letter in *The Times* to-day, I write as one whose morale has not been lowered by the bombing of military objectives in Rome. It is, of course, deplorable that, in the inevitable destruction caused by war, beautiful, sacred, and historic buildings have to suffer, but it would be invidious to try to assess the relative value to human culture of the Basilica of San Lorenzo, Canterbury Cathedral, or Westminster Abbey—all of which have suffered. Buildings, however sanctified by time, are but the creation of man and cannot, to my mind, be compared with the tragic destruction of human lives which war involves.

When one thinks of the courage of those American airmen who went in daylight to bomb military objectives in Rome, after giving due notice to the Roman people of their intentions—thus greatly increasing their own danger—and compares it with the German airmen who, in daylight, without warning, machine-gunned English schoolchildren in their playground, I could wish that his Holiness the Pope had expressed his Christian solicitude more openly on that occasion.
I am yours truly, EMILY LUTYENS
13, Mansfield Street, W.1

JULY 24

Sir,—A word of explanation may forestall many bitter words. The Pope
has a threefold office. He is Head of the Catholic Church, Primate of Italy,
and Bishop of the Diocese of Rome. When speaking as a diocesan bishop (as
in the present instance) he makes that fact clear by addressing himself to his
Vicar-General—a purely diocesan official.

To have expressed no sympathy for the people of his diocese mourning
the death of relatives and the destruction of the last resting place of
generations of the poor of Rome, would have been, to say the least,
unfatherly. The Bishop of Rome did no more and no less than the
Archbishops of Westminster and Cologne in similarly tragic circumstances.

The Holy Father has made frequent protest, in his capacity of Father of
Christendom, against the bombing of homes and monuments in any part of
the world. It should not escape notice that in the latest protest the Pope uses
language no stronger than on the occasion of the bombing of Malta by
Italian aircraft. He also pays incidental tribute to the careful though
inadequate precautions taken by the airmen who bombed the Eternal
City.

I am, &c., JOHN C. HEENAN

The Presbytery, Little Ilford Lane, Manor Park, E.12

JULY 24

Sir,—Surely Mr. Desmond MacCarthy cannot seriously mean to compare
the bombing of Hamm, which took place during the time of our weakness in
the air and can have done small damage, with the raid on Rome in which
500 modern bombers took part? The bombing of Rome was not undertaken
as an attack on Italian morale but to protect our forces in Sicily from
German reinforcements. It is the Italians themselves who must be blamed
for the bombing, in that they have used Rome for military purposes instead
of declaring it an open city.

Yours, &c., GORDON JACOB

75, West Street, Ewell, Surrey

JULY 24

Sir,—I should like to reassure Mr. Desmond MacCarthy. If the Italian
compares the precautions taken by the allies before and during the bombing
of Rome with the precautions taken by the Axis before and during the
bombing of Guernica, Rotterdam, Belgrade, London, Coventry, Exeter,
and Abyssinia, his morale will hardly be fortified by the thought that he
stands for all the holy things and his enemy for all the unholy things. And
the morale of Russia, of our soldiers who are hazarding their lives, and of all
the tortured and enslaved peoples of the occupied countries will be

strengthened by the knowledge that we are really engaged on a war of liberation, not on a sentimental pilgrimage.

Yours, &c., A. A. MILNE

Cotchford Farm, Hartfield, Sussex

Sir,—It is a palpable exaggeration to talk of "the bombing of Rome" when all that has been bombed is the rail and air systems on the extreme south-west of the city and, in large part, entirely outside it. Is it to be laid down as a law of this war that the railways at Rome and Cologne must be immune from attack on the ground that a splinter might damage a church? If "cultural monuments" are to be spared, *que messieurs les assassins commencent.*

Yours truly, GEORGE SAMPSON

33, Walsingham Road, Hove 3, Sussex

WAR-TIME MANNERS

◄────►

A number of correspondents deplored what they considered a war-time deterioration in the customary good manners of the British. Many, however, reported happier experiences.

Sir,—When recently in the course of my military duties I was making a tour of the British Isles, I was disturbed by a growing lack of consideration and courtesy in the ordinary relations of civilian life.

Parents, for instance, thoughtlessly allow children in railway carriages to take up the room of an adult, while women with babies and soldiers with full equipment stand in the closely packed corridors. It frequently happens that youths on holiday will occupy first class seats with third class tickets, while women who may well have made a sacrifice to buy the extra comfort of first class accommodation have to crouch on their suitcases until the ticket collector arrives when perhaps two-thirds of the journey are over. I have noticed, too, in some cases in the shops a marked deterioration in the hitherto high standard in the manners of shop assistants, particularly in relation to goods that are in short supply. All this adds needlessly to the stresses and strains that the civilian population is suffering so patiently as the fifth winter of war approaches.

Is not this a subject to which the Ministry of Information might turn its attention? At the beginning of the war there were admirable posters stressing the importance of "your courage and your resolution." Might it not be an opportune moment to call attention in a similar manner to the need for "your courtesy and your consideration?" I am convinced that it is only a minority who are at fault, and that it only requires a little judicious propaganda to shame them into mending their manners to the benefit of the whole community.

I am, Sir, your obedient servant, ROBERT BERNAYS
House of Commons

SEPT. 25

Sir,—I would like to corroborate what Mr. Bernays says in his letter on the deterioration of the present-day manners. It should be taken in hand without delay, in the homes, in the schools, and perhaps by the help of the B.B.C. I have often noticed in the buses that the parents of children never tell them to give up their seats to elderly tired women who have to remain standing. The child cannot understand, but surely the mother can do something about it.

As we have so many foreigners in our midst these days it is rather sad that we should be so much less courteous than they are themselves. More than once have I had a seat offered me by a foreign officer while English young men have remained seated. I feel sure a little direction and education would, before long, make an improvement in our manners.

Yours faithfully, ETHEL RUMBOLD
Royal Cottage, Kew, Surrey

SEPT. 25

Sir,—May I be allowed to add something to your correspondent's letter in to-day's issue? There must be many older women like myself who have to do more travelling than they would choose these days; and were it not for the unfailing courtesy of all ranks of the United States services in offering us their seats, the journeys often would be more arduous than they are.

Usually we have to start out already tired from hurried work, and the prospect of long standing appals us. We have become accustomed in these latter years not to expect from men, other than the older generation, much courtesy while travelling, and therefore it comes as an added surprise and pleasure when it is shown us by a younger generation, and then by that of our great ally.

Yours, &c., B. MORGAN
Oxford

SEPT. 28

Sir,—Are not your correspondents Lady Rumbold and Miss Morgan merely reiterating the usual feminine claim both to have their cake and eat it? Some decades ago women importuned the community with their demands for equality. Now that they have it they want more.

I have the honour to be, Sir, your obedient servant, C. A. BRANSTON

30, Thompson's Lane, Cambridge

Sir,—Must women have it all their own way, as Miss Morgan and Lady Rumbold suggest?

Were I a man I should very much resent being expected to give up my seat to someone who, in all other matters, cried out that she was my equal, if not my superior. Women must choose between chivalry and equality—and not expect both.

Yours faithfully, JANET GREEN

118, Hill View, Henleaze, Bristol

Sir,—Before leaving home this morning I read *The Times* and noticed the two letters under the title of "War-Time Manners." On going to catch a bus I found myself the last in a fairly long queue. When the next bus arrived I boarded it, but it was evidently full, and there was some question as to whether I was entitled to remain on it. I offered at once to get off.

I am an old and lame man, and two ladies insisted on getting off so that I could remain. A boy, perhaps 14 years of age, seated next to the entrance insisted on giving me his seat so that I should not have to stand. I have also to make many journeys on another route which serves a large industrial area, and the passengers, mainly working people, seeing that I am lame, show me the greatest possible service in giving me their seats. I have also much railway travelling to do, and the same experience applies there also.

I submit therefore that the war-time manners of the British are by no means as bad as the two letters referred to suggest.

Yours faithfully, NOTTINGHAM CITIZEN

Sir,—No one who goes about much in London can fail to observe the deterioration in manners spoken of by your correspondents. In particular one notices, as Lady Rumbold says, the mothers who allow, and encourage, their children to sit while tired women stand.

An incident which occurred recently exemplifies this. As I was travelling home by bus from my work a timid little boy offered me his seat and received a smart cuff from his mother for so doing. He certainly will never be guilty again of such politeness.

This country has shown itself very responsive to propaganda. Surely it would respond again if appealed to in the right way.

Yours faithfully, GWLADYS CLIFTON-MOGG
49, Addison Avenue, W.11

SEPT. 29

Sir,—One of our pupils last week at the town bus centre gave up his seat in a bus to a lady. The bus filled up, and, as there were then too many standing, the conductor ordered the boy off. He had an hour to wait for the next bus, and, as he had a long journey, did not arrive home till late.

Yours faithfully, T. GARETH THOMAS
Dumbarton House School, Swansea

SEPT. 29

Sir,—May I be allowed to put another point of view from that expressed by your correspondents with regard to present-day manners? It has fallen to my lot to do a good deal of travelling in train and omnibus during the last two years, and the difficulties experienced by every one have for me been greatly lessened by the unfailing and generous help and consideration of fellow-travellers, particularly by girls and men wearing his Majesty's uniforms.

Their vision of the needs of others seems to be increased and not diminished by the anxieties and fatigues common to all. To an elderly woman their behaviour has been a constant inspiration, and to them I am happy to express my gratitude.

I am, Sir, faithfully yours, LUCY GARDNER
11, Alexandra Terrace, Exmouth

THE POPULATION OF BRITAIN

◆

The Beveridge Report for post-war social security, published on 2 December 1942, provoked many letters over the following months. But not all correspondents favoured such pampering or the means by which it was to be funded.

OCT. 1

Sir,—Does not the decline in British population lie much deeper than Canon Shillito suggests in your issue of September 25?

Fifty years ago in this part of the country, which I assume to be typical, a family was an economic necessity to the working man. As he and his wife grew older and less able to work the children helped in the house and brought home their earnings. There was a recognized obligation that, in return for their early maintenance and education the children should protect their parents from want and sickness and old age. Must we not face the fact that as the State undertakes the obligations of the children so the incentive to beget a family vanishes?

It seems axiomatic that every advance in social security will show a corresponding decline in the birth rate unless the whole plan of security is designed to make a family a personal asset rather than an inconvenient liability.

Yours faithfully, L. H. STRAIN

Ladyburn, Maybole, Ayrshire

OCT. 1

Sir,—Mr. W. R. Darwin's suggestion that the bachelor ought to be "really worse off than the married man" appears to bristle with tyrannies. Does he refuse to believe that any one could conceivably think that there are quite enough people in the world as it is; or that any one could hold it not necessarily benevolent to introduce any more children into life as man has made it? Further, does he consider it fair to penalize those who have either not met the suitable partner or, having met her, have been assured that her ideas were far otherwise? One is very happy to read of married bliss in the lives of others, but it is a little difficult to see why the unmarried should be expected to pay for it.

Yours, &c., PAUL NICHOLS

Great Crosby Vicarage, Liverpool, 23

WAR CRIMES

◆

A conference of Allied governments, meeting in London on 13 January 1942, had announced that Axis war criminals were to be tried and punished after the war. But how was this to be legally done, since preparing for war and crimes against humanity, the two main charges to be brought, had not before been recognised in International Law?

DEC. 14

Sir,—Do my eyes or do my senses deceive me? At Moscow it was decided that war criminals should be taken back to the land where their crimes were committed and there tried. In your issue of to-day I read: "Lord Cecil said one international Judge should sit as a member of the Court set up. That would establish a guarantee that nothing grossly unfair would be done. One of the best British Judges should be included."

Such interference would be an insult to our allies, and I do not doubt that they will reject it as such. Who are we, who have not shared their sufferings, to meddle with their justice on the suggestion that it will be "grossly unfair"—before it has even begun? This savours of the Bishop of Bradford:—"What I dread more than anything else is, what is going to happen the week after the war comes to an end—what those who are oppressed and tortured are going to do when the means of revenge and the worst impulses of vindictiveness are put in their hands." Cannot we restrain these wounding insularities and imputations, which seem to show more concern for the oppressor than for the oppressed?

We hear much of avoiding hatred in Germany. (The victors will of course be hated anyhow.) We hear nothing of avoiding odium in Europe. Yet the danger is there. Germans used to attack us for having a "governess mind." Don't let us encourage our allies to think likewise.

Yours truly, VANSITTART

Denham Place, Denham, Bucks

DEC. 16

Sir,—Lord Vansittart says that I have "a governess mind." May I very respectfully say that it is better to have the mind of a governess than the mind of a fanatic? The worst of a fanatic is that, though he may be on occasion quite right, yet he is apt to put his case with such violence that people think he is wrong. It is that danger which Lord Vansittart runs.

As to his particular charge against me, because I said that when the war criminals are tried it would be desirable to have an international Judge in the Court, I see nothing to object to in that. The object of the trial of war criminals is not only to punish them but also to demonstrate to the world that the Germans have been guilty of terrible crimes. Until the Germans are convinced of that, there is no hope of their "re-education." But if the criminals are taken to the country where they committed the crimes and are tried by a Court consisting entirely of fellow-countrymen of the victims, it is impossible to expect that the proceedings will be regarded as conclusive demonstrations of German guilt.

If I mentioned an English Judge it was only because in England we have been so very lucky as not to have had any of the worst crimes committed in our land. I cannot believe that even the most sensitive foreigner listening to what I said could have thought that what I said was "wounding." It is only people like Lord Vansittart who detect a hostile meaning in words that are intended to be perfectly friendly. By doing so he creates an insult where none was meant.

Yours faithfully, CECIL

16, South Eaton Place, S.W.1

Sir,—Does not Lord Cecil fall into the very error which, with his fair, judicial, and impartial mind, he is so scrupulously anxious to avoid? He refers to "the trial of war criminals." Our system of criminal jurisprudence proceeds on the principle that the accused is *prima facie* innocent until he is proved guilty. If before or during the trial he is already to be termed the criminal the trial is waste of time.

Imagine the outcry from the judicial bench if counsel for the prosecution in a murder charge referred to the accused as the "murderer in the dock."

Your obedient servant, CHARLES L. NORDON

Winchester House, 100, Old Broad Street, E.C.2

Sir,—The correspondence in your columns between Lord Cecil and Lord Vansittart concerning the trial of war criminals has served the useful purpose of bringing this subject to a head. M. Camille Huysmans's letter is a warning that if this question is not handled with care, grave offence may be given to our allies.

The difficulty is that, although we are all agreed that the war criminals should be punished, we are not clear what procedure can be adopted to accomplish this object. The problem may, however, be clarified if we divide the acts which we wish to treat as punishable into two categories: (*a*) those which fall outside the established criminal law of the individual States, and (*b*) those which constitute ordinary crimes. As the Lord Chancellor pointed out in his speech in the House of Lords on December 7, the ordinary process of a trial is not as appropriate for those whose policy has brought on this war as it is for those who have committed particular crimes.

The ordinary legal process is not appropriate to the first category because these acts of policy, however terrible in their effect, are not covered by any existing body of law, whether civil or international. It is open to the gravest doubt whether an aggressive war is illegal under international law as it stands at present, but even if it were, that system provides no penalty for the individual and no court where he could be tried. This does not mean, however, that the men guilty of this wrong against the world ought to escape unpunished, because the obvious answer is that they can be punished by a political Act of State. The correct procedure was adopted in the case of Napoleon, for he was dealt with by direct State action. The Government of that day was wise in not adopting the suggestion that he should be tried legally, as he could have raised the objection that such a trial had no basis in law. It has been argued that a judicial trial is necessary so as to convince the Germans of their guilt, but when in history has a trial of this nature ever succeeded in convincing anyone?

The second category covers acts which are crimes in the true sense, for they are acts in violation of existing State law. They are called "war crimes" because they are committed in the course of a war, but they do not differ in essence from ordinary crimes. The laws of all States recognize that in certain circumstances war provides a justification for acts which would otherwise be criminal, but acts which fall outside these circumstances are not protected. Therefore, if a German soldier, when landing in England, kills a British soldier this is not murder, because it is a legitimate act of warfare; but if he deliberately shoots a civilian this is murder, and he can be tried, convicted, and ordered to be hanged by an ordinary English court of justice. There is no need here for any international tribunal. The same principle must, of course, apply in the case of our allies, and therefore every person who has committed a crime in the occupied countries should be tried by the courts of those countries, and by those courts alone.

There is much to be said for the view that the British and the Americans should concern themselves only with the trials of those who are charged with having committed crimes against their own nationals, except in so far as they can help the other allied countries in making the necessary arrests and in establishing the evidence. In English law a prisoner is tried at the place where the crime has been committed, and there seems to be no sound reason why this principle should not be followed in the case of war criminals.

I am yours, &c., A. L. GOODHART
University College, Oxford

400,000,000 CIGARETTES

◆

Far from being advised to refrain from smoking, war-time servicemen were actually encouraged to do so by receiving millions of free cigarettes from the Over-Seas League Tobacco Fund.

DEC. 20

Sir,—Four hundred million gift cigarettes have now been sent by the Over-Seas League Tobacco Fund to men in all the services, in every battle area, and in every lonely garrison—to the fighting men, to the wounded, and to our men in prisoner-of-war camps. The comfort and good cheer these cigarettes have brought to them is pictured in many and many a touching letter from the men themselves, and from their commanding officers, their welfare officers, and their padres. "Something to smoke" —something good to smoke—is what they all want.

In the operation of the Tobacco Fund we promised to every contributor that each pound sent to the fund would provide 1,000 duty-free cigarettes. Actually, we have been able to exceed our published promise considerably. We have managed, through economical working, to dispatch no less than 76,000,000 more cigarettes than we had promised.

The need goes on. It increases with every new battle front. When the "big offensive" comes—and who can say when this greatest military effort of all will start?—the need will be far greater than ever. So I do hope that your readers will again be generous. Reply postcards will be enclosed with each package giving the name and address of the donor, so that the men can send their grateful thanks direct to those who have contributed. Our address is:—Over-Seas League Tobacco Fund, St. James's, London, S.W.1.
Yours very truly, MARIE WILLINGDON, President,
Over-Seas League Tobacco Fund

A MATERNITY HOSPITAL

Then, as today, there was general affection for nurses and concern for their welfare. A circular from a London maternity hospital, stating that the nurses' home had been requisitioned, led to a correspondent demanding that the bureaucrat responsible should be sent to the stake.

DEC. 10

Sir,—Many of your readers will have received the circular letter from the Secretary-Superintendent of Queen Charlotte's Maternity Hospital with this astonishing passage:—

Incredible as it must seem, our partly built nurses' home was requisitioned for storing bombed-out furniture, and our nursing staff has to occupy in the hospital itself space urgently needed for mothers (half of them wives of serving men). We are turning away expectant mothers at the rate of 2,500–3,000 a year—because we cannot accommodate them!

If this is not true it should be officially denied at once. If it is true the responsible culprit should surely be roasted without delay, and in public.
Yours obediently, CHRISTOPHER STONE

LOST LUGGAGE

To all the numerous vexations of daily life in Great Britain was added the perennial problem of lost luggage on the railways.

Sir,—Is it not time that some clear and emphatic warning was given to passengers who travel with luggage which they are not able to keep under personal supervision?

On September 24, having to come to London from the West Country on urgent business, I dispatched a trunk containing all the clothes I should need for a stay of three months—locked, labelled, and sent "luggage in advance." From that time to this no trace of the trunk has been found. Nearly a month elapsed before the railway authorities thought it desirable to report the matter to the police, and in the meantime I received reiterated assurances that the luggage would turn up before long. I am given to understand that after a further substantial interval I may expect to receive compensation; but I cannot wait for that and must at once replace the essential items of my wardrobe, a great part of which is really irreplaceable.

If this were an isolated happening one would have no right to complain in present conditions, but a number of my personal friends and acquaintances have lately suffered in the same way. In some cases the luggage, sent in advance, has disappeared, in others it has been found missing from the van on arrival at the destination. So numerous are these occurrences that they strongly suggest the activities of an organized gang. As the railways are greatly understaffed it is impossible for their overworked officials to exercise adequate supervision, and the inevitable sense of grievance and hardship which results from these losses would be much reduced if passengers were clearly informed of the risk and advised to insure any luggage of value which they are unable to keep under their personal control.
Yours, &c., OLWEN LAWSON
13, St. Peter's Square, W.6

Sir,—I sent a bicycle as luggage in advance from High Wycombe to Wantage Road Station recently. For over three weeks it vanished; then it was discovered at a station to which it was not addressed, all the labels being intact and clear.

Nobody knew how or when it arrived there, and I was not asked for a signature before removing it.
Yours faithfully, JEAN HUGH-SMITH
Denchworth Manor, near Wantage, Berkshire

Sir,—As a fellow sufferer with your correspondent, may I trespass on your columns to take the matter one point further? My case was exactly the same as that described in her letter. I lost clothing to the value of 128 coupons, but all I have been allowed by the Board of Trade officials is 20 coupons. Surely, as a matter of elementary justice, the position of anyone losing luggage should not be made worse from a clothing point of view by an action that is entirely outside his control.

I might add that I found the railway company most anxious to help. They accepted full responsibility and met my claim fairly and promptly.

Yours, &c., ROLAND B. WORTH

Chadstowe, Corbett Avenue, Droitwich, Worcestershire

RURAL NEEDS

As the nation entered its fifth year of food and fuel rationing, certain persistent administrative anomalies were continuing irritants. The farmers were not alone in feeling that something more could be done to ease the situation.

DEC. 10

Sir,—"Grow more Food" is a slogan which the Agriculture and Food Ministries have so usefully persisted in during the past four years. Another slogan has invited farmers to get rid of vermin, such as rats, rabbits, pigeons, and other destructive creatures. Some dare-devils have even run in the face of the sporting world by inviting the ruthless extermination of foxes!

I am one of those strange people called property-owners, no matter how much or how little it may be. Among my iniquities is the possession of a wood of some 40 acres. In the halcyon days of peace it produced a certain modest income. Now, in war-time, its only industry is maintained by a couple of quite decent poachers, who, I am told, are garnering profits from their pillage enough to project them soon into the proprietorial classes. Even a rabbit's paw now fetches some 10 times the pre-war price, with the superstitious folk who still believe in charms. Otherwise my wood is populated by rats, hares, half-wild pheasants, pigeons, jays, magpies, and other food robbers. Mr. Hudson at the Ministry exhorts us all to "Grow more Food."

The farmers are perplexed. They dislike traps, because traps are cruel and they take time to set and place. The snare is a delusion and ——! The only recourse is a good old 12-bore hammer gun. There are plenty of these on the farms, but no cartridges to meet the occasion, as neither the Agricultural Mogul nor the Food Fairy will lift a trigger finger to secure a few more fives or sixes to "Shoot for Food." Would it not be possible for Sir James Grigg to loosen up a trifle on the clay-pigeon shooting by trainees, most of which is literally waste of powder and shot? "Give us the tools," say the farmers, "and we will finish the job and give you more to eat at home."

Another thing. In my wood, besides pixies, which do not eat, there are some foxes and one particularly prolific vixen. What is their daily ration of chickens, young and boilers, ducks, geese, and Christmas turkeys? Could not we have a respite from *noblesse oblige* towards Reynard till peace comes, and then, "View Halloa" again up hill and down dale as of yore? In the meantime "Grow more Food for Home Consumption."
Yours, &c., R. D. BLUMENFELD
Muscombs, Great Easton, Dunmow

DEC. 30

Sir,—A constituent of mine, discharged recently on medical grounds after three years' active service in the Royal Navy, invested part of his savings in a second-hand car with a view to earning his living by plying for hire. There is no other car for hire in the parish in question and local bus service is severely restricted. The Essex County Council gave the necessary licence, but the Ministry of Fuel and Power refuse to allow him to buy any petrol.

The fact that if it were not for men like this in the Royal Navy there would not be any petrol for the Ministry to control appears to have escaped their attention. I feel that further comment is superfluous.
Yours faithfully, OSWALD LEWIS
House of Commons

1944

A TRINITY JUMP

Field Marshal Montgomery's father, later a bishop but at the time an undergraduate, once jumped the eight hall steps of Trinity College, Cambridge, in a single bound. This considerable feat brought a large correspondence on athletic prowess, including that of an elderly captain who would on occasion spring straight from the floor onto his chimney-piece and then stand there. To what purpose was not disclosed.

MARCH 16

Sir,—On a recent visit to Cambridge, General Montgomery, on entering the Great Court at this college, pointed to the hall steps and said to me, "Those were the steps my father jumped up at one bound." The general's father, Henry Hutchinson Montgomery, afterwards Bishop, was an undergraduate at Trinity from 1866 to 1870. He came here from Dr. Butler's Harrow with a great reputation as a runner and jumper.

The feat of leaping up the eight steps at a single bound has often been attempted by athletes, hurdlers, and jumpers without success. The only person to succeed of whom I know was the gigantic Whewell, when he was Master of the college; he clapped his mortar-board firmly on his head, picked up his gown with one hand, and leapt. The late Sir George Young, Bt., saw him do this, and many years later told his son Geoffrey Winthrop Young, who allows me to make this statement.

I have heard that the feat was accomplished once or twice in this century; once, I was told, an American succeeded, but I have not the facts or names. It has certainly been done very seldom.

Now we have a fully authenticated case of which I had not heard. Bishop Montgomery himself told his son the general, and the story was often told in the family. The general has asked me to send the facts to you in the hope that publication may elicit further facts.

Yours, &c., G. M. TREVELYAN
The Master's Lodge, Trinity College, Cambridge

MARCH 23

Sir,—When I was a boy at Cheltenham during the last war, the late Prebendary H. W. Webb-Peploe once preached in the college chapel. He told us, if I remember rightly, that as an undergraduate he had leapt up the hall steps of Trinity Great Court at a single bound. I am pretty sure that this is correct, for my father was afterwards told by my housemaster's wife that the impression left by the sermon on the minds of some of the boys was that the good Prebendary had been boasting.

Yours, &c., W. H. OSWALD

MARCH 23

Sir,—With reference to the recent letter from our Master in *The Times*, we would like to point out how remarkable a feat Whewell's jump up the steps to Hall must have been. That great Master of Trinity was born in 1794, and Sir George Young, who saw him do it, came up to Trinity at the end of 1855. In those days, no doubt, sexagenarian dons were more athletic.

Yours truly, R. W. CAHN, OSCAR HAHN

Trinity College, Cambridge

Sir,—Some of my older friends in Newmarket have told me of the exploits of the late Captain Machell, who when well in the fifties would take a flying leap and jump on the mantelpiece and stand there. Is there something sprightly in the East Anglian air?

Your obedient servant, STANLEY AUSTIN

Withersfield Rectory, Suffolk

MARCH 24

Sir,—The acumen of Messrs. Hahn and Cahn has enabled them to perceive the point of my father's story—that Whewell, when he jumped up the hall steps, was old. It would not have been memorable of him in youth. For that he would have had to jump over the hall.—LORD KENNET, Adelaide House, King William Street, E.C.4

MARCH 24

Sir,—Among unofficial athletic feats accomplished within the walls of Trinity may be counted a great kick by C. M. Wells (double Blue, 1st class Classical Tripos, and later Eton master). Going through to the Backs one day Wells, on being dared to, punted the Rugby ball he was carrying clean over the far tower of New Court. This was told me by St. John Parry, afterwards Vice-Master, who kept in New Court. The tower must be some 40ft. high and has the width of a large set of college rooms.—SIR JOHN POLLOCK, The Athenaeum, S.W.1

MARCH 24

Sir,—We in this small parish are the proud possessors of a rector who jumped the Trinity steps from bottom to top from standing position. This is

Canon Hugh Le Fleming, and he performed the feat in or about 1892 when at Clare and president of the C.U.A.C. and a high-jumping and hurdling Blue. I was not a witness, but as we were passing the steps two years ago he told me that this was his only claim to fame, and he thought it was a record.—MRS. A. G. WADE, Bentley, Hants

MARCH 24

Sir,—In January, 1934, J. B. Luddington, an undergraduate of Jesus College, agreed, for a wager of £30, to walk from Cambridge to Mill Hill and back (101 miles) in less than 24 hours and spend the next day in the hunting field. He accomplished the walk in 21 hours, reaching Cambridge at 3 a.m., and spent most of the rest of that day "whipping-in efficiently," thus winning the wager.—MR. F. BRITTAIN, Jesus College, Cambridge

A "NO TREATING" ORDER

War-time conditions led to an increase in alcohol consumption. This was deplored in a letter from a number of Congregational ministers, who urged that there should be a 'no treating' order (a ban on buying rounds) in public houses.

MARCH 25

Sir,—The undersigned are Congregational ministers, most of them of very long service and experience, who are deeply concerned by the increase of the alcoholic habit, especially on the part of the young people of the country.

We recognize the peculiar situation set up by war-time conditions, and it is for this reason that we write to urge only one measure of very urgent reform. We beg the Government to consider most seriously and immediately the issue of a "No-Treating" order, to be effective throughout the country and throughout the services.

This simple measure, so effective during the last war, will provide an excellent brake upon the present rather stupid development that is occurring. The strain and stresses of this war are in many ways more novel and greater than in the previous struggle, and hence recourse to stimulants is more prevalent and frequent, and the use of alcohol tends to an increasing recklessness to other and worse temptations.

We are, Sir, yours most faithfully, JOHN BEVAN, E. E. JOHNSON, SYDNEY CAVE, T. WIGLEY, F. CHALMERS ROGERS, W. J. COATES, A. D. BELDEN, NORMAN COCKS, R. MORTON STANLEY, E. J. BARSON, W. ARCHIBALD DAVIES, IDRIS EVANS, W. SELBY STEYN, EBENEZER REES, FRANK H. BALLARD, WILL SIMPSON, J. P. STEPHENS

Sir,—As an advocate of moderate drinking, for reasons of health and fitness rather than of religious principle I should like to support the plea of the Congregational ministers which appears in your columns to-day for the speedy introduction of a no-treating order.

Last summer, while spending a week at the seaside, I joined the local club. It was obvious that the atmosphere, friendly and sociable above the ordinary, had not been impaired by this self-denying ordinance. Indeed, it seemed to have had the opposite effect for, unlike most clubs or, for that matter, public houses in wartime, there was always plenty of alcohol available for those who needed it. I was told that this happy state of affairs had been accompanied by a *per caput* decrease in consumption amounting to about 50 per cent.

Young people are notoriously the slaves of fashion. It is the fashion to-day to stand drinks to your friends, including your girl friends, at fantastic prices, five-sixths of which go straight to the Exchequer. I believe that a no-treating order would change this. I am not impressed by the argument that such an order could not be enforced, because we are a law-abiding nation and because I am convinced that vast numbers of people would welcome a measure that would enable them, without loss of face, to spend their money to better purpose or better still to save it and make it fight for victory.

Yours faithfully, TOM WICKHAM
House of Commons

Sir,—May I suggest that the Congregational ministers who are calling for this impracticable order to be brought into force again should make some inquiry as to its working during the last war, and they might also get a hint or two by referring to my letter on the subject in *The Times* of November 9, 1942. Among the many incongruities it became illegal for a man to give money to his wife for the purchase of alcoholic liquor. Where do they expect to get the necessary army of police spies?

Yours, &c., C. L'ESTRANGE EWEN
31, Marine Drive, Paignton

Sir,—The interesting correspondence on "treating" has more than two sides to it, I think. Logically, the demand for a non-treating order is fair enough. Treating has been proved to increase drinking expenditure, especially among the young and alcoholically inexperienced. People in groups also drink about 10 per cent. faster than solo drinkers.

Sociologically, the demand is less firmly based. The pub is above all else a fundamental British social organization—the only simple, public, informal, communal unit still freely available to anybody every day. It serves alcohol among many other things. The biggest other thing is company, comradeship, and good cheer. Treating and toasting are the symbols of public friendliness. It has been so for centuries, and bans on those customs —always unsuccessful—go back to Charles II, Pope Innocent III, and the 1356 Council of Cologne. A new attempt, in these democratic days, would probably lead to mass evasion, unless there were a complete new inspectorate to ensure enforcement. But if successfully applied, would such an order not knock one more nail into the coffin of private liberties and of positive social groups?

Moreover, while the solitary drinker goes more slowly and quietly, there is much to suggest that he or she is the one who, chatterless, anchorless, private, carries on into the area of extremism—drunkenness. Whereas the friendly, noisy, treating group go off to the dance or the whist drive, at least keeping each other on the rails.

These are at least points worthy of consideration. So often in the past our social habits have been altered by sincere but one-sided legislative action which has inhibited traditions integral in our way of living.

Yours, &c., TOM HARRISSON

82, Ladbroke Road, W.11

"A JOLLY FACTORY"

Some advertisements soliciting labour were not always considered appropriate in war time.

JUNE 17

Sir,—Immediately after listening to the broadcast of invasion news the other night I caught sight of the following advertisement in a provincial paper:—

Girls age 14–17. If you want big money and clean, light essential work that does not soil your hands, in a jolly factory with music, hot dinners, and every freedom, free overalls, no Sats. and no overtime, you can get over £2. 14s. per wk. of five days, provided you are reasonably intelligent and prepared to concentrate on the work.

That any firm in this country should be capable of making an appeal of this kind to anybody, let alone to young people, is surely outrageous.

Yours, &c., H. C. A. GAUNT

Malvern College, Headmaster's Office, 5, High Street, Harrow-on-the-Hill

JUNE 22

Sir,—Your correspondent Mr. Gaunt seems to find it "outrageous" that a good job should be offered in what appears to be a well-run factory. Perhaps he would approve if the advertisement were redrafted.

If you want little money and dirty, heavy, unessential work that soils your hands, in a dismal factory without music, food, or freedom, providing your own overalls, working Saturdays and overtime, you cannot earn £2 14s. per week, and you must be unintelligent and not prepared to concentrate on your work.

Does Mr. Gaunt think that our soldiers are fighting for this sort of thing after the war?
Yours faithfully, JOCELYN WALKER, Chairman, Walker's Dyers and Cleaners, Limited, Leyton, E.10
Wellingham Vane, near Lewes, Sussex

FLYING BOMBS

The British, accustomed to earlier air raids, were subjected to V-1, 'doodle-bug', attacks in 1944. The warning siren caused some annoyance.

JULY 8

Sir,—Would it not be possible to reduce the duration of air raid warnings from sixty seconds to thirty or forty? We all know the sound perfectly well by now, no one takes half a minute to distinguish an alert from an all clear, in fact there are complaints on all sides that the sound goes on too long and gets on the nerves. I have also noticed several times that it drowns the noise of an approaching bomb.
Yours faithfully, RUPERT GLEADOW
33, Cheyne Walk, S.W.3

JULY 8

Sir,—Isn't it obvious that some warning should be given to the public in the streets of the imminent approach of flying bombs? At present people indoors are aware of the imminent danger by hearing the throbbing note of the approaching object and can immediately take cover, but people in the streets are deafened by the noise of the traffic and have no possible means of knowing there is immediate danger. Surely some special signal could be devised whereby people in the streets could take cover for a few minutes when approaching craft are overhead.

Further, would it not be a public benefit if firms who have warning bells

for their staff could have them connected with a bell ringing in the street, thereby warning passers-by that an enemy aircraft is directly approaching?
Yours faithfully, HENRY OSCAR
Theatre Royal, Drury Lane, W.C.2

JULY 12

Sir,—To many others like myself, who are responsible for the safety of children, our task would be made very much easier if it were possible to forbid all low flying of aircraft (except, of course, in cases of urgency) over the area threatened by air-bomb attack. It is especially difficult to differentiate between the noise of some light training aircraft and that made by these infernal machines.
Yours faithfully, PAUL GRIFFITH

JULY 13

Sir,—Would it be possible to send a message to that R.A.F. pilot mentioned in Saturday's paper? The incident to which I refer was one of which it was said that:—

An R.A.F. pilot, at considerable personal risk, prevented a flying bomb from crashing on houses. After he had fired at it, the bomb went towards the houses. The pilot, seeing the danger, gave it another burst of fire at close quarters . . .

We, who live in one of those houses, would feel it a privilege if we could be allowed to express our deep gratitude to that pilot, and I am sure our neighbours feel the same. Under God, we feel we owe him the lives of those near and dear to us, as well as our own lives and homes. And we can never thank him enough for his courageous, daring action.
Yours sincerely, IRENE M. ALLDER

AUG. 30

Sir,—Hitler of the *Hunnenvolk* has made a miscalculation similar to that of the Baron van Coehoorn, 250 years ago. This Dutch military engineer, who receives notice in every good encyclopedia, English, French, and German, invented a little, easily carried mortar which bears his name (two were produced for trench warfare in 1914).

In sieges in which he took part they were employed in mass, a hundred or more at a time. He calculated that, judiciously aimed and shifted about, their bombs would by a succession of salvos infallibly destroy any fortress and its garrison in a short time. The bombs "troubled" (Enc. Brit.) the French, but did not achieve the results which he expected.
I am, Sir, your obedient servant, ARCHIMEDES

A CITY HOARDING

Though Allied victory was assured by 1944, the final, supreme effort remained. Some able-bodied men, however, were thought to be frivolously employed.

JULY 14

Sir,—Recently, in the fifth year of this war, much timber has been used and several men have been employed for several weeks in erecting and painting a huge, elaborate hoarding on Ludgate Hill, advertising "Wonder Tablets" for the blood. The future historian of our civilization may be interested to have a record of this astonishing fact.

Yours, &c., V. A. DEMANT

3, Amen Court, E.C.4

RABBITS

The problem of pest control, or indeed of pest consumption, lingered on . . .

JULY 20

Sir,—It is strange to read that over 1,000,000 frozen rabbits are imported from New Zealand when a similar number, very much unfrozen, are consuming the food we try to grow in Herefordshire.

Yours faithfully, SHEILA WENHAM

Brook Farm, Kingsland, Herefordshire

THE HOME GUARD

The Home Guard was seemingly redundant by the autumn of 1944 and would shortly be disbanded. But how best were the men to be informed of this? Should they be awarded medals? And could they keep their army issue boots?

SEPT. 18

Sir,—It would be interesting to know who has been responsible for the present anomalous position in which this force now finds itself. Last

Sunday I explained the position to the four platoons in my command at the last compulsory parade, and everywhere I found the same expression of opinion from officers, n.c.o.s, and men.

What is generally resented is the feeling that after four years of keen and unpaid service Britain's "cheapest army" is to be allowed to fizzle out. It is generally agreed that a reduction in the hours of training is overdue, but there is no doubt that the vast majority of the men would have preferred to have continued a limited number of parades until those in authority felt that the final "stand down" could be ordered. Very strong resentment was also felt that orders for the discontinuance of compulsory parades should have been given over the radio instead of through the proper military channels.

Yours faithfully, COMPANY COMMANDER

SEPT. 23

Sir,—Does "Company Commander" really believe that the rank-and-file of the Home Guard are so devoted to military etiquette that they resent receiving orders otherwise than through "the proper military channels"? The great majority approved both the matter and the manner of Sir James Grigg's announcement. "Company Commander's" men, if they persuade him to the contrary, must be a very exceptional, or very tactful, body. In any event, as they are all so eager for more parades, how will the abolition of compulsion do them any harm.

Yours faithfully, C. WHIBLEY
406, Duncan House, Dolphin Square, S.W.1

SEPT. 23

Sir,—As a Home Guardsman I read with astonishment the letter from "Company Commander." Most of us are greatly relieved that the H.G. is to be allowed to "fizzle out," if in fact such is the case. We find our time very fully occupied and have no desire whatever for any parades that are not essential.

So far from feeling any resentment that the discontinuance of compulsory parades was announced by radio, we are very glad that it was announced in this speedy manner. Sir James Grigg evidently knows the feelings of the majority of the H.G. better than "Company Commander."

Yours faithfully, G. D. MILLWARD
1, Arbrook Lane, Esher, Surrey

SEPT. 23

Sir,—Your correspondent "Company Commander" is right. Bitter disgust and a sense of frustration have been the results of the recent treatment of the Home Guard, and now it appears that a force which has been second to none in keenness and dutiful service may be entirely disbanded before the cessation of hostilities in Europe. So, when the day of rejoicing comes, instead of taking our place with the other armed forces, we shall be standing as civilians on the pavements, watching our comrades in arms go by.

If the authors of recent pronouncements think that, on that day, they can induce an already disbanded Home Guard to put on its uniform and parade with the rest—assuming that the uniform is not already rotting in store—let them remember that a clock without a mainspring still looks like a clock, but it is only a shell without a heart. Our mainspring was our duty, and now we are told that there is no duty left for us and are kicked on to the dust heap at a moment's notice.

Yours faithfully, ORIGINAL L.D.V.

SEPT. 27

Sir,—Now that the standing down of the Home Guard cannot be far distant it would be an act of grace on the part of the Government to allow every man to retain his boots and greatcoat.

These articles would be of immense value to the men, especially to those living in country districts, and such a grant would be a token of appreciation of the work of those who have freely given their services and deserved well of their country.

Your obedient servant, W. R. P. HENRY, Lieut.-Col.

Rathburne, Duns

SEPT. 29

Sir,—Colonel Henry will find, in the Army Council Instruction of December 18, 1940, No. 1542, permission granted to the Home Guard to purchase their boots for the sum of 22s. 6d., less one shilling for each month of use; a man, therefore, who has served 23 months is entitled to retain his boots.

Yours, &c., R. B. RAMSBOTHAM

Cromwell's House, Woodstock, Oxfordshire

OCT. 2

Sir,—Mr. R. B. Ramsbotham will find that ACI 1542/40 was cancelled by 1038/42, which was in turn cancelled by H.G. Regulations, Vol. II, para. 114(c).

A man may not retain his boots, no matter how long he has served, except in case of boots made to special measurement.

Yours, &c., J. H. KNIGHT, Kent Home Guard

Woodside, Sevenoaks

OCT. 3

Sir,—I should like to endorse Colonel Henry's letter on Home Guard greatcoats and boots. I have felt so strongly about it that I have asked my local M.P. to take the matter up, which he has promised to do whole-heartedly.

It may not be realized in the towns of what great value these articles would be to men working on the land, as practically the whole of my company are. And I think that the Home Guard deserve some practical recognition after the many hours' free and willing service they have given in the last four years. I can think of no better way of giving this than by allowing them to keep, at least, these things.

Yours, &c., ESSEX

Throope Farm, Bishopstone, Salisbury

OCT. 6

Sir,—I have read with pleasure the letters which you have published recently on the subject of Home Guard clothing, and particularly boots. One important aspect of the matter has not been touched upon—namely, the fact that during the early and most strenuous months of the force men wore out their own clothing and boots on regular patrols and exercises. Surely the authorities should consider this and make reasonable restitution by permitting retention of part-worn clothing and boots now in possession of men?

I am, Sir, your obedient servant, J. LOGAN STRANG, Lt.-Col., H.G.

1, North Charlotte Street, Edinburgh, 2

NOISE OF AIRCRAFT

The approaching war's end brought other hopeful prospects to readers' minds.

SEPT. 12

Sir,—I shall probably be absolved from any charge of wishing to disparage the art of human flight, especially at a time when our very gallant airmen are giving of their best to achieve such a victory in Germany as will bring this war to a speedy end.

It was odd nevertheless to sit recently in the sunshine of an Oxfordshire garden not far from the quiet Thames with so great a roar of aircraft flying overhead in their great formations as to make conversation on anything less than shouting terms an impossibility. Soon, I hope, those haunts will resume their peaceful life, but never will they be forgetful of that din of war which deafened them in the last phases of the greater world war. Much is endured, and even welcomed, in time of war which would not be tolerated in times of peace. After the war civil aircraft will no doubt be on their good behaviour, knowing that if they break seriously into the peace of the countryside public action will be swift.

Yours faithfully, H. E. WIMPERIS

The Athenaeum, Pall Mall, S.W.1

A SERVICE CLUB SIGN

By late 1944, an element of irritation, induced by fatigue, is evident in letters, many of which became spitefully quarrelsome. The erection of a service club sign caused friction, notably between Sir Thomas Moore and H. G. Wells, residents of Hanover Terrace, Regent's Park.

SEPT. 27

Sir,—Some months ago Lady Sinclair, wife of the Secretary of State for Air, opened a club for the services in a house in Hanover Terrace, Regent's Park. Its purpose was to provide rest, relaxation, and food for all service men and women, but more especially for the large number of R.A.F. cadets in the neighbourhood. It has fully fulfilled its purpose.

As the owner and his wife, although having spent all their married life there, could no longer live in it, they were very happy to let this home of theirs at a nominal rent to the Salvation Army for the purpose specified. Since the house is set back from the public road and somewhat sheltered from view by trees and shrubbery, the Salvation Army, with the owner's concurrence, erected a signboard (on the same level as the notice boards "To Let" and "For Sale" near by) intimating the existence of the club. This sign caught the eagle eye of a quaint body termed the Crown Estates Paving Commission set up by Act of Parliament 122 years ago for the purpose of supervising the amenities of Regent's Park (Hitler's arrival was not then anticipated).

This active body immediately drew the attention of the other residents in the terrace to this board and asked them if it had their approval. Two out of the 20 residents objected. Their names, as subsequently revealed in the Press were Mr. J. Harrison and Mr. H. G. Wells. The commission thereupon ordered the owner to remove the board. The owner refused on the grounds that without the board the people for whom the club was intended would have no means of knowing that it was a club. After this refusal the commission baled the owner to court, where he was found guilty and fined £2, with £5 5s. costs. An airfield, however, in Southern England, some of whose staff and crews had happy memories of the club, made a collection and substantially reduced his outlay.

As the reasons for which the board was originally put up still remain good the owner has kept the board in position until this day. Now he has been informed by this same Paving Commission that unless he removes it within 14 days they again intend to use the Act of William IV and will institute proceedings against him.

Our men and boys are being killed, mutilated, and burnt daily for the safety and freedom of all of us, including Mr. Harrison and Mr. H. G. Wells. Why therefore this concern about the cheapening of this select residential neighbourhood? Hitler has already cheapened it much more effectively than either the Salvation Army or the owner, who is

Your obedient servant, THOMAS MOORE

House of Commons

SEPT. 28

Sir,—I do not see that it is any affair of mine that Sir Thomas Moore sees fit to break the contract under which he secured possession of No. 1, Hanover Terrace. The matter lies between him and the Crown Estates Paving Commission.

Sir Thomas talks of the safety and freedom the tenants of the terrace enjoy, thanks apparently to his unnamed associates who are being "killed, mutilated and burnt daily." I apologize to him for not having so strenuous a daily routine, but at any rate I have faced the risk of it and Sir Thomas and his wife have not. Regent's Park, so far from being a haven of safety and freedom, has suffered more than any other part of North London from bombing. Anyone who chooses can walk along it and note the devastation its tenants (who also include the Master of the Rolls) have endured.

Most of those who have gone have simply been bombed out. It has apparently been too dangerous for the occupation of Sir Thomas Moore, who, for reasons best known to himself, maintains a campaign of insult and misrepresentation against me.

Yours faithfully, H. G. WELLS

13, Hanover Terrace, Regent's Park, N.W.1

SEPT. 29

Sir,—In answer to Mr. H. G. Wells I can testify that Sir Thomas Moore has commanded a battalion of the London Home Guard for more than four years, and lived at No. 1 Hanover Terrace throughout the blitz of 1940–41, which he left late in that year owing to lack of domestic help. Since then he has resided continuously in a top-floor flat in the same locality.

Incidentally, the immediate neighbourhood of this house has long been gay with the signs and flags of American clubs, Fighting French hostels, and the like, without exciting the permanent residents to vituperative combat.

Yours faithfully, G. K. M. MASON
17, Ennismore Gardens, S.W.7

Sir,—Mr. H. G. Wells is quite enthralling when he allows his imagination to play with fancy, but he is apparently quite irresponsible when he allows it to play with facts. I suppose it is now too late to suggest that before making dogmatic and slanderous assertions he should verify his assumptions, but for his information and yours, Sir, I would only say that Colonel Mason's statement is quite correct and that I have lived continuously in Regent's Park, or near by, from September 3, 1939, until this day.

Ignoring Mr. Wells's somewhat obscure gibe about my associates, lads who die for him and me, I would briefly answer his petulant charges of misrepresentation and insult. Does he deny his written words that on May 31 this year he stated that he was "entirely hostile to this needless cheapening of one of the best sites in London"? That quotation I suggest covers his charge of misrepresentation.

On the question of insult, I have had ample reason and opportunity both to criticize and insult Mr. Wells, but have hitherto imposed a self-restraint which he might care to imitate.

Yours faithfully, THOMAS MOORE
House of Commons

Sir,—Mr. H. G. Wells may be interested to know that since my last letter the anonymous mother of an airman who apparently had some happy hours in the Hanover Terrace Club has sent me the money to pay my next fine.

It may of course be Brixton for me if the Crown Estates Paving Commission and Mr. Wells have their way, but that would not lessen my gratitude to the kindly donor.

Yours faithfully, THOMAS MOORE
House of Commons

Sir,—I have no desire to renew this controversy with Mr. H. G. Wells and therefore do not propose to reply to his misleading and somewhat involved letter published in your issue of the 14th instant.

I must, however, repeat that the signboard to which Mr. Wells and his associate took exception remains in place and with the assent of the Crown Estates Paving Commission. I would not have announced publicly the

amicable settlement of my dispute with the Commission but for the fact that
I had no other way of notifying my many generous but unknown friends in
various parts of the world that I had no longer any need of their financial
assistance to meet the costs of the further proceedings threatened against
me.

Yours faithfully, THOMAS MOORE
House of Commons

POULTRY KEEPING

*The war had been waged for more than five years, but even in
October 1944 bureaucracy was still frustrating the poultry
keeper.*

OCT. 5

Sir,—It will I think be interesting and also surprising to poultry keepers
who contemplate removal to hear that in that event they are unlikely to
receive an allowance of food for their stock.

I reside in Surrey and for the last five years have kept about 30 head of
poultry producing eggs for home consumption and supplying the remainder, in accordance with the present regulations, to the local committee for
distribution. Being about to remove to Dorset I applied to the War
Agricultural Executive Committee, Dorchester, for the necessary allowance of foodstuffs. In reply I am informed that the ration I at present
receive belongs to the holding I occupy and will pass to my successor (who,
incidentally, may not wish to keep poultry) and that as my new holding of
19 acres does not carry a basic ration it is regretted that the allowance
cannot be continued.

As I have pointed out to the bureaucratic officials, who appear to govern
us in these days, my only course now is to slaughter my poultry, in other
words to "kill the goose that lays the golden eggs"—such is the encouragement we receive when we endeavour to produce food as asked by the
Government.

Yours truly, LEONARD WELLS
76, Southwark Street, S.E.1

OCT. 9

Sir,—I am particularly interested in Mr. Leonard Wells's letter in *The
Times* to-day. I venture to write as my experience is the exact opposite.

We came here 16 months ago, and were told by the W.A.E.C. that the previous owner, who had kept poultry here, was entitled to have, and had had, his allowance of foodstuffs transferred to his new farm. Therefore it was regretted it was not possible to issue one to us. It would appear that either a mistake has been made in Mr. Wells's case or ours, or that the Government wishes to reduce the supply of fresh eggs for the public still further.

It would be interesting to know which of the W.A.E.C.s concerned has interpreted the regulations correctly.

Yours truly, P. H. BEEVOR
Cooks Mill, Lexden, Colchester

OCT. 11

Sir,—The letter from Mr. Leonard Wells in *The Times* of October 5 prompts me to give a similar illustration of bureaucratic ineptitude.

I, too, live in Surrey, and my wife (wishing from patriotic motives to begin keeping fowls for food production, as recommended) approached the local food authority and was informed that the first step was to procure the hens and then apply for the necessary form for authority to purchase the required food, and that this consent might possibly be received within about a month after application.

What was to happen to the fowls during that month was left to conjecture. In these circumstances the idea was abandoned in disgust.

Yours truly, F. ROWLAND
56, Moorgate, E.C.2

OCT. 17

Sir,—Your correspondents should do what I did last year when buying a large number of pure-bred hens from a farm that was being sold. I applied to the Hampshire War Agricultural Executive Committee to have the ration that had been allotted to the farm transferred to me, with the proviso that should the person taking over the particular ground apply for its ration, then I should have to give it up as he would have priority.

The trouble is that the Ministry never has realized the potential value of poultry in wartime; and it will take many years under the present system for our poultry to be even a fraction of what it was before the war.

Yours, &c., WALTER HUTCHINSON
Stanbridge Earls Estate, near Romsey, Hampshire

OCT. 20

Sir,—Has Mr. Hutchinson overlooked the letter in *The Times* of July 4, 1941, from Mr. Howard Marshall, Director of Public Relations, Ministry of Food? He says:—"The whole matter, however, can be condensed into the fact that scientists have advised the Government that the hen is the most extravagant converter of feeding-stuffs into human food."

Yours faithfully, W. W. ELDERS
25, Carew Road, Eastbourne

HORSE MARINES

'Slang' phrases were a recurring part of war-time conversation.
'Tell it to the Marines' was one such.

OCT. 18

Sir,—I regret to see your crossword of last Friday endorsing the phrase "Tell it to the Marines," which has occurred several times in recent broadcasts. "Tell it to the Infantry" or "Tell it to the Cavalry" would do just as well and be equally pointless. The correct version is, surely, "Tell it to the Horse Marines"—there being no such persons.

Your obedient servant, STICKLER

OCT. 19

Sir,—I am sorry, but "Stickler" is wrong. Throughout my service in the Royal Navy the expression "Tell it to the Marines" was an undeserved joke about the alleged thickheadedness of a magnificent body of sea-going soldiers.

I am, Sir, yours, &c., STRABOLGI
House of Lords, S.W.1

OCT. 20

Sir,—It is unfortunate that this saying has been twisted so as to impute credulity to the Royal Marines. The undernoted extract from Burton Stevenson's Book of Quotations should correct the popular idea:—

"Mr. Pepys, from the very nature of their calling, no class of our subjects can have so wide a knowledge of seas and lands as the officers and men of our royal maritime regiment. Henceforth, whenever we cast doubt upon a tale that lacketh likelihood, we will tell it to the marines. If they believe it, it is safe to say it is true."—Charles II, as recorded in Pepys' diary.

The tale that had tested the king's credulity was one about flying fish, which his Colonel of Marines assured him was true.

Yours faithfully, JOHN R. McLAREN
The Drove Way, Buxted, Sussex

OCT. 21

Sir,—I think the inventor of the crossword may be justified. The "Horse Marines" is of course an expression known for long among sailors, but the correct proverb is surely "Tell it to the Marines, for the sailors won't believe it!" That is how I heard it 60 years ago from my father, who commanded the old Blackwall frigate Superb.

Yours faithfully, JESSE BERRIDGE
Little Baddow Rectory, Chelmsford

OCT. 25

Sir,—Lord Strabolgi says I am wrong. But I don't think I am. Neither, of course, is he. My version comes down from Scott, Marryat, and the general usage of the nineteenth century: and all I contend is that it is a pity that the newer version should have lost its point.

Yours, &c., STICKLER

1945

IDENTITY CARDS

◆

National Registration identity cards were tolerated, even welcomed, during the war years. But should they be compulsory in peace?

DEC. 27, 1944

Sir,—While obtaining, recently, a National Registration identity card for my small daughter, I remarked that it was pleasant to think that all this bothersome business would soon no longer be necessary. I was blandly informed by the clerk that my expectation was quite wrong, since registration was to continue after the war. On looking at the card in my hand, I discovered that it was valid until 1960.

I do not know, and have no means of finding out, whether the statement made to me was the product of ignorant dogmatism or was based on facts. If it was true, then I think it is time that the public should be informed of these facts and have the opportunity to express an opinion on them: I do not think there is very much doubt what that opinion would be.

I am, Sir, yours, &c., ANTONY WELLS
3, Prospect Place, Hampstead, N.W.3

DEC. 29, 1944

Sir,—Referring to Mr. Antony Wells's letter in *The Times* of to-day, it would be interesting to know his objections as a law-abiding citizen to the continuance of identity cards after the war. To some they seem to be one of the few war-time measures worth retaining.

Some relaxation will be possible in peacetime in the regulations concerning them, but I foresee many citizens voluntarily carrying these cards, just as the foreign traveller used to provide himself with a passport where one was not legally required. In many ways they will always be a safeguard to the individual as well as a valuable administrative adjunct.

I am, Sir, yours faithfully, A. J. R. FRASER TAYLOR
42, Selborne Road, Hove, 3, Sussex

DEC. 29, 1944

Sir,—If the use of identity cards is to be continued after the war, I should like to put in a plea for a more robust and compact construction. The authorities were more happily inspired when they designed the driving licence for motorists. The *Cedula de Identidad* (for example), as used in the Argentine, has a stiff cover of about the same size and shape.

I am, &c., J. WARDALE

Ardingly

JAN. 1

Sir,—Mr. Fraser Taylor feels that the continuance of identity cards after the war would be a safeguard to the individual.

A safeguard against what? Against arrest on a charge of being unable to prove his identity? Against refusal by a shopkeeper to sell him a box of matches without proof of his right to buy one? Against refusal of admittance to a public meeting? Against some bureaucrat's doubt of his right to exist?

Are these the essential liberties for which we shall have fought and toiled?

I am, Sir, yours, &c., SINCLAIR WOOD

Reform Club

JAN. 1

Sir,—The diffidence of the identity card magnates in not bluntly stating their intention to survive is not shared by our war agriculture committee which, taking the bull by the horns, has already dropped the word "War" and now boldly parades itself on its invoice forms as the "Surrey Agricultural Executive Committee."

Yours, &c., JULIAN D. MARKS

Snoxhall, Cranleigh, Surrey

APRIL 10

Sir,—May I, through your columns, express the earnest hope that friends of liberty will unite to resist the continuance of identity cards in time of peace? Such cards may seem only a small inconvenience, but they are seriously dangerous to liberty in two ways:—First, they facilitate all sorts of further regimentation of citizens, and that is, of course, why it is desired to retain them; secondly, they have a most mischievous moral effect in treating the individual as a numbered item in the aggregate which makes up the State. There lie before us two alternative conceptions of the State: it may be thought an organization useful to individuals and essentially their servant, or it may be thought a pagan demigod for whom the individual exists, whose service is his greatest glory and whose supremacy is without limit.

The ideas of Fascism will certainly not be killed by the war. They will persist and attract and make proselytes just as democratic ideas did after

1815. We have to fear an Anglicized totalitarianism, humane and benevolent, but essentially destructive of personal liberty and initiative; and there will be a strong coalition of philanthropists and bureaucrats eager to regulate their fellow-citizens. We must be jealous for our liberties, and to begin with must resist being numbered like convicts in order to facilitate our servitude.

I remain yours faithfully, QUICKSWOOD
16, Beechwood Avenue, Bournemouth

APRIL 16

Sir,—Has not Lord Quickswood misconceived the purpose of the identity cards, to which he so much objects? I myself like them and have always regarded them as something of a safeguard for the holder. On the Continent they were a commonplace in peace-time and were, I think, liked by all respectable members of the community and only disliked by those who wished to conceal their identity and their actions.

I fail to perceive that these cards are in any way "seriously dangerous to our liberty," and I am quite sure that my card has never had any "mischievous moral effect" either on me or anybody else, although Lord Quickswood contends that both of these results must inevitably follow.

Yours truly, F. B. ADAMS
Rudhall, Brackendale Road, Camberley

BOARDING THE BUS

Public transport, despite operating under difficult conditions, was the object of repeated criticism. The 'bus service did not escape censure.

APRIL 14

Sir,—It is surely time that the responsible authorities put an end to the dangerous and persistent habit of the London bus conductors in giving the starting signal while passengers are still attempting to board the bus. I have twice recently seen women fall because the starting signal was given when they were only half on; in both cases the conductor was on the lower deck and perfectly able to see that the passengers were not on, and such instances could be duplicated many times over.

Complaint to the L.P.T.B. is met by the invariable reply that the public asked for faster buses, and has got them; hardly an adequate answer to a continual infringement of the safety margin, and curiously forgetful that the first object of a bus service is to convey passengers, not leave them behind.

Yours faithfully, C. B. ACWORTH

Flat 3, 14 Pembridge Crescent, W.11

Sir,—All bus users will be grateful for the publicity given to a dangerous practice in the letter "Boarding the Bus" which appeared in your issue of April 14. The conductors are apparently unaware that elderly persons are usually not active enough to board a bus which starts when they have one foot on it. It is quite frequent for conductors on the upper deck, without troubling to look down the gangway, to give the starting signal by stamping with their feet, and a person half-boarded gets, or barely escapes, a nasty fall.

Complaints to higher authorities are usually not made because the replies are perfunctory. As means of other locomotion are restricted and there is in fact no competition, the only remedies would appear to be for the Ministry of War Transport to employ a few officials whose business it would be to travel on buses and report dangerous practices, or for all bus travellers to form a protective association.

Yours faithfully, FRANK DE MONTE

21, Tanza Road, Hampstead, N.W.3

Sir,—The route I travel by bus daily to a railway station is the last stage of its journey and on my return homewards it is the first stage. In the morning the bus almost invariably crawls along, and on occasions stops altogether while the conductor and driver go into conference to consider how long they have before they are due at the terminus. The result is that one cannot gauge the amount of time that should be allowed to catch a train, and often it is missed because of this. What a difference on the return journey! The bus has only just started from the terminus and the driver is apparently anxious to get as much time in hand as possible. I have observed all that Mr. Acworth described in his letter recently, with the added annoyance of people signalling the bus at request stops which the driver ignores.

It is evident that the bus crews are more concerned with running to schedule than anything else, and the conveyance of passengers is of small consequence.

Yours faithfully, A. G. RANSLEY

55, Blenheim Terrace, St. John's Wood, N.W.8

HITLER

The Times *obituary of Adolf Hitler provoked comment.*

MAY 5

Sir,—A slight correction of statement is necessary in your obituary notice of Adolf Hitler to-day. It was not in a Berlin hospital, but in a hospital at Pasewalk, in Pomerania, that Hitler learned of the November revolution of 1918.

On hearing, from the padre, that Germany had lost the war he had a recurrence of his blindness of a month previous, thus showing that he had a tendency to hysteria. As he himself wrote in "Mein Kampf" (s. 223 in the German edition) *"Während es mir um die Augen wieder schwarz, wurde, tastete und taumelte ich zum Schlafsaal zurück."* ("While darkness again settled in my eyes, I fumbled and stumbled my way back to my ward.")
Yours faithfully, WILLIAM BROWN
The Athenaeum, Pall Mall, S.W.1

MAY 7

Sir,—Two short footnotes to your obituary of the Führer. The often alleged change of name by Hitler's father amounts to this:—Austrian peasants have regularly two names, one derived from the name of their freehold —the "house name" (*Hausname*)—transmitted from owner to owner in case of inheritance or sale of the property, the other the family name a man signs on documents (*Schreibname*). A man is "called" (*heisst*) by his house-name as long as he dwells there and owns his place; he signs himself (*schreibt sich*) with his family name. The change from the one to the other is evidence of the sale or cession of property-rights to a new owner. *"Hitler"* (from *Hütte, Hitten*, diminutive *Hittel*) means "small cottager" or "little cotman," and is originally an expression of contempt on the part of the bigger landowners in the neighbourhood. So is *Schicklgruber*, "the owner," "the man of the chequered pit"—*i.e.*, a low-lying patch of land, piebald with sandy patches and dark scrub.

Hitler "drank in the pan-Germanism of" Georg von Schoenerer, not "of Luege." Dr. Karl Lueger was the great leader of the Christian-Socialist Party, a fervent Austrian, and an enemy of Pan-Germanism.
I am, Sir, your obedient servant, ROBERT EISLER, late of Dachau and Buchenwald
Oxford

MAY 7

Sir,—I read with interest your article on Hitler's career, and I came across a slight inaccuracy in your description which might seem quite insignificant, but which you may perhaps allow me to point out in a few words. You say that Hitler obtained the rank of corporal in the German Army in the last war. This is not correct. In fact, he was only lance-corporal (*Gefreiter*, a rank which is not that of an n.c.o. in the German Army). I was told by the German officer in whose company Hitler served throughout the war that on more than one occasion when necessary promotions to n.c.o.s were discussed in his battalion Hitler was turned down as altogether too empty headed and irresponsible to be trusted with the job of an n.c.o.

I am, Sir, your obedient servant, S. E. MICHAEL
98, Park Lane, Croydon

EIRE AND HITLER

On Hitler's death, the Prime Minister of Eire, de Valera, saw fit to have himself driven to the German Embassy in Dublin to sign the book of condolence. His outing prompted several indignant letters.

MAY 7

Sir,—May I call attention to two extracts from *The Times* to-day? The first is the last sentence of your leading article on Adolf Hitler, the second is an item of news.

"For the moment it is more than enough to know that the world is rid of its worst and most dangerous malefactor."

"Mr. de Valera, accompanied by Mr. J. P. Walshe, Secretary to the Department of External Affairs, called on the German Minister in Dublin last evening to express his condolence on Hitler's death."

Your obedient servant, LESLIE HOUSDEN
3, New Street, Basingstoke

MAY 15

Sir,—The publicity given to the visit of condolence on the death of Adolf Hitler, paid by the Prime Minister of Eire, accompanied by the Secretary to the Department of External Affairs, to the German Minister in Dublin, calls for Irish comment which would have preferred silence regarding this strangest day in Irish history.

Irish people may view the tragi-comedy of Portuguese diplomacy with some detachment. But to those of Irish Nationalist traditions, educated in passionate love of freedom and championship of oppressed peoples, that day on which the Premier of Eire who made his last stand with the cause of freedom and small nations with his 1940 denunciation of the violation of

Holland and Belgium, now, with the evidence of Buchenwald and the rest freshly before him to reinforce what he has always known, gave fullest honour to an expression of condolence on the death of the symbol of these crimes, must remain the strangest of all the strange pages that Mr. de Valera has written in Irish history. The name Hitler, as the head of the force responsible, stands for the breaking of the world's heart and life. The latest evidence before Mr. de Valera, whether or not his censorship has permitted it to reach the people within Eire, proves also what would have been the fate of many of those had Hitler triumphed.

In this hour thousands of Irish homes mourn their contribution to the world's liberation and the ending of those horrors in Europe. Thousands more wait for news from the Far East. The living Irish volunteers have been among the liberators and carriers of merciful relief to stricken populations and torture camps; and Irish prisoners of war are now home-coming, telling what their eyes have seen of the horror of the treatment of the Poles and others. I would ask English people and the people of the United Nations not to forget these facts.

English people may view the tragi-comedy enacted in Dublin with some detachment. Such detachment is not possible for those of Irish traditions, who, regarding it, may find their sense of humour as much in abeyance as that of the Prime Minister of Eire when he performed the strangest act in Irish history.

Yours, &c., PAMELA HINKSON
London

MAY 15

Sir,—Much abuse has been showered on Mr. de Valera for his action in tendering the condolences of his Government to the German Minister in Dublin on the death of Hitler. In common fairness it should be pointed out that this was strictly in accordance with diplomatic usage.

Whenever the head of a State dies, the heads of all other States who maintain diplomatic relations with her, as also their Foreign Ministers, invariably tender their condolences to the Ambassador or Minister as the case may be: to fail to do so would be regarded as an act of gross discourtesy. I have no admiration for Mr. de Valera or his Government, but we should remember that they are neutrals and must be expected to act as such.

Yours faithfully, A. MacDERMOTT, Commander, R.N.

MAY 18

Sir,—The correctness of the Taoiseach's action when the death of the head of the German State was reported has been vindicated by Commander MacDermott. But his letter does not cover the whole story. In 1943 the allies called upon the neutrals to deny asylum to Axis refugees, described for the occasion as war criminals. Portugal refused. The rest took it lying down, except Mr. de Valera. He replied that Eire reserved the right to give asylum when justice, charity, or the honour or interest of the nation required it. That is what all the neutrals ought to have said; and Miss Hinkson, as an Irishwoman, will, on second thoughts, be as proud of it as I am. The voice of the Irish gentleman and Spanish grandee was a welcome relief from the chorus of retaliatory rancour and self-righteousness then deafening us.

I have not always agreed with the Taoiseach's policy. Before the ink was dry on the treaty which established the Irish Free State I said that if England went to war she would have to reoccupy Ireland militarily, and fortify her ports. When this forecast came to the proof the Taoiseach nailed his colours to the top gallant, declaring that with his little army of 50,000 Irishmen he would fight any and every invader, even if England, Germany, and the United States attacked him simultaneously from all quarters, which then seemed a possible result of his attitude. And he got away with it triumphantly, saved, as Mr. Churchill has just pointed out, by the abhorred partition which gave the allies a foothold in Ireland, and by the folly of the Führer in making for Moscow instead of for Galway.

Later on I hazarded the conjecture that Adolf Hitler would end in the Dublin Vice-regal Lodge, like Louis Napoleon in Chislehurst and the Kaiser in Doorn. If the report of the Führer's death proves unfounded this is still a possibility.

It all sounds like an act from Victor Hugo's *Hernani* rather than a page of modern world-war history; but Eamon de Valera comes out of it as a champion of the Christian chivalry we are all pretending to admire. Let us recognize a noble heart even if we must sometimes question its worldly wisdom.

Faithfully, G. BERNARD SHAW

ITALIANS AND MUSSOLINI

Mussolini's death was not allowed to pass without comment either . . .

MAY 7

Sir,—Are not the mob who have been photographed by our Press kicking and spitting at corpses in Milan exactly the same type of *canaille* as screamed "Duce, Duce, Duce" in delirious ecstasy when their triumphant dictator was trampling upon their own liberties and those of others?

I am, Sir, your obedient servant, A. E. E. READE, Capt.
Travellers' Club, Pall Mall, S.W.1

TOO TRUE TO BE GOOD

Inflation, then as now, was a political and personal problem.

JUNE 13

Sir,—Cheap food was indeed one of the lesser glories of Victorian days. In Liverpool in the early nineties three kinds of oysters were on sale at 6d., 8d., and 10d. a score. But in April, 1898, I stayed, with three companions, at a small hotel in Switzerland where full board and lodging cost 2s. 9½d. a day. The only extra was coffee, which was served every evening in two huge jugs and cost 20 centimes a head, or less than a penny a cup. Can anybody beat that?

Yours faithfully, C. E. STEINITZ

Chichester

JUNE 15

Sir,—I fancy Mr. Steinitz can be beaten. Early this century full board and lodging could be had in Vienna, never a cheap city, for 4s. 2d. a day; in country parts of Austria for half that sum. Just before the last war a family of four, real *gourmets*, lived in Bordeaux for 8s. 4d. a day, including *foie gras*, game, lobsters, &c. Wine there cost 3d. a litre, red/white, 4d. At Arcachon Portuguese oysters were 2d. a dozen; flat oysters, 3d.

In a country less blest than France by Nature I remember this meal at Malinne: *quatre bons plats* (as on the menu), each a substantial course of meat or fowl, following *hors d'oeuvre* and soup, and followed by salad, dessert, and cheese, wine and coffee included—total, 10d.

Your obedient servant, JOHN POLLOCK

The Athenaeum, Pall Mall, S.W.1

JUNE 15

Sir,—In Victorian days a substantial piece of cheese could be had in the Middle Temple Hall for 1d. No charge was made for bread or barley water. Thus impecunious law students could, and did, lunch sufficiently for a penny.

Yours truly, EDWARD HARRISON

Old Stones, Ightham, Sevenoaks, Kent

JUNE 18

Sir,—Some three years ago, when swimming in Parson's Pleasure at Oxford, the custodian told me that as a young man, at the beginning of the century, he could go out on a Saturday night with sixpence and buy a pint of beer, an ounce of tobacco, a clay pipe, a box of matches, and bread and cheese.

Yours faithfully, HENRY MORRIS

The Granary, Newnham, Cambridge

JUNE 18

Sir,—May I, as an uncomplaining sufferer from the rations of the present, beg you to refrain from publishing any more letters on the meals that could be had early in this century for a few pence?

Yours, &c., R. H. YELDHAM

A RAILWAY POSTER

◆

Waste again—but a new culprit: public transport. A certain railway poster was considered by many to be a scandalous waste of paper.

JULY 2

Sir,—May I protest in your columns about the shocking wate of paper by the four railway companies by the exhibition of their latest poster. This poster contains the phrase, "In War and Peace—we serve"—a Union Jack, a picture of a railway train, and the initials of the four companies.

In a quick walk round Victoria Station I counted 67 of these posters, size 20in. by 30in. They are also to be seen in various quantities on every railway station in the kingdom. One would have no objection if the poster served any useful purpose, but to use this vast quantity of paper merely to inform a long suffering travelling public that the railways serve in war and peace, seems the height of wasteful absurdity.

What else, may I ask, would the railways be doing? Standing in the sidings? Sleeping in goods depôts and booking offices? No, of course not, they would be serving. It is their natural and only function. They could not exist if they did not serve. I might just as well state that "In war and peace—I breathe." It is natural for living persons to do so, but there is no need to waste the country's sparse stocks of paper to announce the obvious.

This waste is all the more serious because I know how difficult it is to obtain even small stocks of paper to print catalogues for oversea circulation to encourage our much needed export trade.

Yours faithfully, C. D. NOTLEY, Managing Director

Cecil D. Notley Advertising Ltd., 43, Hertford Street, W.1

Sir,—The poster which Mr. Notley dislikes was printed for exhibition on VE Day, owing to the impossibility of obtaining flags and bunting to decorate railway stations.

Yours faithfully, G. H. LOFTUS ALLEN, Chairman, British Railways Advertising and Public Relations Committee

Euston Station, N.W.1

Sir,—Mr. Loftus Allen's explanation of the railway posters which Mr. Notley so rightly deprecated would have been more appreciated had they contained flags only, instead of including the reference to serve in peace and war—obviously advertising propaganda—in which the railways did such good work, but not they alone.

Your obedient servant, W. J. L. STRIBLING

Seaford Cottage, Oxted, Surrey

Sir,—The poster complained of by Mr. C. D. Notley in his letter which appeared in to-day's issue of *The Times* had quite the opposite effect on me when I first saw it at Victoria Station. To-day as I travelled on the Southern Railway I felt that it was a pleasant contrast to what we had been accustomed to for the past few years; and to me it was a timely reminder that service is needed as much in peace as in war.

Yours faithfully, W. HERBERT WARD

Fairholme, Leap Cross, Hailsham, Sussex

THE EXECUTION OF GERMAN BOYS

There was considerable concern over how the Germans should be treated after the Allied victory in Europe. The war crimes commission would deal with the Nazi ring-leaders, whilst a programme of denazification was introduced to purge German society of its ills, allowing the nation to be brought back into the fold of a new Europe. However, the Allies would have to guard against the temptation for revenge and vindictiveness. The execution of some Hitler Youth adherents brought the problems into focus.

JUNE 2

Sir,—May I offer you a pair of quotations, suitable, I think, to serve not merely as a postscript to the series which you have recently brought to a close, but also as an echo to the words in which the Prime Minister has described the frame of mind in which we should discharge the responsibilities imposed upon us by victory?

Inflexible in our resolve to mete out justice to the German nation, and in particular to its leaders, high and low alike, would not we, and our allies, do well to bear in mind the words of the Emperor Marcus Aurelius—himself a conqueror of barbarian German armies?

"See that you do not feel towards the inhuman what the inhuman feel towards mankind."

And

"The noblest kind of retribution is not to become like your enemy."

I am, Sir, your obedient servant, JOHN SPARROW

All Souls College, Oxford

JUNE 8

Sir,—You published the other day a letter in which two maxims from Marcus Aurelius were quoted for the guidance of the allies in the treatment of Germany. One of these read:—"The noblest kind of retribution is not to become like your enemy." When I read in the paper this morning that two German boys, aged 17 and 16 respectively, had just been executed for spying upon the Americans in February last (*i.e.*, while the war was still in progress) I wished that the president of the Military Court which passed the sentence had borne the above maxim in mind. Surely we and our allies are strong enough to establish order in Germany without resorting to the shooting of children?

I am, Sir, your obedient servant, HUGH MONTGOMERY

Oswaldkirk, Yorkshire

JUNE 12

Sir,—In your issue of June 8 a letter-writer raises objection to the shooting of German spies aged 16 and 17. May I remind him, first, that the British "Manual of Military Law" lays down: "neither age nor sex affords any immunity from the laws with regard to espionage and treason."

Secondly, that about two-thirds of the lower ranks of the four new German Reserve corps which fought us at "First Ypres" in 1914, were lads, schoolboys, and university students (the matter is dealt with in the British Official History, "1914," Vol. II, pp. 123–4). I saw some of the prisoners taken; all were young, and one looked so young that I asked his age; which was 14. The Germans themselves speak of this battle as "Der Kindermord von Ypern"—they did the murder. If therefore German lads shoot and spy in war, may we not shoot them without any qualms of conscience? Their own nation considers them of military age.

I am, Sir, your obedient servant, J. E. EDMONDS

JUNE 12

Sir,—Many will agree with the letter from Mr. Montgomery in your issue of to-day, especially after the "cease fire" has sounded, but more will be shocked by the pictures of the execution that appeared in some other papers. What is the object of such pictures, and why should photographs be permitted of such distressing scenes, or published, in any case, in Britain?

Yours, &c., PARMOOR

The Queen's College, Oxford

JUNE 12

Sir,—About a fortnight ago I fell into conversation with a soldier returned from the Continent, where he had been since D-Day. He said: "The German soldiers were good fighters, and, so far as I could see, they kept the conventions of war. But the boys under 20 were just vermin that should be exterminated. They murdered prisoners and wounded, fired on stretcher-bearers and burial parties. We lost a lot of stretcher-bearers and suchlike that way."

If all the crimes of these youths are to be passed over on the grounds that "boys will be boys" we shall have another outburst of Hitlerism 20 years hence. A Judge in this country recently remarked that local courts which treat robbery by youths as just a joke are rapidly manufacturing a generation of criminals.

Yours faithfully, J. CHARTRES MOLONY

Dorchester House, Seaford, Sussex

JUNE 14

Sir,—Under British civilian law it is illegal to condemn to death a criminal under 18. Why is a procedure, which in peaceful times is considered highly unjust and inhumane, regarded as just and expedient in exceptional circumstances?

These two boys were four and five years of age at Hitler's advent to power, thus being incapable of resisting any influence, good or evil, which might be brought to bear on them. Would any English boy and girl have withstood such an influence?

We protest strongly against this outrage on justice and humanity. Is this what the democratic nations have been fighting for six years to bring about?

Yours faithfully, DORA GERRETT, MARGARGET C. GARDNER (Students at University College, London)

Gower Street, W.C.1

JUNE 14

Sir,—Does Brigadier-General Sir J. E. Edmonds think that he can quiet a national conscience by the quoting of the British "Manual of Military Law"? If so, then we can no longer condemn the action taken by Germany's military commanders in the case of Nurse Cavell.

Yours faithfully, ANNE HARRINGTON

Brantwood, Rolleston on Dove, Staffs

NOT ON THE REGISTER

◆

Following the defeat of Germany, a general election was held in Great Britain. The campaign provoked a number of letters concerning the electoral register and political literature.

JULY 4

Sir,—I have been living at my present address for 18 months and it now appears that I am not on the electoral roll. Since we all hold registration cards and food ration books, the compiling of a register would seem to be a simple, straightforward task. Who, pray, was responsible for this deplorably inaccurate piece of work?

Yours, &c., DIANA BARRACLOUGH

12, North Side, S.W.4

JULY 5

Sir,—A little while ago you published a letter from the Registrary of Cambridge University, asking graduates to make sure that their present addresses appeared in the voting lists. I complied, and the results have been remarkable. I have received (i) three copies of Dr. Pickthorn's election address, on three successive days, (ii) one copy of Dr. Charles Hill's address, (iii) two copies of Mr. Wilson Harris's address, in separate envelopes but delivered by the same post, (iv) on the same day but by different posts two voting papers. None of these documents was forwarded from a previous address.

Mr. J. B. Priestley has not, as yet, sought to woo me, perhaps because he thinks that I know him well enough already, and Air Commodore Howard-Williams is still only a name so far as I am concerned. If either of these candidates desires my support, I beg him to ask me for it once only. I cannot avoid a wistful remembrance that some of my books are out of print because of a shortage of paper.

Yours, &c., EDWARD SHANKS

P.S.—I reopen this letter to record that I have just received, by the same

post in separate covers, two copies of Air Commodore Howard-Williams's address.
Kilve, Park Copse, Dorking

JULY 6

Sir,—I have been living at my present address for 16 years, and it now appears that my name has been taken off the electoral roll and that of my housemaid, aged 16, substituted in its stead.
Yours, &c., RICHARD, Archbishop of Liverpool
Archbishop's House, Liverpool

JULY 6

Sir,—It has been a difficult task, with almost no paid labour and with amateur labour much limited for free time, to get election papers out to 43,000 voters, a high proportion of whom have no addresses in the register, some 5,000 of whom have appointed proxies, and another high proportion of whom have changed their addresses. I am sure all the candidates have tried hard to see that not more than one communication is sent to each elector, that being both our legal duty and our interest. The particular case of Mr. Shanks and the three copies of my address is easy to explain. He had not till very lately "made sure that his present address appeared in the voting lists." It is known to two members of my family, who, noticing his name unprovided with an address, each unknown to the other directed an envelope. Meanwhile, Mr. Shanks sent his address to the registrary, who put it on the list of new addresses, and a third envelope must have been addressed. The failure to check is regretted; it is believed that in the circumstances some such failures were inevitable.
Yours faithfully, KENNETH PICKTHORN
Corpus Christi College, Cambridge

JULY 6

Sir,—If Mr. Edward Shanks will spare me one of his three copies of Mr. Pickthorn's election address, for which I have long been waiting, I will call personally and relieve him of the duplicate copy of my own address which was sent him inadvertently.
I am, Sir, yours, &c., H. WILSON HARRIS
Foxhole, Abinger Common, Dorking

JULY 7

Sir,—The voting paper handed to me this morning had a printed number on the back. This number corresponded to a printed number on the counterfoil. Before the voting paper was detached from the counterfoil the clerk in charge wrote on the counterfoil my number on the electoral register. Could not this procedure conceivably be used to violate the secrecy of the ballot?

Yours faithfully, S. W. FISHER
32, The Crescent, Barnes, S.W.13

JULY 7

Sir,—I have been rector of this parish and a ratepayer and taxpayer for nearly 10 years; I also hold a national card (WLCB 60/1) and food ration card; my wife is on the register; my name is omitted.

I also would ask: Who is responsible?

Yours faithfully, EDWARD S. DANIELL, Canon
Little Cheney Rectory, Dorchester, Dorset

JULY 7

Sir,—I hope that whatever Government be elected it may have sense of humour enough to refrain for some little time from urging the general public not to waste paper.

DOROTHEA SHAW
Cranleigh, Surrey

TRUNK CALL DELAYS

Making a trunk call was not always a simple or speedy matter.

JULY 17

Sir,—Having arrived in London last night by train too late to catch the last train to Cambridge I was anxious to inform my wife of what had happened.

I dialled Trunks and heard the ringing tone, but this went on unanswered from 10.25 p.m. till 11 p.m. I then dialled O and got the local exchange, which was sympathetic and promised to try to help but was diffident of success. After waiting about five minutes I again dialled Trunks and except for another short interview with the local exchange kept the ringing tone going until 11.45 without getting any reply. A third conversation with the local exchange assured me that my difficulty was not unique, that every night Trunks have many more calls than the staff can deal with, that the local exchange is as powerless as the private subscriber, but that at 12 o'clock all outstanding calls would be cancelled and if I rang again then I might have some chance of success. I rang from 12 to 12.15 a.m. without success, had a bath, returned to the charge at 12.25 and got an answer from Trunks after two hours' work.

The situation is preposterous. My call was a reasonably urgent one, my

wife having been ill. But however urgent it might have been I was assured by the local exchange that I could have done absolutely nothing about it. It is time the Postmaster-General looked into the situation.
Yours faithfully, ALEX WOOD
Emmanuel College, Cambridge

VICTORY BROADCASTS

On the day of Japanese surrender, both the King and the new Prime Minister, Clement Attlee, broadcast to the nation and empire. Mr Churchill, apparently, was not invited to do so.

AUG. 15

Sir,—It has been stated that, on the day of victory, broadcasts will be given by both the King and the Prime Minister. May we be bold enough to ask for a broadcast also from the Leader of the Opposition?

Whatever the mistakes of a party which has consequently been swept out of power, Mr. Winston Churchill cannot but remain the man who led this Empire's part in the final overthrowing of Japan. There is no other man more eminently qualified to speak in celebration of the occasion.
I am, Sir, yours faithfully, G. SPENCER BROWN, Schoolmaster, Royal Navy
Priors Mount, Great Malvern

AUG. 20

Sir,—Few if any of us are so fortunate as to have lived long in this world without having to look back on scenes or incidents that we would wish to have ordered otherwise. "If only I had thought of this!" "If only I had not said that." But sometimes our regret may be almost equally keen on behalf of some other person's missed opportunity.

I wonder how many people while listening to the Prime Minister's historic message at midnight on Tuesday strained their ears and longed for a reference to Mr. Churchill, but for whose incomparable leadership the victory could almost certainly never have been achieved. But the opportunity was not taken. If only it had been! How Mr. Attlee's own stock would have risen!
I am, yours faithfully, GEORGE A. FALK
Bristol

AUG. 20

Sir,—In this time of thanksgiving and rejoicing there must be millions of people who would love to hear just now above all other voices that of the late

Prime Minister, the wise and brave man who has cheered us in our struggles and under Providence led us to victory. Can anything be done about it?
Yours faithfully, SIDNEY H. BROWN
Flagstones, Sevenoaks

WAR DAMAGE INSURANCE

◆

Despite the war's end in Europe, certain bodies, insurance companies among them, found it expedient to combine playing safe with making a profit.

JULY 6

Sir,—For how long shall we have to pay the War Damage "Contribution"? I have just received a demand for this, as being due and payable on July 1, 1945. Is not the European war over?—or are the Japs likely to raid over here?
Yours faithfully, RICHARD CLOUGH
The Downs, Woodwater, Exeter

JULY 6

Sir,—House owners are now receiving demand notices for War Damage Insurance. Hostilities in Europe are at an end, and with them risks of war damage. The demand would therefore seem to be in the nature of taxation rather than of insurance. Is this to become a new imposition on property owners?
Yours faithfully, HOUSEOWNER

EPILOGUE

◆

British idiosyncrasy, of which many of these letters give proof, was remarked upon. Let Messrs. Potter, Dugdale and Larby have the last words.

JULY 27

Sir,—Is it not now time that we received some direction as to what to do with our gas masks?
Your obedient servant, GEORGE RICHARD POTTER
21, Stayleigh Lane, Sheffield

MAY 12

Sir,—Truly we are an odd race. Having read that churches would be open on VE Day for thanksgiving, I went to St. Paul's Cathedral at 2 p.m. on Tuesday and found the entrance steps thronged with people listening to a Guards band seated below who at that moment were giving a spritely rendering of "Roll Out the Barrel." Excusable perhaps, but hardly the place even on VE Day.

Yours, FRANK DUGDALE
Sanderstead, Surrey

MAY 17

Sir,—In Warwick Lane to-day two able-bodied men are burning waste timber from bombed buildings—just that and nothing else. Thousands of us cannot get hold of any kind of wood for lighting fires, if we are lucky enough to have some coal! We certainly do strange things at times.

Yours faithfully, ERNEST W. LARBY
9, Old Bailey, E.C.4

"Strange" the British might be, but they won nonetheless.

INDEX OF
SUBJECTS

Alcohol	46–48, 183–185; cost of, 207–208; *see also Temperance, Brewing*
Aircraft	in combat over Channel, 75–79; low flying, 187; noise, 191–192
Air raid precautions	*see ARP*
Air raids	81–86; on Rome, 166–169; *see also Flying Bombs*
Air raid warnings	21, 26; by pheasants, 26; annoying sirens, 186–187
Aliens	incarceration of, 59–63
Army	management of, 97–101; employment of soldiers on leave, 121
ARP	18–22
Athletic prowess	181–183
Baths	*see Rationing*
Bats	getting rid of, 36–37
BBC	67, 69, 75–79, 118, 127–131, 170
Beggars	52–53
Binoculars	donation to Government of, 94–95
Birds, rare	as food, 107
Birth-rate	*see Population*
Black-out	18–25, 55–56, 156–157
Bombing	*see Air raids*
Brains Trust	on employment, 159
Brewing	and distilling, 48
British	Empire, 56–57; spirit of the, 76, 81–86; Summer Time, 105–106
Broccoli	nutritional value of, 161
Brothels	licensed, 155
Buses	crawling, 164–165; manners on, 170–172; boarding of, 201–202
Cameras	illegal carrying of, 33
Cars	accidents during black-out, 22–25, 156; camouflage of, 80–81; wasteful use of, 116–117
Cats	tax on, 73–75; for vermin control, 74–75; in preference to terriers, 74–75; diet, 134–135; "doing their bit", 134
Censorship	33, 122
Chickens	food for, 102–105, 148–150; egg supply, 104–105, 148–150, 195–197
Children	dirty, verminous, 28; during evacuation, 27–29; bedtime for, 106
Chimneys	sweeping, 21–22; soot, 163
Chrysanthemum leaves	for smoking, 110
Churchill, Winston	pronunciation of foreign words, 49; broadcasts, 163–164, 215–216
Cigarettes	duty-free allowance, 34; cartons, 58; price of, 79–80; smoking on trains, 111–112; gift of 400,000,000, 176–177; *see also Smoking*
Cinemas	closure of, 15–17; filming the war, 155–156
Clothing	recycling, 40–41; coupons, 135; unnecessary, 136–138; *see also Rationing*
Coltsfoot	for smoking, 110–111
Conscientious Objectors	114–115

Cooking — 27, 30–31; with sugar and butter ration, 50–51; alternative food, 54–55

Cricket — flannels, 41

Crosswords, *The Times* — 17–18; essential to war effort, 17; 197

Customs — restrictions, 33

Distilling — *see Brewing*

Dogs — terriers and rats, 74–75; as vermin killers, 147; in the Blitz, 147; licences, 164

Domestic staff — 27, 29

Eggs — *see Chickens*

Election, General (1945) — 212–214

Employment — 121, 159, 185–186

Evacuation — 26–29

Flowers — aesthetic appeal of, 32; municipal gardens, 32; window boxes, 32; rather than vegetables, 144–146

Flying Bombs — 186–187

Food — *see Rationing*; illegal possession of, 114; hoarding, 138–139; price of vegetables, 161–162; shooting for, 179–180; cost of, 207–208

Gas-masks — 19, 25, 115, 216

German Youth — fanaticism of, 43–45; execution of, 209–212

Glamour girls — 71

Göring, Field-Marshal — bombs Buckingham Palace, 86; claims descent from Henry II, 101–102

Graf Spee — 41–43, 93

Grass-mowings — as food, 55

Haw-Haw, Lord — 43; accent of, 49

Hay-box cookery — 30–31

Hess, Rudolf — 118–119

Hitler, Adolf — and *Graf Spee*, 42–43; oratory, 43; as God, 44; keeping us guessing, 58, 61; proclamation of peace, 68; triumphal visit to Britain, 86; and Hess, 118–119; compared with Lucifer, 160; birth place, 203; blindness, 203; origin of name, 203; rank in Great War, 204; and Eire, 204–206

Home Guard — 63–68; uniforms, 67–68; allowance, 67–68; organisation of, 70–71; disbandment of 188–191

Horses — homesick, 34–35; racing, 68–71, 108–109

Hygiene — 27, 142–144

Identity Cards — 199–201

Ink — economy in use of, 162–163

Jelly, medlar — 50–51

Jervis Bay — 92–95

Kangaroo hunters — 64

Kilts — infestation of, 37–40

LDV (Local Defence Volunteers) — *see Home Guard*

Lice — *Pediculus vestimenti*, 37–40; head lice, 142–144

Lighting restrictions — *see Black-out*

Luggage, lost — *see Trains*

Manners — on public transport, 169–172

Michaelmas daisies — 31

Mosley, Sir Oswald — arrest of, 72

Mothers — during evacuation, 27–29; and maternity hospitals, 177

Mussolini, Benito — compared with Machiavelli, 71–72; death, 206

Nazi — pronunciation of, 49; regime, 59–63; as readers of *The Times*, 67; the Hess affair, 118–119

Paper — waste of, 29–30, 57–58, 112–114, 139–141, 208–209, 212–214

Paratroops — invasion by, 63–66; as big game, 64

Petrol — see Rationing

Pheasants — see Air raid warnings; half wild, 179

Pigs — domestic, 72–73

Pigswill — 112

Population — of Germany, 152–155; of Britain, 172–173

Porridge — 50

Potatoes — in their jackets, 30–31; noses of, 31

Poultry — see Chickens

Rabbits — and Jerusalem artichokes, 55; digestive tract of, 73; as a pest, 107; paws, 179; frozen, 188

Raspberry leaves — for smoking, 111

Rationing — food, 49–51; petrol, 70–71, 116–118; chicken food, 102–105, 148–150; coal, 120, 139, 151–152; clothing, 121, 138; and imports, 131; and hoarding, 138–139; eggs, 148–150; bath water, 151–152

Rats — trench rats, 38; menace of, 74–75, 134–135, 147; shooting, 179

Razor blades — recycling, 58–59

Regulation 33B — see Venereal disease

Religious observance — 15–16, 132–133

Reprisals — for civilian bombing, 86–91; retribution, 210

Rooks — shooting, 54; rook pie, 54

Shooting — rooks, 54; parachutists, 64; for food, 179–180

Slang phrases — 151, 197–198

Smoking — 34; attendant waste, 58–59; price of, 79–80, 207–208; substitutes for tobacco, 110–112; giving up, 111; on trains, 111–112, 176–177

Snow pancakes — 55

Snuff — efficacy of, 80

Taxis — during black out, 56, 125–126

Telephones — 214–215

Temperance — 46–48, 183–185

Theatres — closure of, 15–17

Tobacco — see Smoking, Cigarettes

Trains — during black out, 156–157; smoking on, 111–112; saving ink, 162; manners on, 169–170, 173; lost luggage, 177–179; wasteful poster, 208–209; 214

Treating — see Alcohol; "No-treating order", 46–47, 183–185

Trinity (College, Cambridge) Jump — see Athletic prowess

Venereal disease — 152–155

Waistcoats — wind-proof, 40–41

War crimes — 173–176, 209–212

Waste — 29–30, 57–59, 112–114, 208–209; of effort, 166

Wives — sale of, 35–36

INDEX OF
CORRESPONDENTS

Acworth, C B, 202
Adams, E W, 141
Adams, F B, 129, 201
Addison, W, 37
Aldridge, J, 147
Alison Phillips, W, 123
Alker Tripp, H, 125
Allder, Irene M, 187
Allen, C K, 150
Ames, P R, 156
Archibald Davies, W, 183
Archimedes, 187
Armstrong, H W, 161
Ashton-Hopper, H, 73
Athill, A K, 116
Atkins, J B, 47
Austin, Stanley, 182
Baily, F E, 71
Ball Dodson, R, 58
Ballard, Frank H, 183
Bancroft, Monica C, 85
Barber, Donald, 137
Barham, Ruth, 117
Barr, W J, 66
Barraclough, Diana, 212
Barson, E J, 183
Batchelor, Veronica S, 52
Beaman, Lieutenant-Colonel
    A A H, 101
Beaumont, O, 85
Beaumont, Oliver, 109
Beerbohm, Max, 123
Beevor, P H, 196
Belcher, E A, 146
Belden, A D, 183
Bell, C M E, 50
Bell, Clive, 20
Bell, F E, 56
Bernays, Robert, 170
Berridge, Jesse, 198
Betts, The Rev H P, 36
Bevan, John, 183
Bingham,
    Lieutenant-Colonel R C,
    98
Bingley, 95
Birdwood, F M, 63
Birmingham, E W, 132
Black, F A, 111
Blaikley, Ernest, 163
Bland, J O P, 112

Blumenfeld, R D, 180
Blundun, Jessica, 136
Bolton, Geoffrey, 92
Botley, Cicely M, 36
Branson, J R B, 55
Branston, C A, 171
Brittain, F, 183
Brooks, H, 58
Brown, H, 54
Brown, Sidney H, 216
Brown, William, 44, 203
Brownrigg, Beatrice, 119
Bryan, Herbert, 112, 133
Buckston Browne, FRCS, 80
Cadell, G L, 32
Cahn, R W, 182
Campbell, Olwen W, 118
Carlos Clarke, Major C L,
    115
Carter, F W P, 137
Carter, Henry, 48
Cave, Sydney, 183
Cazalet, V A, 87
Cecil, 174
Chalmers Mitchell, P, 107
Chalmers Rogers, F, 180
Chartres Molony, J, 211
Childs, Mrs E B, 41
Childs, R E W, 45
Civval, Lewis, 64
Clarke, H C, 152
Clarke, The Ven C P S
    Clarke, 51
Clerk, George R, 44
Clifton-Mogg, Gwladys, 172
Clough, Richard, 216
Coates, W J, 183
Cockin, F A, 86
Cocks, Norman, 183
Comyn-Platt, T, 52
Corbett Ashby, Margery I,
    155
Cotterill, H S, 35
Coxwell, C B, 18
Creed, F G, 25
Crick, Walter, 72
Crofton, Beatrix, 29
Croxton Smith, A, 74–75
Curtis, E M, 27
Daniell, Canon Edward S,
    214

Darroch, J M, 72
Davey, Norman, 124
Dawnay, Guy P, 75, 77
De Monte, Frank, 202
De Pree, H, 21
Decies, 18
Demant, V A, 188
Denne, Alured, 132
Desborough, Ethel, 82
Dill-Russell, M C, 148
Dobson, F, 161
Doherty, J W, 24
Dolby, J, 122
Dolphin, Arthur H, 54
Donnison, E, 36
Dowsett, Colonel E B, 37
Drake, Lieutenant-Colonel
    R J, 83
Drummond, Cyril A, 121
Dudman, N A, 80
Dugdale, Frank, 217
Edmonds, J E, 211
Eisler, Robert, 203
Elders, W W, 197
Eltisley, 65
Elverson, J H, 148
Eperson, D B, 149
Ervine, Leonora M, 83
Espir, H, 126
Essex, 191
Evans, Idris, 183
Fairweather, W L, 99
Falk, George A, 215
Ferguson, Millicent, 78
Fisher, C, 76
Fisher, H Frank T, 59
Fisher, S W, 214
Foley, F C, 23
Frank, Fritz, 61
Fraser Taylor, A J R, 199
Gampell, Sydney S, 131
Gardener-Smith, P, 116
Gardner, Lucy, 172
Gardner, Margaret C, 211
Gareth Thomas, T, 172
Garland, S T, 114
Garwood,
    Lieutenant-Colonel H P,
    17
Gaunt, H C A, 185
Geden, Margaret, 148

Gerrett, Dora, 211
Gildroy, A J, 20
Gleadow, Rupert, 186
Godfrey, William M, 156
Golding-Bird, Bishop Cyril H, 82, 132
Goodchild, R, 118
Goodhart, A L, 176
Gordon Hassell, J, 115
Gosse, Philip, 39
Graves, P P, 62
Green, Janet, 171
Green, T R L, 138
Gregory Pearce, H, 140
Griffith, Paul, 187
Hahn, Oscar, 182
Haldane, M M, 40
Hardie, Martin, 163
Harrington, Anne, 212
Harrison, Edward, 207
Harrisson, Tom, 185
Harrod, R F, 153
Hart, E P, 111
Hawkins, R H, 75
Headley, Lady Catharine, 55
Healy, Maurice, 85
Heenan, John C, 168
Henry, Lieut.-Col. W R P, 190
Hensley Henson, Bishop H, 100
Hensley Henson, H, 160
Henvey, R, 78
Herbert Ward, W, 209
Herd, Harold, 113
Higson, W, 105
Hill, A V, 124
Hill, Leonard, 142
Hillyard, A W, 165
Hinkson, Pamela, 205
Hoare, J B, 22
Holloway, E A, 129
Hooper, Captain C W R, RIN, 58
Hornby, Claude H, 88
Housden, Leslie, 204
Howard Badger, W, 25
Howard, Brigadier-General Thomas, 65
Howard, Francis, 67
Hudson, R C, 56
Hugh-Smith, Jean, 178
Hughes, Hector, 42
Humphery, Selwyn W, 81
Hurd, Archibald, 117
Hutchinson, Walter, 196
Jackson, Philip H, 140

Jacob, Gordon, 168
James, Lionel, 119
Jamieson, John R, 151
Jessop-Hulton, Mrs, 54
Johns, Charles R, 147
Johnson, E E, 183
Johnstone, Gilbert, 109
Jones, Frank H, 81
Jones, Roderick, 152
Kay, P C, 146
Keay, William, 151
Kennet, Lord, 182
Kent, C S, 125–126
Kent Wright, R, 148
King-Hall, Stephen, 84
Knight, J H, 190
Koe, Brigadier-General L C, 51
L'Estrange Ewen, C, 184
Lampson, A C, 161
Lancaster, John de B, 23
Larby, Ernest W, 217
Law, Colonel W H P, 121
Lawson, Olwen, 178
Leather, Colonel Gerard F T, 100
Lees, J V E, 145
Lewis, Oswald, 180
Lightbody, D M, 26
Lloyd, R E A, 90
Lloyd Davies, M H, 22
Loftus Allen, G H, 209
Logan Strang, Lt.-Col. J, 191
Loring, John H, 106
Lumley-Kelly, Vera, 125
Lutyens, Emily, 167
Lyle, R C, 70
Lyttelton, Edward, 89, 112
Macaulay, Rose, 49
MacCarthy, Desmond, 167
MacDermott, Commander A, 205
Mackay, Dr M R, 39
MacKay, M R, 23
Mac Kinnon, F D, 120
Malden, R H, 93
Mallett, Will C, 150
Mamhead, 132
Mangles, Brigadier General R H, 66
Marillier, H C, 78
Marks, Julian D, 200
Marsden, Canon E L, 37
Mason, G K M, 194
Mathieson, D, 60
Matthews, F R, 18
McAllister, J, 157

McConnell, E, 22
McLaren, John R, 197
McNally, R J, 20
Meade Fetherstonhaugh, Admiral H, 92
Medley, D C, 53
Mellanby, Kenneth, 144
Michael, S E, 204
Millward, G D, 189
Milne, A A, 169
Montgomery, Hugh, 210
Moore, Thomas, 193
Mordaunt Burrows, O, 108
Morgan, B, 22, 170
Morgan, Robert H, 54, 134
Morrell, Philip, 20
Morris, Henry, 208
Morrison, Ronald, 102
Morton Stanley, R, 183
Moule, Mrs E C, 37
Muirhead, Thorburn, 165
Muspratt, A, 106
Naish, Roy L, 64
Nelson Heaver, A, 89
Neville, W, 143
Newcombe, Luxmoore, 93
Newton, Robert G, 17
Nichols, Paul, 173
Nordon, Charles L, 175
Northcote, Canon A F, 35
Notley, C D, 208
O'Connor, Donald M, 43
Oates, Violet E, 27
Offer, A R, 50
Ogilvie, F W, 77
Oldham, E C W, 51
Orr, J B, 104
Oscar, Henry, 187
Oswald, W H, 182
Oved, Mosheh, 138
Owen, A S, 68
Oxford, Margot, 16
Paley Scott, C, 90
Palmer, Gerald, 127
Palmes, Olave N, 30
Parker, R G, 111
Parmoor, 211
Pearson, Mrs M M, 50
Pendred, Loughlan, 122
Penton, Lady, 31
Percival Westell, W, 108
Perrin, Eric, 162
Phillips, E J, 130
Phillpotts, Eden, 128
Pickthorn, Kenneth, 213
Piekarski, J, 93
Piercy, Selden, 119

Pigg, C H, 98
Pile, John W, 69
Pinkney, K T, 59
Pocock, R I, 134–139
Pollock, John, 207
Pollock, Sir John, 182
Pollok-McCall,
  Brigadier-General J B, 59
Poole, F R, 68
Potter, George Richard, 216
Pritchard, H, 156
Probert, Charles, 20
Purcell, Ethel A, 41
Putnam, J Eric, 34
Pye, H M, 103
Queenborough, 94
Quickswood, 201
Ramsbotham, R B, 190
Ransley, A G, 202
Rathbone, Eleanor F, 113
Reade, A E E, 206
Redmayne, E R, 120
Rees, Ebenezer, 183
Reeve-Flaxman, D, 114
Reeve Wallace, W, 123
Reid Moir, J, 24
Richardson, Alec B, 145
Richardson, E C, 73
Richard, 213
Ridge, Mrs John, 30
Robertson Scott, J W, 48
Robinson, E Keith, 74
Rogers, M I, 61
Rowland, D, 135
Rowland, F, 196
Rumbold, Ethel, 170
Russell, Claud, 124
Russell, Conrad, 106
Ryan, A P, 79
Sainsbury, John, 164
Sampson, George, 78, 169
Sandeman, H F, 58
Sandwith, Mrs Cecil, 34
Sargent, Malcolm, 160
Saunders, Mrs Iris M, 50
Sayers, Dorothy L, 16
Scarborough Johnson, Mrs,
  35
Scholey, G J, 26
Schrijver, Herman, 137
Scott, F C, 141
Scott, Francis, 57
Selby Steyn, W, 183
Shanks, Edward, 212
Shaw, Dorothea, 214
Shaw, G Bernard, 16, 206
Shaw Scott, G, 140

Shaw-Stewart, Hugh, 134
Shepherd, C J, 103
Silver, Mrs D M, 30
Simpson, Helen, 16
Simpson, Will, 183
Sinclair Rohde, Eleanour, 31
Sitwell, Osbert, 124
Slade Baker, A, 77
Smith, F E, 94
Smith, H A, 67
Smith, Nowell, 90
Sparrow, John, 210
Spencer, J G C, 51
Spencer Brown, G, 215
Stedman, H J H, 37
Steegman, John, 165
Steele, Captain R V, 39
Steinitz, C E, 207
Stephen, Lady, 31
Stephens, J P, 183
Stephenson, T, 49
Stewart, Dr J A, 110
Stokes, Simpson, 34
Stokoe, F W, 89
Stoll, Oswald, 15
Stone, Christopher, 177
Strabolgi, 197
Strachey, James, 131
Strain, L H, 173
Strauss, Henry, 79
Stribling, W J L, 209
Summers, M W, 159
Summerskill, Edith, 155
Symns, J M, 110
Tallents, Stephen, 110
Tatchell, Sydney, 141
Teale, The Rev Kenneth
  W P, 72
Tennyson Jesse, F, 29
Thomas, L I M, 130
Thompson, Alan, 149
Thompson, Malcolm, 43
Thomson, William, 149
Threlfall, H M, 33
Thursfield, H G, 101
Toppin, Heather M, 154
Townshend, C A H, 122
Trevelyan, G M, 63, 181
Turle, H B, 128
Turton, P H J, 143
Vanier, George P, 85
Vansittart, 174
Wade, Albert, 36
Wade, Mrs A G, 183
Walker, Jocelyn, 186
Walmisley-Dresser, Brenda,
  105

Ward, T J, 162
Wardale, J, 200
Warner, G R, 163
Warwick, Geoffrey, 80
Washington, C H, 41
Weller, Samuel, 82
Wells, Antony, 199
Wells, H G, 193
Wells, Leonard, 195
Wenham, Sheila, 188
Wharncliffe, 140
Wheatcroft, Harry, 145
Whibley, C, 189
White, Sarah A, 31
Whitehead, W, 35
Whittington, Alan R, 55
Whitton, C A, 56
Whitwell, Dr J R, 26
Wickham, Tom, 184
Widdowson, Mrs Mary, 31
Wigley, T, 183
Wilkinson, Guendolen, 32
Williams, R A, 91
Williams, T, 105
Willingdon, Marie, 177
Wilson, H A, 91
Wilson Harris, H, 213
Wimperis, H E, 192
Withers Green, P, 39
Wood, Alex, 215
Wood, Sinclair, 200
Wood, Sylvia M, 36
Wood, Walter, 124
Woodham, Ronald, 25
Woolley, Mabel F, 161
Wootton-Davies, J H, 166
Worth, Roland B, 179
Wyatt, Canon R G F, 111
Yeldham, R H, 208